Praise for *Don't Let Us Win Tonight*

"A modern-day, single-team cousin to the classic 1966 *The Glory of Their Times,* the key literary effort of the first half of baseball's history.... Stokes your capacity for sports-based wonder.... The beloved '04 Red Sox now have the first important book to document their achievement, efficacy, and, really, folklore.... The archival stuff is a delight.... Reading along to testimony of one sports miracle after another, you become dubious that all of this actually could have happened."

Colin Fleming, *Boston Globe*

"Lovingly constructed...quotes that get into the heads of the players and manager—not to mention the GM, owners, medical staff, and even the bat boy. Through their testimony, the smaller dramas behind the series all coalesce into a broader overarching story about grit, determination, and sheer boneheaded luck. You know exactly what's going to happen, and yet you still feel the bumps rise on the back of your neck.... [M]uch more than a souvenir for Sox fans, it's a historical document that, behind all the game-time drama, reverberates with a love of the sport that would resonate with any baseball lover. Maybe even a Yankee fan."

Pete Chianca, Gatehouse Media (Danvers, MA)

"Rather than simply write a dry synopsis of each game, the authors chose to incorporate a vast quantity of quotes by those who were there: the players, coaches, front office, the medical staff, and members of both the Yankees and the Cardinals. A few paragraphs of text, then it's on to the comments from those who lived each moment.... The reader comes away with a true sense of the strategies behind various decisions, what the players were thinking, play by play, the tension, stress, anxiety, and best of all, the relief and elation. *Don't Let Us Win Tonight* should be added to every Sox fan's library!"

The Feathered Quill

T0037721

"The authors seem to have left no stone unturned in researching *Don't Let Us Win Tonight*.... The result is a wealth of detail that enhances, but never detracts, from the incredible story. I would say the same of their prose. Wood and Nowlin let the tale tell itself.... Description of the game action is both concise and precise, and they typically use quotes to highlight the drama and significance of plays.... I'll be passing on my copy to my daughters, and then they will know what it was like to watch those games."

Andy Kirkaldy, *Addison (VT) Independent*

"Dave Roberts doesn't just steal second base in Game 4 of the ALCS; Wood and Nowlin recreate the entire scene using narratives from Roberts, Kevin Millar, Bill Mueller, Terry Francona, Joe Torre, and even Chris Cundiff, the Red Sox bat boy. Through their words, you can almost feel the cold air of that October night, see the clock inching just past midnight, hear the fans cheering, and see Roberts taking off for second as Mariano Rivera makes his move to the plate, on his way to igniting the comeback.... Even though we know how the tale ends, with Boston enjoying its first World Series championship in 86 years, we still feel the tension and emotion channeled through the anecdotes and observations that pepper each page, making it an easy and enjoyable read not just for Sox fans but for all baseball fans."

Jeff Moon, Fenway Fanatics

"*Don't Let Us Win Tonight* by Allan Wood & Bill Nowlin celebrates and re-creates the 2004 incredible playoff run of the Boston Red Sox. Carefully crafted, filled with succinct and insightful interviews, the terrific tome is just perfect for all Red Sox fans and for that matter all sports fans."

Dr. Harvey Frommer, Sports Book Shelf

"Historic pennant races make for compelling narratives, none more fantastic than the fairy tale 2004 Red Sox season.... Memories of David Ortiz's slugging heroics, bourbon fueled pregame rituals, Dave Roberts' stolen base, Curt Schilling's blood-stained sock, and Kevin Millar's manic enthusiasm all recall the most profound championship by the long benighted Red Sox."

Robert Birnbaum, The Daily Beast

"A gripping read.... Wood and Nowlin connect the narrative with a perfect sense of transitional phrasing, all the while keeping the reader engrossed in the action.... A must-read for members of Red Sox Nation."

Mike Olmstead, *Newport (VT) Daily Express*

"Captivating.... An outstanding oral history.... Relive the baseball party of a generation, all over again, in the pages of *Don't Let Us Win Tonight*."

Don Laible, *Utica Observer-Dispatch*

"Reliving the Red Sox's successive triumphs in the 2004 postseason never seems to get old for their fans, and a new book is out doing just that—reliving 2004. It is named *Don't Let Us Win Tonight* by Allan Wood and Bill Nowlin, perhaps the best of the many Red Sox historians through the years."

Bill Ballou, *Worcester Telegram & Gazette*

"Allan Wood and Bill Nowlin, who have written several books each, [have] scored a hit.... Red Sox fans will certainly be happy to relive October 2004 all over again, and *Don't Let Us Win Tonight* doesn't disappoint in that sense. Just keep away from Yankee fans."

Budd Bailey, Sports Book Review Center

"Ten years after the Sox creamed the Cardinals in the World Series, two sportswriters look back on how a team that hadn't won a championship in almost a century raced to the top of the heap. Wood and Nowlin mined accounts from everyone involved, from players to administrators to the doctor who saved Curt Schilling's ankle."

Boston Magazine

Don't Let Us Win Tonight

An Oral History
of the 2004 Boston Red Sox's
Impossible Playoff Run

Allan Wood and Bill Nowlin

TRIUMPH
BOOKS

Library of Congress Cataloging-in-Publication Data available upon request.

This book is available in quantity at special discounts for your group or organization. For further information, contact:

    Triumph Books
    814 North Franklin Street
    Chicago, Illinois 60610
    (312) 337-0747
    Fax (312) 280-5470
    www.triumphbooks.com

Printed in U.S.A.
ISBN: 978-1-63727-393-7
Design by Sue Knopf

For every fan who kept the faith

Contents

Preface

THE 2004 RED SOX rewired my brain. There may be no scientific evidence that those whiskey-sipping idiots performed some type of telepathic neuro-plasticity by winning Boston's first World Series championship in 86 years, but I know *something* astonishing happened, although it took nearly a year before I realized it.

It was perhaps an hour after Boston had been swept in the 2005 American League Division Series by the Chicago White Sox, although the Red Sox would remain the official defending World Champions for another 19 days. I was walking my dogs in a light evening rain when I realized I was neither angry nor frustrated that Boston's season was over. Watching your team lose a postseason series is never *fun*, of course, but I wasn't upset, which was surprising and a bit mysterious. But I wouldn't truly grasp the power of 2004's ripple effect for another two years.

During the 2003 and 2004 seasons, I was a much different person. My Red Sox fandom (which began in 1976 in northern Vermont) was at its peak, as was the rivalry between the Red Sox and New York Yankees. The various machinations of both clubs during the winter between those two seasons made the 20 months from March 2003 to October 2004 feel like one continuous season. In that time, the Red Sox and Yankees met an astounding 57 times. I watched or listened to almost every game, pored over print and online media, and participated in discussions at several message boards, where every bit of news, every managerial decision, was analyzed as if the fate of the season hung in the balance. Because maybe it did.

The outcome of each game felt crucial. If the Red Sox lost a game they should have won, I'd be furious afterward, as if personally wronged, sometimes even waking up the next morning still fuming. When my partner questioned why a loss in May or June should cause such an intense reaction, I would explain: If the Red Sox end up missing the postseason by one game, *that* might have been the game.

I desperately wanted to see my team win a World Series championship. I wasn't greedy. Just one in my lifetime would be enough. Boston often had a mediocre or bad club, so when the Red Sox did have a chance at contending for a title, I wanted them to be in the best position to win every day. If a single game could be the difference between making the postseason or not, then to my mind, the outcome of the season was in jeopardy every single day.

During the 2003 and 2004 seasons, the Red Sox excelled at putting their fans through a dizzying gauntlet of emotions: relentless intensity, unbridled joy, crushing sadness, furious anger, lingering doubts, and suspensions of disbelief, both positive and negative. When things were not going well, there was the nagging question of why I was devoting so much time and emotion to something over which I had no control. But it was extremely important to me, whenever the Red Sox finally won a championship, to know I had followed that team as closely as I could and been involved from the first day of spring training. In the late '90s, while working on a book about the 1918 Red Sox, I knew that if the Red Sox won the World Series before my book came out, absolutely no one would give a damn about 1918. In a bizarre twist, I feared my team would *break my heart by winning*. Thankfully, that did not happen, and the book was published in 2001. Now, since I had no idea when this magical season would arrive, what choice did I have? Obsession was the only option. In 2003, despite living in New York City, I had access to every Red Sox game for the first time in my life, thanks to MLB.TV.

The ending of the 2003 ALCS was soul-crushing. The next day, I began a post on my blog (The Joy of Sox): "Numb. Shell-shocked, angry, disbelieving, and impotent." (Fun Fact: Game 7 was played on my 40th birthday!) Sometimes it's a blessing the body is unable to fully recall the pains of the past. But this is important context—along with the prior seasons of heartbreak; the older you are, the more you've experienced—for what happened the following year.

When the 2004 Red Sox began spring training, expectations were extremely high. The team hired a new manager (who, unlike his predecessor, was a sentient being) and acquired two key pitchers. If you were too young to experience the 2004 season as it unfolded, you should know that for more than half of the season—14 weeks, from May 1 to August 6—the Red Sox were a .500 team. After winning 15 of their first 21 games, they went 43–43. By that first week in August, I was sure this was the most frustrating Red Sox team I had ever seen. But then, on August 16, everything suddenly clicked. The Red Sox became virtually unbeatable, winning 16 of their next 17 games and going 40–15 for the rest of the regular season, showing everyone—especially their long-suffering fans—exactly what they could do.

"GO YANKS!" was plastered on the front page of the *Boston Herald* on the morning of October 8. "We Want To Kick Your Butts On Our Way To The Series!" At the time, the Red Sox hadn't yet won the ALDS (though they did later that day). The Yankees, then tied 1–1 with the Twins, also obliged by winning their next two games.

This was what we had wanted all year long: an ALCS rematch with the Yankees. But everything fell apart. The Yankees won the first three games, including a 19–8 rout in Game 3. Every sportswriter in the country had already ushered the mighty Yankees into yet another World Series. While Kevin Millar ran around before Game 4 warning, "Don't let us win tonight," my only thought was, *Just don't get swept. Please.*

The investment disclaimers warn that past performance is not indicative of future results. The Red Sox won Game 4. The Red Sox won Game 5. The Red Sox won Game 6. The Red Sox won Game 7. Boston played and won those four games within a span of only 72 hours. And so the Red Sox were in the World Series for the first time since 1986. They swept the Cardinals in four straight games. What I imagined the Red Sox winning it all would look and feel like bore no resemblance to what actually happened. I saw it coming days ahead of time, and so I was well-prepared, but no less happy. (When Doug Mirabelli walked into Yankee Stadium's visitors' clubhouse in April 2005 for Opening Day, he said, "It still smells like champagne in here." I suspect that's the real reason they tore that stadium down.)

Even after 20 years, a feeling of unreality surrounds the 2004 postseason. *Did that really happen?* I don't expect that feeling will ever go away. But why? I don't feel that way about 2007, 2013, or 2018. What makes 2004 so different? Here are two possible reasons. It was the first championship Red Sox fans had experienced after many near-misses. This was the one we thought we might never see. There's also the unprecedented comeback, winning four do-or-die games against the Yankees, pushing the Yankees to collapse in a way that was far worse than anything any Red Sox team had ever done. We can watch the DVDs over and over, but we're still pinching ourselves: *How did that happen?*

After eight straight seasons of finishing in second place, the Red Sox dropped to third in 2006, but rebounded in 2007 and won the AL East for the first time in 12 years. In September, when Boston's division lead shrunk from seven games to 1½ games (due in part to a three-game sweep by the Blue Jays in Toronto, every annoying pitch of which I witnessed in person), I was unperturbed. That's when I realized the rewiring of my brain wasn't a lingering effect of 2004. It was permanent. Panic seemed unwarranted; winning felt inevitable. The Red Sox sprinted through the ALDS and beat Cleveland in the first game of the ALCS—and then lost the next three games. It didn't matter. There was no cause for alarm.

In the early 1990s, I was living in the Washington Heights neighborhood of New York City, reading newspaper articles about a high school phenom named Manny Ramirez, who was drafted, spent time in the minors, and was called up by Cleveland in September 1993. His second major league game was at Yankee Stadium, and he had a lot of friends and family in the stands. Manny hit two home runs and a double, his first three major league hits. After the 2000 season, when Ramirez signed with the Red Sox, I was beyond thrilled. The guys I had seen for years in my neighborhood wearing Cleveland caps had switched to Boston caps. In 2007, Manny hardly spoke to the media, but when the Red Sox were down 1–3 to his old team in the ALCS, he suddenly became a chatterbox. "If it doesn't happen, who cares? There's always next year. It's not like the end of the world or something…. If we go play hard and the thing doesn't come like it's supposed to come, we'll move on."

Most Red Sox fans did not appreciate hearing one of the team's stars say, "Who cares" and "It's not the end of the world." I understood that. Manny's choice of words was not ideal, but I heard his comments a little differently. Ramirez wasn't saying he didn't care if the Red Sox won or lost, he was attempting to explain his mindset. Manny knew, from years of practice, that having thoughts about previous at-bats or future games swirling around in his head was a recipe for failure. He had no control over the outcome of a game, so why worry about it? Keeping his mind free of all extraneous thoughts was an essential part of focusing only on what he could control, on *now*. Achieving that level of concentration is far more difficult than it looks.

Manny's teammates may have adopted his view of things, because the Red Sox won the next three games by a combined score of 30–5 and went on to sweep the Colorado Rockies in the World Series. Coming back from the dead had become a new Red Sox tradition. Kevin Millar said he was unimpressed. "This group had it easy. They had already won a game. We were down 0–3."

The Tampa Bay Rays won the AL East in 2008, with the Red Sox finishing two games behind. The two teams met in the ALCS, and the Red Sox found themselves in a familiar spot—trailing 1–3. However, from where I sat, the Rays, who had won the last two games by a combined score of 22–5, were three games away from elimination, just as Cleveland was the year before. As we have all learned, past performance is absolutely indicative of future results.

It was getting late in Game 5 at Fenway Park. Tampa Bay led 7–0 in the seventh inning. At that point, the Rays' win expectancy was 99.4 percent. However, the Red Sox, in front of their increasingly bonkers fans, rallied for eight runs—the greatest comeback by any team facing postseason elimination and the second biggest comeback in postseason history—sending the ALCS back to Florida. Winning Game 6 was almost too easy. The Red Sox's

4–2 win was their ninth consecutive victory in an ALCS elimination game. But they would not win a 10th. Although Boston had a lead after only six pitches in Game 7, the Rays prevailed 3–1.

The 2010s was a strange decade for the Red Sox. They had an ugly collapse in 2011 and missed the postseason by going 7–20 in September, which led to the firing of manager Terry Francona. For the next seven seasons, the Red Sox either won the division or landed in the basement. From 2012 to 2018, it was first or fifth—and during that time, the Red Sox captured two more World Series titles.

No major league team finishing a season with a winning percentage as low as .426 had ever won the World Series the following year—until the 2013 Red Sox. From a 69–93 record in 2012, the franchise's worst in nearly half a century, Boston won 97 games with many players growing enormous beards, each of which came with its own nickname—e.g., The Siesta, The Ironsides, The Wolf. Back in 2009, I thought David Ortiz had reached the end of his career. I did not mind being completely wrong. Big Papi's grand slam against the Tigers turned the ALCS around, and in six World Series games, Ortiz made only five outs—and on one of them, he was robbed of another bases-loaded home run. His teammates began calling him "Cooperstown."

The 2018 season was nonstop fun. The Red Sox were relentless, winning 17 of their first 19 games, eventually setting a franchise record with 108 wins. They never lost more than three games in a row. In the postseason, the Red Sox shoved the Yankees aside while sticking them with the most lopsided postseason loss in their history (16–1), bulldozed the Astros, and dominated the Dodgers. Boston's one loss in the World Series (Game 3) set numerous records, including the longest World Series game by innings (18) and the longest postseason game by time (7:20; only two regular season games have lasted longer). In fact, when I looked at the box score for the first time in several years, I initially thought the time of the game must be a typo. The Dodgers' Game 3 win took 15 minutes longer to play than the entire 1939 World Series!

Don't Let Us Win Tonight exists because I wanted to know everything about the Red Sox's 2004 postseason. When Bill told me he had scheduled an interview with Orlando Cabrera, I said there was one question he *had* to ask. In ALCS Game 6, during the delay after Alex Rodriguez slapped the ball out of Bronson Arroyo's glove, a few Red Sox players were standing on the infield dirt. Cabrera looked toward third base and flashed seven fingers, then he mimed crying. He was likely telling someone, *We're gonna be playing Game 7*, but the Red Sox dugout was on that side of the field. And what about the crying? This was my only chance to learn the whole story after wondering for nine years. I explained all of this and emailed Bill two screenshots from the broadcast. A few days later, he reported back, "Cabrera remembered everything without even seeing the pictures." You'll find the answers nowhere else but in this book.

Bill spends a lot of time at Fenway Park and during this project he happened to chat with the distributor who brought the 10 cases of champagne the Yankees expected to spray around the locker room after winning Game 4 (or Game 5). The story of what happened to those bottles is one of my favorite parts of this book.

While thinking about this anniversary edition of *Don't Let Us Win Tonight* and what effect the 2004 Red Sox had on me, I wondered if that season was the dawning of a golden age for Red Sox fans. Four World Series championships *(four!)* in a span of 15 seasons is remarkable for any team, but could an authentic golden age include three last-place finishes and a span of six years in which the team made the postseason only once? That's a decision best left up to each fan. I'm far more confident in stating that there has been no greater time to be a Red Sox fan than the past 20 years. Who among us could possibly say otherwise?

Allan Wood

EVERY RED SOX FAN who lived through the 2003–04 stretch and a good number of years before and after had a different experience—and yet we also share so much.

I'd been through a lot by 2003. I was out of state with relatives for Game 7. Inured to Red Sox disappointments, I had to shrug off yet another lost season. After all, I'd been at Fenway in 1978 when the Yankees crushed the Red Sox in a tiebreaker for the pennant despite having been shut out for the first six innings. It wasn't like losing to the Yankees was anything new. It was an all-too-familiar state of affairs. It was the way life was for Red Sox fans.

Sure, we rooted for the Red Sox, but since well before I was born, they seemed doomed to lose—and more often to the Yankees than to any other team. Should you have forgotten it for a moment, a Yankees fan would probably have reminded you. All they needed was four syllables in a little singsong chant: "19-18." That was the last time the Red Sox had won a World Series.

I grew up in Lexington, Massachusetts, where the first battle of the American Revolution took place, and I was a guide on the Battle Green all through high school and college. I had a deep interest in history, so I knew that Boston had won the very first World Series and a total of five times in the first 18 years of the new American League. One might deem it the first dynasty in A.L. history.

After 1918, there followed decades and decades of disappointment. Fifty-nine games out of first place in 1927. Sixty-four games out of first in 1932. There was a whole decade (1924 through 1933) in which the Red Sox averaged a full 40 games behind the first-place winners. None of us had to suffer those 10 years.

One might argue that we suffered worse—from time to time, we harbored hope. Only for that hope to be dashed, time after time.

OK, they had been the first dynasty, but what good did that do me? The Yankees won it *five times in a row* when I was a kid (1949, 1950, 1951, 1952, and 1953). Born in 1945, I can't say I was aware of any of those. But I was certainly aware of Yankees World Series wins in 1956 and 1958, 1961 and 1962, 1977 and 1978, 1996, and then three in a row in 1998, 1999, and 2000.

The Red Sox had won pennants in 1967, 1975, and 1986 and valiantly took each World Series to a final Game 7. But then they lost. Each time. There had been magical moments. I'll forever be glad I saw Carlton Fisk's home run in Game 6 in 1975; I had to shrug off the next night's experience. They lost again, just as they had lost the pennant on the final day of 1948 and the final day of 1949. They had lost as well in 1972—eliminated on the next-to-last day of the season.[1] And the tiebreaker in 1978.

When Dan Shaughnessy wrote *The Curse of the Bambino* (1990), the notion that the Sox were cursed resonated with just about every baseball fan in New England (and many who had fled). There had to be some reason the Red Sox lost, and lost, and lost, teased their fans, and then lost again. Right?

It's different to finish in third place, or fourth, or last. But to see your team take it to the final World Series game three times, and lose each time, it can deaden the spirit. No doubt some Sox fans jumped ship at different points along the way.

After 1986? The 1988 Red Sox made the playoffs but got swept.

In 1990? The Red Sox made the playoffs but got swept.

In 1995? The Red Sox made the playoffs but got swept.

In 1998? The Red Sox made the playoffs and won the first game handily, beating Cleveland 11–3. But then lost the next three games and went home for the winter.

In 1999? The Red Sox won the first round, this time beating Cleveland in the division series. After two one-run losses to the Yankees, they beat them in Game 3 13–1...then lost the next two.

Does anyone detect a pattern here?

It builds character, those of us who remained steadfast counseled each other. Counsel and consolation are different matters. I'm not sure it made us feel much better. But it gave us some shred of something or other to hold onto.

We knew that Chicago fans had been waiting even longer—the Cubs since 1908 and the White Sox since 1917. But they didn't have the same tantalizing torturous history. The Cubs lost Game 7 of the 1945 World Series. Remember that? I didn't think so. Come the year 2001, there were

---

[1] This was the year in which they played one fewer game than the triumphant Tigers. One more win might have made all the difference. There had been a players strike earlier that year, though, and a late start and it seemed as though fate conspired against them.

rather few Cubs fans bearing emotional scars from 1945. The Cubs didn't even get to the World Series again until 2016.[2]

As we transitioned to the 21st century, the years the Yankees *didn't* win a World Series in which they took part were notable ones—1997 and 2001. But who won those series? The Florida Marlins in 1997 and the Arizona Diamondbacks in 2001. The Marlins had played their first season in 1993 and their fans had to watch in agony as they progressed ever so slowly up the ladder—finishing sixth, fifth the next year, fourth in 1995, and third in 1997. Think of it—Marlins fans had gone *five full seasons* without winning a world championship! A freshly minted 13-year-old Marlins fan in 1993 might have finished high school before seeing their team win it all.

Diamondbacks fans didn't have to wait quite that long. They launched in 1998 and placed last that first year. They finished first in 1999 but were knocked out in the NLCS. In 2000, they plunged to third place. After putting in *three entire seasons* of rooting—the anguish!—D-backs fans were finally rewarded with a World Series championship in 2001.

They both won, and in 2003 the Marlins won yet another championship, this time beating the Yankees to do so. Viewed through a 2003–04 Red Sox lens, it's of note that the 2003 Marlins didn't even have to go to a Game 7; they took the Yankees in six.

And it's safe to say that most Red Sox fans likely rooted for them to do so. The rivalry with the Yankees runs so deep, and with sufficient bitterness, that rather few Sox fans were rooting for the American League team to prevail in 2003. Enough about those teams.

Red Sox fans had cowboyed-up in 2003 and enjoyed a nice run. The team hadn't been in first place since June 11, but they hung in there. They had taken on Oakland in the division series and won it in the fifth and final game. That gave Red Sox fans of a certain age some feeling of satisfaction, knowing how the Athletics had swept the Red Sox in 1988 and swept the

---

2 In 1984 and 2003 the Cubs got to the final game of the NLCS but lost both times. Most Red Sox fans saw Cubs fans as kindred spirits, though they hadn't suffered nearly so many agonizing last-minute defeats.

Red Sox again in 1990, winning eight postseason games in succession from Boston.

But then the 2003 Red Sox were head-to-head with the Yankees—for just the second time since that 1978 playoff. There was still some scarring from 1999 when the Yankees took four of five from the Red Sox in that year's ALCS.

There was hope. What was the point of being a fan if you didn't have hope? And the Red Sox won Game 1 of the 2003 ALCS. And then Game 4. And Game 6. All they needed was to win Game 7 and they would have been back in the World Series.

But there was also realism. And, as stated, losing to the Yankees wasn't anything new.

Then we came to 2004. A rematch—the same two teams head-to-head again in the ALCS. Anything was possible—in theory, at least. But the Yankees won the first game 10 7 and it looked like Boston's ace, Curt Schilling, was hurt and out for the duration. And the Yankees won the second game 3–1 with fellow Sox ace Pedro Martinez pitching well, but unable to hold back the New Yorkers. With the next three games to be played in friendly Fenway, yes, there was hope the Sox could win a couple and get back in it. But they were clobbered—obliterated, crushed, beaten to a pulp—call it whatever you want. They lost 19–8. It was as demoralizing a defeat as one could dream up. Or "nightmare up," if you were a Red Sox fan.

Some of us who were at Game 3 left early. Some of us who had tickets for Game 4 simply sold them off. We didn't want to have to see it happen—see the Red Sox swept by the Yankees. There was nothing but doom and gloom—except in the hearts of Red Sox players like Kevin Millar, who uttered his famous words: "Don't let us win tonight."

Well, they did win. And then won again, and won Game 6 and won Game 7. This brought the St. Louis Cardinals to Fenway Park for the World Series. It was the Cardinals who had beaten the Red Sox in the 1946 World Series and it was the Cardinals who had beaten the Red Sox in the 1967 World Series, each time taking it to Game 7 and each time taking the trophy, while Red Sox fans bore more postseason defeats.

They build character, though.

So, what happened to Red Sox fans when the Red Sox finally did win it all in 2004—so improbably beating their rivals, the Yankees, and then actually sweeping the Cardinals? What happened to all that character that had been built?

First of all, for anyone who had lived through the years from 1967 onward, it didn't seem real. It just didn't seem real. Over the next three or four mornings when I woke up, I truly had to convince myself that it really had happened. I was 59 years old, and the Red Sox really had won the World Series.

We'd been accustomed to losing. It was, in a way, "our thing." How could we handle winning? It turned out to be pretty easy. Some sent messages to Cubs fans, letting them know that most BoSox fans hoped they could come to enjoy what we had just experienced. Most did hold back from taunting Yankees fans. After all, Yankees fans did have a slight 16–1 edge should one tabulate World Series wins from the end of World War II through 2004.

But it was nice just to relax a bit and savor the moment.

As it happens, the Red Sox won another World Series just three years later—in 2007. After that one, some of us felt compelled to warn, "Don't crow. Bear the wins proudly but graciously, with the sort of humility that one might suggest by looking at the long run." Winning twice in 89 years was, well, nice but...

Then the Red Sox did it again in 2013 and 2018. Oddly, the wins came during a stretch when they sometimes finished in last place, as they had in both the year before and after the 2013 win—worst to first, then worst again.

With the 2018 win, were Red Sox fans satiated? Perhaps to a degree. Imagine being just a bit older than that 13-year-old Marlins fans imagined above—born in, say, 1991. You got to see the Red Sox on top of the world at age 13, age 17, age 22, and age 27. How does that warp one's perspective? What happens to one without "character" being built? Might one develop a sense of entitlement? Might one grow up something like a—gasp—Yankees fan of days gone by?

Here we are with the 20th anniversary of the 2004 Red Sox season on the horizon and the Red Sox have won more world championships than any other team in the current century. Yankees fans can sigh, "Well, we'll always have 2009."

What happens next?

It's hard not to have it cross one's mind as we look ahead to the 2024 season that the Red Sox haven't won since 2018. Five full years without a championship! But the number 18 leaps out.

In the first 18 years of the 20th century, the team had won four World Series (their predecessor 1903 Boston Americans had won the first World Series). In the first 18 years of the 21st century, the Red Sox have won four World Series. Will we ever see another one? Will there be an 86-year wait until the next one?

It is our hope that not one reader of this book will have to wonder about the answer to that question for very long.

It was our pleasure to interview more than 30 players and coaches from the 2004 Red Sox as well as a number of executives and staff and others who contributed to that very special championship season.

The 2004 season is a gift that keeps on giving. No baseball team ever did what that team did—coming back from a three-games-to-none hole in a championship series and coming out on top.

That team refused to give up. Neither curses nor the accumulated weight of 86 years nor the crushing 19 runs scored against them in Game 3—nothing could hold them back. It was, and remains, inspiring.

It might not be too much of a stretch to say that when we prepared the first edition of *Don't Let Us Win Tonight*, the Boston Red Sox's victory in the 2004 World Series was still reasonably top of mind. And though nearly a decade had passed, it was perhaps even still a bit unreal.

As we wrote in the introduction to the first edition of this book, any screenwriter who had pitched a script that had the 2004 season unfold as it did might well have been laughed out of Hollywood. It took us a long time to process—yes, that really did happen!

Some fans declared, "Now I can die in peace." But it didn't stop there. Indeed, in the first two decades of the 21st century, the Red Sox have gone on to considerable success. They did win the World Series again in 2007, in 2013, and yet again in 2018.

It felt very good when the 2021 Red Sox beat the Yankees in the wild card game that year—an exorcism of sorts for those of us who were at that 1978 game.

But for those of us who suffered through decades of losing, there's a lingering worry. A cloud of consciousness that has perhaps never entirely dissipated. The first two decades of the 20th century were great for Red Sox fans; they ended in an "18" year. Does this portend another drought?

Perhaps the spirit of the 2004 Red Sox will prevail.

Bill Nowlin

Foreword

By Kevin Millar

"Don't let us win tonight!"

It was the morning of Game 4. We got beat really bad in Game 3, 19–8. We're down 0–3, we're down to the mighty Yankees. You can't win four in a row against the mighty Yankees. Here we are in this postseason battle, and that morning Dan Shaughnessy wrote an article that really offended me. He called us "a pack of frauds." Now I don't get offended that often, but I'm sitting there that morning, I was in a good mood, we got another baseball game—and I'm thinking *Frauds?* No one in that clubhouse was a fraud. Are you going to look at Bill Mueller and think of him as a fraud? Or Trot Nixon, or Johnny Damon, or Jason Varitek, or Pedro Martinez? That's a big word to use. And I was pissed off and thinking, *All right, that's it.*

I got to the clubhouse early. I was fired up, having fun, making sure the boys aren't hanging their heads and feeling sorry for themselves. We're down 0–3, but nothing has changed. The music was still going. And then Shaughnessy walked in, and that's when it started. I was yelling at him, calling him out because he was in our space. That led to the scene that everyone knows about—out on the field before the game. MLB had me wired during batting practice. And I told him, "Don't let us win tonight." If the Yankees are going to win this series, it better be tonight. Because if we win, then Pedro Martinez is pitching Game 5, Curt Schilling is coming back in Game 6, and in Game 7, anything can happen.

I was saying that to everyone. My plan was to get my teammates to drink the Kool-Aid. Because this wasn't crazy-ass Millar talking shit anymore. I wanted them to really believe it. If we could get by as a group, find a way to win that game, trust me, we had a big-time shot. But there has to be some foundation when you're saying something that crazy, right? It's like when you go into the manager's office to argue why you're not in the lineup, you need a good reason why you should be playing. He's going to say you're not in the lineup because of X—and you better have something else.

My thing was don't let us win tonight and if the guy says, "What do you mean?" Well, let me tell you why. Pedro Martinez and Curt Schilling in Games 5 and 6—are you going to take it? That was my reasoning. That was the method to my madness, just yelling that all day long, "Don't let us win tonight." And I wasn't just saying it to say it. I truly believed it. There's nothing fake about me other than my highlights.

There was never any panic because at that point, we had nothing to lose.

The 2004 Boston Red Sox were a talented ballclub, but we were also scrappy. And we were relentless. We were a bunch of guys that cared. In this generation, it's hard to find a team that cares about each other, and this group of guys cared about each other. This group of guys played the game with the fear of losing their jobs. It was refreshing, because in this generation we don't have that. There's so much money that goes in and out of hands, and so many guaranteed contracts, but this team, they played with a fear, almost like their hair was on fire.... Even though some of us didn't have hair.

The rivalry with the Yankees was fun, but we respected them. We also knew they kind of wanted to be us, if that makes sense. We had facial hair, we were able to be who we were on the field, we didn't have to wear the same pullover. We were the kind of team that you looked over at and thought, *Man, how fun would it be to play with them?* And we showed that you could win a championship being who you are.

That team had so many different personalities. Trot Nixon was our Sunday Bible studies guy, but you get him on the field and he'd eat your lunch. Pedro Martinez to Manny Ramirez to Mike Timlin. Bottom line, you have to tip your hat to Theo Epstein. Back in 2003, he went out and got a bunch of players that no one really wanted: myself, David Ortiz, and Bill Mueller. And then he brought in some other guys in 2004. Mark Bellhorn—who the hell was that? And then we make the Nomar Garciaparra trade and you bring in Orlando Cabrera. Papi turns into Papi, Cabrera turns into the energy of the club halfway through the season, Bellhorn hits two of the biggest home runs the organization has ever seen. And Mueller wins a batting title! Everything Theo touched turned to gold.

There is something unique about Boston. When you take the field every day in Fenway—you can't describe it until you're part of it. When you're a visiting player and you travel to Fenway, you're looking forward to that trip. There are certain cities that are awesome to play for, and Boston is one of them. It's not for somebody soft, but if you play the game hard and play the game right, you're loved. We broke through that miserable black cloud and now we're folk heroes and we've got 3.7 million at the parade.

Once I was part of Boston, it was like home. With Red Sox Nation, once you're in, you can't get out. I've always embraced it, and they are always going to be part of my life, no matter what. Hell, I came back in 2007 while still playing for the Orioles and threw out the first pitch of a playoff game! That was one of the quirky things that makes it so much fun. I joke around with Tom Werner and John Henry and Larry Lucchino like I'm the fourth owner. I just don't have the finances they do.

I have a great piece of my heart with all of the teams I played with, but the Red Sox is who I am.

Acknowledgments

AUTHORS WOULD LIKE TO THANK the following Red Sox players for granting interviews: Terry Adams, Mark Bellhorn, Ellis Burks, Orlando Cabrera, Alan Embree, Keith Foulke, Adam Hyzdu, Gabe Kapler, Curtis Leskanic, Derek Lowe, Dave McCarty, Ramiro Mendoza, Doug Mientkiewicz, Kevin Millar, Doug Mirabelli, Bill Mueller, Mike Myers, Trot Nixon, David Ortiz, Pokey Reese, Dave Roberts, Curt Schilling, Mike Timlin, Jason Varitek, Tim Wakefield, and Kevin Youkilis.

Thanks for interviews are also extended to Marilyn Bellhorn, Uri Berenguer, Billy Broadbent, Galen Carr, Joe Castiglione, Tom Catlin, Ben Cherington, Joe Cochrane, Gary Cormier, Chris Correnti, Chris Cundiff, Walt Day, Skip Dervishian, Christian Elias, Theo Epstein, Stan Grossfeld, Ron Jackson, Bill James, Dave Jauss, Lynn Jones, Dana LeVangie, Randy Marsh, Tom McLaughlin, Gary McNally, Dave Mellor, Brad Mills, William Morgan, Brian O'Halloran, Euky Rojas, Jim Rowe, Bob Tewksbury, Tom Tippett, and Tom Werner.

Thank you to Dick Bresciani, John Carter, Kevin Gregg, Pam Kenn, Jon Shestakofsky, and Leah Tobin of the Boston Red Sox. Thanks, as well, to Terry W. Adams Sr., Louis Barricelli, Joe Bick, Frank Bokoff, Greg Bouris, Peter M. Collery, Katie Cabrera, Peter Case, Paula Dawson (Auburn University), Jim Dumm (Tara Hall), Vince Gennaro, David Holtzman, Tom Hufford, Joe Jareck, Jeff Lantz, Rachel Levitsky (MLBPAA), Cynthia Mendoza, Nick

Moulter, Jim Prime, Jean Rhodes, Bob Schwartz (Boston Duck Tours), Chaz Scoggins, Jayson Stark, Richard Wang, and Jason Zillo.

Allan Wood would like to acknowledge the personal support of Laura Kaminker, and the online community of The Joy of Sox, where the water is always dirty.

Bill Nowlin would like to congratulate the 2007, 2013, and 2018 world champion Red Sox teams.

Finally, thanks to Tom Bast and Michelle Bruton at Triumph Books.

The material for this book was obtained from interviews conducted by the authors, and from newspapers, books, and magazines. In some cases, quotes were edited for readability, or reorganized and combined to present the information in a coherent manner. Our aim was to present a complete overview of the 2004 postseason in the words of the players and others who were there. In every case, we remained faithful to the individual's own language and recollections, although it was sometimes necessary to make superficial alterations for stylistic reasons.

Introduction

IT WAS LATE AFTERNOON AT FENWAY PARK on Sunday, October 17, 2004, and the city of Boston was in shock. The hometown Red Sox trailed the New York Yankees in the American League Championship Series, three games to none.

The previous autumn, the Red Sox had lost the ALCS to the Yankees in seven grueling games, a devastating defeat that had crushed the spirits of Red Sox fans around the world. Now, exactly one year later, the team was on the brink of being swept by its bitter rival. No baseball team had ever battled back from 0–3 to tie a seven-game series, let alone win one.

The sports media in both cities had written off the Red Sox as a bunch of frauds, unable to muster even a perfunctory fight against the mighty Yankees. The 2004 Red Sox's dismal performance was yet another in the long line of late-season collapses for the chronically underachieving franchise. Boston—as almost everyone knew, baseball fans or not—hadn't won a World Series since 1918. Red Sox fans were weary of the media-driven idea that a "curse" haunted the team.

Yet in the Red Sox clubhouse, the players were loose and loud, seemingly unconcerned. The night before, they had been humiliated 19–8—and were now just one loss away from a long, cold winter—yet the atmosphere was no different than it had been during a stretch in late August when they won 20-of-22 games. Music was blaring, players laughed, joked, and milled about, convinced everything would be all right.

First baseman Kevin Millar insisted to anyone who would listen—sportswriters, teammates, early arrivals at Fenway Park who gathered behind the Red Sox dugout—that if the team could win Game 4, the Yankees were in trouble.

"Don't let us win tonight! Don't let the Sox win this game!"

Other teammates said to focus on this one game. The Sox didn't have to win four games. They only had to win that evening's game…and worry about tomorrow, tomorrow.

At 8:18 PM, the Red Sox took the field with Derek Lowe as the starting pitcher. Less than two weeks before, Lowe had been demoted from the starting rotation and sent to the bullpen. Now it was up to him to save the Red Sox's season and extend this playoff series one more day.

What happened next was gut-wrenching, nerve-wracking, euphoric, heroic, and unprecedented. Over the next 76 hours, the Boston Red Sox won four consecutive must-win games—two marathons in Boston and two games on enemy turf in the Bronx—and became the first team in major league history to win a seven-game series after losing the first three games. And they had done it against their longtime rivals, the team that always seemed to come out on top when everything was on the line. Then the Red Sox kept winning, sweeping the St. Louis Cardinals in the World Series, and winning their first title in 86 years. Any screenwriter pitching such a scenario as fiction would have been laughed out of Hollywood.

The final out at Busch Stadium set off hundreds of celebrations in New England and throughout Red Sox Nation. Champagne sales in New England no doubt soared during the last week of October. In the weeks following the championship, people paid visits to gravesites, leaving caps and notes on the headstones of relatives and friends who had lived and died without seeing a championship.

This is that story, in the words of the Red Sox players themselves. We interviewed nearly everyone on the Red Sox 2004 postseason roster. We talked to coaches, scouts, umpires, and even Duck boat drivers who were a part of the party that followed the 2004 World Series championship. We also gathered voices from familiar—and not so familiar—media. *Don't Let Us Win Tonight* offers the best perspective on what really went on during those magical three weeks in October, 20 years ago.

1

Setting the Stage

ANY ACCOUNT OF THE 2004 RED SOX must begin on the night of October 16, 2003, when the New York Yankees capitalized on one of the most egregious managerial blunders in baseball history.

The Red Sox had come into Yankee Stadium needing two wins to capture their first American League pennant since 1986. They rallied in the late innings to win Game 6, setting the stage for a winner-take-all Game 7 with a matchup of Pedro Martinez versus Roger Clemens, a former Boston pitching star now toiling for the enemy. Martinez had the upper hand that day, pitching seven innings and walking off the mound with his team ahead 4–2. Pedro's teammates congratulated him with hugs and high-fives, and pitching coach Dave Wallace told his ace he was done for the night. The Red Sox added an insurance run in the top of the eighth—and fans prepared to watch the Boston bullpen, utterly dominant in the playoffs, nail down the final six outs.

Everyone was stunned when Pedro returned to the mound. Even as Martinez was mentally coming out of the game, manager Grady Little asked him for an additional inning. That decision cost Little his job. It's never been fully explained why Little went against the clear instructions of Boston's baseball operations people about Martinez's use, or why he ignored the lights-out performances of his bullpen. Readily available statistics showed that once Martinez passed 100 pitches, he was much more vulnerable. Little had been reminded before the game not to push Pedro past that limit. Through seven innings, Martinez had thrown exactly 100 pitches.

The Yankees promptly scored three runs off the fatigued Martinez to tie the game and won the pennant on Aaron Boone's 11th-inning home run. The Red Sox seemed to have had victory in their hands, but now their season was over.

It was a crushing blow to everyone affiliated with the team. Red Sox Chairman Tom Werner said he was "devastated" and "comatose" for a couple of months. Principal owner John Henry spoke for millions of Red Sox fans when he said he had no interest in watching the Yankees and Florida Marlins in the World Series.[1]

> **JOHN HENRY,** *principal owner*:
> I thought New Englanders would just finally throw up their hands. But their level of commitment and resolve is astonishing and deserves our full attention. ... It shows you how little I know about the toughness of this region. And it shows me how tough I need to be in making sure we accomplish our goals.[2]

Boone's shot both ended the Red Sox's 2003 season and signaled the beginning of the 2004 campaign.

Building a Winning Team

When John Henry and his group of investors (which included Tom Werner and Larry Lucchino) purchased the Red Sox in the spring of 2002, the team was under new ownership for the first time in nearly 70 years. Tom Yawkey had purchased the club back in 1933, and for nearly seven decades, either Tom, or his wife, Jean, or the Yawkey Family Trust had run the team. The Red Sox had gotten to Game 7 of the World Series four times—1946, 1967, 1975, and 1986—but had come up short each time. Those years and many other near-misses, such as 1948, 1949, 1972, 1978, and 1999, were burned into the consciousness of diehard Red Sox fans, whether or not they were old enough to have actually experienced them. The number of times the team had fallen short seemed improbable and led many fans to see the Red Sox as perennial also-rans—especially when compared to the Yankees.

The Henry-Werner-Lucchino trio may have been initially considered outsiders in New England, but each had a deep baseball background. They said all the right things about being humble stewards of the Red Sox franchise, showing a reverence for a team that was steeped in tradition.

After the 2002 season—a summer of transition between the old regime and the new group—the trio brought in a new general manager, Theo Epstein, who at age 28 was the youngest GM in the history of the game. His baseball operations group used sabermetrics and their own progressive analysis to identify undervalued players in the market. To those ends, they hired baseball iconoclast Bill James as senior baseball operations advisor. Henry applied the same fact-based theories to baseball that he had used in his investment businesses.

JOHN HENRY:
All investment decisions should be based on what can be measured rather than what might be predicted or felt. People in both baseball and financial markets operate with beliefs and biases. To the extent you can eliminate both and replace them with data, you gain a clear advantage.[3]

The leadership group was new, but many of the pieces needed to contend in 2004 had been put in place by Dan Duquette, the previous general manager. Duquette traded for Pedro Martinez in 1997 and signed him to a long-term contract. He brought in free agents as disparate as Tim Wakefield and Manny Ramirez and traded for Derek Lowe and Jason Varitek. Only weeks before he was cut loose, Duquette signed free-agent outfielder Johnny Damon. And under Duquette's supervision, the Red Sox farm system produced fan-favorites Nomar Garciaparra and Trot Nixon.

Epstein added several other key pieces to those building blocks, bringing in such undervalued players as David Ortiz, Bill Mueller, and Mike Timlin and jostling Kevin Millar loose from an agreement with the Chunichi Dragons of Japan's Central League. Epstein correctly guessed that besides being productive players, they could withstand—and actually thrive in—the harsh glare of the Boston media and the sky-high expectations of the fan base.

Ortiz, Millar, and Mueller succeeded in Boston beyond all expectations. Once he received regular playing time, Ortiz became a slugging revelation, electrifying Fenway with his big bat and infectious smile and humor. Mueller hit .326, edging out teammate Manny Ramirez (.325) for the American League batting title. And Millar cemented his reputation as a fun-loving, locker-room cutup who rallied the team with the command to "Cowboy Up." The 2003 Red Sox scored 961 runs, 54 more runs than any other major league team. Boston also led all teams in hits, doubles, batting average, on-base percentage, and slugging percentage. In fact, they posted the highest team slugging percentage of all time—.491—topping the .488 mark set by the legendary 1927 Yankees.

Winter Moves

Although there were no games on the schedule, Boston's rivalry with the Yankees raged on through the winter. During the 2003–04 off-season, Epstein made a flurry of moves resulting in three notable additions—and there was one monumental trade that was not completed.

First, there was the matter of getting a new manager. On October 27, two days after the Florida Marlins defeated the New York Yankees in the 2003 World Series, Grady Little's managerial contract was not renewed, and the Red Sox began looking for his replacement. After interviewing several candidates, including Angels bench coach Joe Maddon (who later settled in Tampa Bay), the Red Sox hired Terry "Tito" Francona, a former player who had managed a bad Phillies team for four seasons starting in 1997. In Boston, Francona was fairly unflappable, running the team with a steady hand yet still keeping things light in the clubhouse. He had a warm, easy rapport with his players and the media, a receptiveness to progressive ideas, and a desire to use the information he received.

Epstein was also in touch with teams who were looking to shed some of their more expensive contracts. The Red Sox GM began talking to Arizona Diamondbacks GM Joe Garagiola Jr. about Curt Schilling. The burly right-handed pitcher—the co-MVP of the 2001 World Series—had told the Diamondbacks that he would waive his no-trade clause if he and his new team could agree to a contract extension. Schilling wanted to go somewhere familiar and comfortable, and to a contending team. He mentioned the Yankees and the Phillies (who he had pitched for from 1992–2000), but Schilling said he would not consider the Red Sox.

CURT SCHILLING, *pitcher:*
I'm not going to Boston. I'm a right-handed fly-ball pitcher. In Fenway Park, that's not a tremendous mix.[4]

However, once he learned that Terry Francona was being considered for the manager's job in Boston, Schilling added the Red Sox to his list of possible destinations. A meeting was arranged. The Red Sox presented Schilling with an introductory letter. It stated, in part, "There is no other place in baseball where you can have as great an impact on a franchise, as great an impact on a region, as great an impact on baseball history, as you can in Boston.... The players who help deliver a title to Red Sox Nation will never be forgotten, their place in history forever secure."[5]

The letter emphasized the team's commitment "to create a lineup that would be relentless one through nine" and to create a pitching staff that was similarly relentless. "You are the key to the plan; in fact, you are the plan."[6]

There was the famous Thanksgiving dinner that Theo Epstein and Assistant GM Jed Hoyer had at the Schillings' home in Arizona, where the trade was eventually finalized. Schilling and the Red Sox agreed on a three-year contract with the provision that Schilling would receive a $2 million bonus if the Red Sox won the World Series during any of those three seasons.

CURT SCHILLING:
You come to Boston and win one, there'd be nothing like it on the planet anywhere.[7]

Schilling quickly embraced his new team and its traditions, interacting with fans online and filming a couple of commercials—one in which he practiced affecting a Boston accent and another in which he played a hitchhiker in the American Southwest. Asked where he was headed, he said, "Boston. Gotta break an 86-year-old curse."

A few weeks after trading for Schilling, the Red Sox landed one of the game's elite closers, former Oakland reliever Keith Foulke, signing him to a three-year deal in December. Foulke's 43 saves for the A's led the American

League in 2003; he also had a 2.08 ERA. Foulke already had a relationship with Francona since the new Boston manager had been Oakland's bench coach in 2003.

> **KEITH FOULKE, *pitcher*:**
> When Terry went over there, my agent told me, "Don't be surprised if the team that just beat you [in the 2003 playoffs] is going to be interested." Boston made an offer I couldn't refuse. I'm not going to lie. They made it worth my while.... Just the excitement of playing for a team with this heritage and this history is something I want to do before I retire. I would love to be a part of a championship. Bobby Orr called me and left a message. He said, "You win in this town, you're forever idolized." And that still gives me chills. He called me after I met with the Red Sox. I was too scared to call him back.[8]

> **THEO EPSTEIN, *general manager*:**
> We went after Keith so hard because...he's one of the best pitchers in baseball, who happens to be a closer. He impacts a game or season so much that we view him as a real weapon. He's had five outstanding seasons in a row. He's going to throw 80 outstanding innings for this club, and they're going to be the most important innings of the year for us.[9]

The Mega-Trade That Wasn't

Only two days after saying good-bye to Grady Little, the Red Sox placed left fielder Manny Ramirez, who had made periodic noises about wanting to be traded, on irrevocable waivers, meaning that any of the 29 other teams could have him as long as they assumed the remainder of his contract—five seasons and approximately $100 million. No team filed a claim. Although Ramirez was one of the best right-handed hitters in baseball, the new ownership group believed that the eight-year, $160 million contract Ramirez had signed with the old regime was too expensive.

The Red Sox had also been talking with the Texas Rangers about shortstop Alex Rodriguez, who had been voted the 2003 American League Most Valuable Player. In December 2000, Rodriguez, then only 25, signed a historic 10-year, $252 million contract with the Rangers. Texas had finished in last place during each of the three subsequent seasons, and Rodriguez wanted out. He wanted to play for a contending team.

By mid-December, it was rumored that a trade involving the two dis-
gruntled superstars was all but complete. Boston would send Ramirez to the
Rangers in exchange for Rodriguez, then ship shortstop Nomar Garciaparra
to the Chicago White Sox for outfielder Magglio Ordonez. It would be one
of the biggest trades in the history of baseball. However, the deal fell apart
because Boston wanted to restructure Rodriguez's contract. A-Rod was
willing to accept millions of dollars less to come to Boston, but the Major
League Players Association refused to give its consent, saying the Red Sox
proposal would lessen the contract's overall value.

About six weeks later, the Yankees stunned the baseball world by swoop-
ing in and completing a deal with the Rangers for Rodriguez, countering
Boston's acquisition of Schilling with a mega-trade of their own.

Headlines in Yankeeland crowed that New York had bested the Red
Sox yet again: "Summer Or Winter, The Yankees Show The Red Sox How
To Win" *(The New York Times)* and, "This Rivalry Always Has The Same
Ending" *(Newark Star-Ledger)*. The back page of the *New York Post* boasted,
"A-Rod Steal Is Bombers' Best Move Since Babe."

> **GEORGE STEINBRENNER,** *Yankees principal owner*:
> We understand that John Henry must be embarrassed, frustrated, and
> disappointed by his failure in this transaction. Unlike the Yankees, he
> chose not to go the extra distance for his fans in Boston.[10]

The Yankees also signed free agents Gary Sheffield (outfielder) and Javier
Vazquez (pitcher). Sheffield was confident the Yankees would once again
be playing in the World Series.

> **GARY SHEFFIELD,** *Yankees right fielder*:
> We're not going to lose, you can be assured of that. The Red Sox can
> say what they want, but look at us. Who's going to beat us? Nobody.[11]

The Season

The Red Sox arrived for spring training in a good frame of mind. They
had not forgotten the bitter end of the previous season, but they were
confident that they would be battling the Yankees for the pennant all
summer long.

MANNY RAMIREZ, *left fielder*:
This is the year.[12]

KEVIN MILLAR, *first baseman*:
I honestly believe that we're going to win the World Series this year. I think we still have the better lineup. I can't wait to get after them.... This is a pretty hot rivalry.... And it's going to get even bigger this year.[13]

Was that possible? Could 2004 be more exciting and tension-filled than 2003?

DEREK JETER, *Yankees shortstop*:
Unless it's just brawls every single game we play, I can't see it being any more intense than last year.[14]

Tickets to the first spring exhibition game between the two teams were being re-sold for multiple times their face value. A group of four tickets to the March 7 game—referred to jokingly as "Game 8" in some circles—was listed on eBay with a starting bid of $1,000.

TERRY FRANCONA, *manager*:
I got an idea in spring training when I saw people lining up at 6:00 AM to buy tickets. And then I got yelled at during the game for not playing all of my regulars.[15]

The Red Sox had five key players who were in the last year of their contracts: shortstop Nomar Garciaparra, catcher Jason Varitek, designated hitter David Ortiz, and pitchers Pedro Martinez and Derek Lowe. The window of opportunity to win with this particular group of players was closing.

The team that reported to Fort Myers, Florida, was nearly identical to the offensive juggernaut that had led the major leagues in runs scored by a large margin in 2003. It really only needed some fine-tuning. Bronson Arroyo, a bit player from 2003, would move into the starting rotation. Epstein also signed infielders Mark Bellhorn and Pokey Reese.

POKEY REESE, *infielder*:
I was excited to go to Boston because I always wanted to be part of a team that knocked off the Yankees. Boston was a winning organization, and I thought I had a chance to go to the playoffs—I'd never been in the playoffs—and Boston gave me that opportunity.[16]

Terry Francona had to deal with the possibly bruised egos of Ramirez and Garciaparra, who came to camp knowing their employer had tried to move them. It turned out that Ramirez arrived feeling upbeat and positive.

MANNY RAMIREZ:

I can't be mad at anybody. I'm happy to be back with the guys. What happened in the winter happened, and it's in the past.... Baseball doesn't need me. I need baseball.[17]

Johnny Damon caused a minor stir when he arrived sporting a heavy beard and shoulder-length hair.

KEVIN MILLAR:

He showed up looking like the Wolfman. We call him Jesus, and he's running around sprinkling water on people to end the curse.[18]

Throughout the season, fans calling themselves "Damon's Disciples" would show up at Fenway Park wearing long wigs and fake beards. As the season went on, other players either grew their hair or shaved their heads. No matter what happened in 2004, the Red Sox would not be dull.

The Red Sox began the season strong, winning six out of their first seven meetings against the hated Yankees and ending April at 15–6, the best record in the majors. However, that was followed by three months of malaise.

During May, June, and July, the Red Sox went 41–40, slipping back into second place behind New York. There was not one particular thing wrong with the team; every aspect of their play was inconsistent. While they often showed signs of brilliance, there were just as many nights filled with scattershot fielding, bone-headed base running, and a lack of clutch pitching and hitting.

Injuries were also a problem. Trot Nixon was plagued all season by a herniated disc and a quadriceps problem. Bill Mueller—the reigning American League batting champion—ended up missing roughly six weeks after having arthroscopic surgery on his right knee. Curt Schilling announced in early June that he would need surgery on his right ankle at the end of the season, but he hoped the ankle would not be too much of an issue.

KEVIN MILLAR:
This is what builds you, this is when you are judged and when you are tested because it's easy to come off the field when everything is going right and hunky-dory. These are good times for this team to go through now because this will make us stronger in October.[19]

In late July, on the eve of yet another series with the Yankees, right fielder Gabe Kapler addressed the matter of too many players giving away at-bats.

GABE KAPLER, *right fielder:*
We need to battle a little bit harder. We've had a couple of instances recently where we've gotten behind in a game and have become semi-lifeless, and it's important that we show a little amount of tenacity right now.[20]

After beating the Red Sox on July 23, the Yankees held a 9½-game lead in the American League East. The following day, on a soggy Saturday afternoon, the rivalry erupted, bringing back memories of the contentious 2003 ALCS.

The Fenway Park grounds were soaked from a morning thunderstorm, and it was questionable whether the game would (or should) be played. As the story goes, a group of Red Sox players marched into manager Terry Francona's office and demanded that the nationally televised game go on as scheduled, wet grass and outfield puddles be damned.

That game had it all: a benches-and-bullpen-clearing brawl, triggered when Bronson Arroyo drilled Alex Rodriguez with a pitch and Jason Varitek rammed his catcher's mitt into A-Rod's face; four Red Sox errors (including three on three consecutive plays); New York taking a quick 3–0 lead; Boston coming back 4–3 with four hits on four consecutive pitches in the fourth inning; Francona getting ejected; Boston blowing the lead and trailing 9–4; cutting the gap to 9–8; falling back 10–8; and then winning the game 11–10 on Bill Mueller's two-run home run off closer Mariano Rivera in the bottom of the ninth.

THEO EPSTEIN:
This game had more intensity than most postseason games. This win and the way it happened should prove to be very important to us. It's hard to have a more meaningful regular season victory. We've been kind of waiting to have this feeling all year.[21]

DAVID ORTIZ, *designated hitter:*

I think that's the best thing that ever happened to us. It's the start of something good.[22]

However, if the dramatic victory gave a necessary kick-start to the Red Sox's moribund season, it did not immediately show on the diamond. Boston beat New York 9–6 the following night, but the team continued playing .500 ball during the next two weeks. Nonetheless, most of the players felt that the July 24 win was a key moment in the season.

TIM WAKEFIELD, *pitcher:*

That might have lit a fire under us. It showed we weren't going to be pushed around. A lot of us were tired of being mediocre, even though we were still in the hunt.[23]

DANA LeVANGIE, *bullpen catcher:*

It was an image of our team that we all knew—but we had to show it. And other teams understood that this was what we were all about. We showed up every game, every day, to battle no matter what.[24]

During the postseason, a few reporters caught a glimpse of the screensaver on Jason Varitek's laptop; it was the image of him sticking his mitt in A-Rod's face. There's little doubt that the confrontation provided some lasting inspiration for the team.[25]

DAVID McCARTY, *first baseman:*

When a team struggles and underperforms, it's easy for cliques to form and for bad feelings to develop. Just the opposite occurred with this team. That game got everybody focused on pulling their own weight to reach that ultimate goal. Nothing else mattered.[26]

The team had fought the "25 players/25 cabs" mentality, where each player isolated himself away from the rest of the team, early in the season.

POKEY REESE:

But then we had a big team meeting. We were in Canada, and the whole team went out to a steakhouse, and we said we need to start doing more as a team. That's when things clicked. As the season went on, we came together as one. Jason Varitek. He was the leader.[27]

URI BERENGUER, *Spanish language radio announcer*:
A .500 team for four, four and a half months, isn't necessarily a bad thing. You've just got to keep your head above water. The trade was huge. I think Orlando coming over here had a lot to do with it—the chemistry and energy that he brought.[28]

On the following Saturday—the July 31 trading deadline—Theo Epstein and the Red Sox front office shocked the baseball world by trading Nomar Garciaparra, an idea that would have been unthinkable one year earlier. Garciaparra had been the face of the Red Sox franchise for nine summers, but injuries had blunted his talent, both at the plate and in the field. There were also disagreements with the front office about the size of Garciaparra's next contract.

In exchange for sending Garciaparra to the Chicago Cubs in a four-team trade completed just minutes before the deadline, the Red Sox received shortstop Orlando Cabrera from the Montreal Expos and first baseman Doug Mientkiewicz from the Minnesota Twins. In a separate deal, the Red Sox picked up outfielder Dave Roberts from the Los Angeles Dodgers.

Fans across New England were aghast. Even Paul Epstein, Theo's twin brother, reportedly phoned and said, "That's all you got for Nomar? You're getting killed. People are furious that Nomar was traded for a couple of .240 hitters."[29]

Theo Epstein felt that shoring up Boston's porous fielding, especially in the infield, was essential. The Red Sox had allowed 24 unearned runs in May—more than any team in baseball—and June was even worse with 27 unearned runs in only 25 games. Cabrera and Mientkiewicz had both won Gold Gloves.

THEO EPSTEIN:
If there was a flaw on this club, it was that the defense was not championship-caliber. We might have gotten to the postseason. But, in my mind, we weren't going to win a World Series with our defense the way it was.... I didn't want [the defense] to become a fatal flaw. We've been a .500 team for three months. I liked the club before, but I like it better now. We're a fully functional club.... We need to be able to win the tight, low-scoring games you often have in October. We need to be able to catch the ball.[30]

Expos manager Frank Robinson told Cabrera he'd been traded but wouldn't tell him to which team.

ORLANDO CABRERA, *shortstop*:
Frank calls me. "I'm going to give you five tries, and I'll bet you a paycheck that you will not guess where you got traded." I threw out a bunch of teams, and he goes, "No. Keep guessing." "Frank! If they traded for me, I gotta get going!" He goes, "No, not until you tell me which team." "I have no idea." "You got traded to Boston." I remember sitting down and I started getting mad. "How am I going to play shortstop? Nomar Garciaparra is there." He goes, "No, no. You got traded for Nomar." My heart was pumping. I was like, "What? He died?"[31]

BRAD MILLS, *bench coach*:
Cabby was always an upbeat, high-energy guy. We needed a guy like that at shortstop. He really infused a lot of that energy into the ball club. And he got some big hits for us from the right side of the plate. He plugged in really well.[32]

DAVE ROBERTS, *outfielder*:
Tito brought me into the office and said that Trot's hurt right now so you're going to play right field and once he gets back, you'll be our fourth outfielder and be used situationally. I really appreciated him being forthright.[33]

EUKY ROJAS, *bullpen coach*:
The trades had an impact. We had more speed on the team, and the manager had more choices he could make during a game.[34]

There was a period of adjustment in which Francona tried to get everyone enough playing time. Roberts and Mientkiewicz were regulars who would have to get used to being part-timers. It did not always go smoothly.

The gregarious and energetic Cabrera hit a home run in his first at-bat for the Red Sox. His infectious love for the game—and the creative handshakes he came up with for his teammates—fit right in with the team's image as goofy misfits. Cabrera even took on a leadership role in the clubhouse, taking on Manny Ramirez when the slugger wanted a random day off.

CURT SCHILLING:
One of the most vivid memories I have was the first day back in Boston. Manny was being Manny. Which can mean a lot of things. We had a game, and Manny was a late scratch. Manny didn't want to play that night.... I was actually in the room where Manny's locker was—I was in the hot tub—and Cabrera walked up to him and said, "What the fuck?" And Manny's like, "What's up, Papi?" "Don't fuckin' Papi me! What the fuck? You're fucking playing tonight." Manny's like, "No, no." "No, you're fucking playing tonight! You're fucking with my paycheck now." And I was like, "Okay." Manny played that night.[35]

BOB TEWKSBURY, *mental skills coach***:**
Research talks about team dynamics. There's a storming phase, a norming phase, and a performing phase. The storming phase could be when the players are rejecting a new coach's philosophy or a couple of players are having conflicts with playing time or status or whatever. After a while, things start to normalize—that's phase two—players begin to understand their role within the team. That leads to phase three—the performing phase—which on the outside is described as team chemistry. Winning teams have that; they gel. Teams gain positive momentum. You can tell when teams have it and when teams don't.[36]

The turning point was August 16. The previous day, Boston had lost to the White Sox, dropping the team 10½ games out of first place. In a roundtable meeting between players and management, a promise was made to principal owner John Henry.

KEVIN MILLAR:
We're gonna go on a run. We're gonna win, and we're gonna kick fucking ass starting today.[37]

The Red Sox beat the Blue Jays that night 8–4. The following night, they won again. Boston finished its three-game sweep of Toronto—and then took three in a row from the White Sox. After winning two of three in another series from the Jays, Boston swept four games from the Tigers and three straight from the Angels. They won 16-of-17 games.

CURT SCHILLING:
Plays that weren't made before that became hits are outs now. Ground balls that weren't turned are double plays now. Earlier in the year we were getting 27 outs a night and giving the other team 31. That's stopped. When plays get made, you throw fewer pitches, and when you throw fewer pitches, you go deeper into games, and when you go deeper into games, you don't need to ask so much of your bullpen. It's pretty simple.[38]

Boston went six weeks—August 5 to September 13—without losing consecutive games. They whittled down New York's lead to a measly two games, but that was the closest the Red Sox got to first place. They finished the regular season with a 98–64 record, three games behind the first-place Yankees. It was the most wins by a Boston team since the 1978 club won 99.

RON JACKSON, *hitting coach*:
One of the things that we instilled in everyone is that everybody can get the job done—one through nine. You don't have to go out of the zone to try to make something happen. It's okay to take your walk. That's why we scored so many runs. Let another guy knock him in. When you're on a team with only three or four good hitters, you're going to have to go out of the zone and try to make something happen. But with the Red Sox, we were patient and we got on base—and that's how you score runs.[39]

The Red Sox scored more runs than any team in the major leagues for the second year in a row, averaging almost six runs per game. They had the highest batting average, on-base percentage, and slugging percentage of any team in baseball. They tied the all-time record for doubles and led all teams in total bases.

Ortiz and Ramirez became only the second pair of teammates in 104 years of American League history to hit better than .300 with at least 40 homers and 130 RBIs. The other duo was Babe Ruth and Lou Gehrig.

While the Red Sox withstood injuries to numerous position players, their starting rotation was blessed with remarkably good health all season long. The quintet of Pedro Martinez, Curt Schilling, Derek Lowe, Tim Wakefield, and Bronson Arroyo started 157 of Boston's 162 games. All five starters had 10 or more wins, the first time a Boston rotation had done that since 1977.

Schilling led the majors with 21 wins and finished second in the American League with a 3.26 ERA. Pedro was ninth in ERA in the American League, and Arroyo was 12th.

Red Sox fans had confidence in their team, but they also had questions. Could the team stay hot for another three weeks? Would there be another white-knuckle showdown with the Yankees for the right to go to the World Series? And after 86 years of angst, frustration, and heartache, would this finally be *the* year?

2

American League Division Series Preview

TIM WAKEFIELD:
We still have a little unfinished business to take care of.[40]

CURT SCHILLING:
Anything short of being in the World Series this year means that we have fallen short.[41]

KEVIN MILLAR:
I feel we're five outs better this year.[42]

KEITH FOULKE:
I want to be part of the future here, not part of the past.[43]

MAJOR LEAGUE SCOUT:
The Red Sox are the logical pick, except for one thing—they're the Red Sox.[44]

The Boston Red Sox clinched the 2004 American League wild card on September 28 when Kevin Millar's 11th-inning home run gave them a 10–8 win over the Tampa Bay Devil Rays. It would be another four days before the Red Sox learned the identity of their Division Series opponent because the Anaheim Angels and Oakland Athletics were tied for first place going into the season's final weekend. "We're going somewhere," said first-year Red Sox manager Terry Francona, "and we're going to play someone. So we're okay."[45]

The schedule pitted Anaheim and Oakland against each other in what would essentially be a best-of-three playoff to make the actual playoffs. Anaheim blew out the A's in the first game 10–0 and clinched their first divisional title in 18 years with a 5–4 victory on October 2. The other Division Series featured the New York Yankees and Minnesota Twins.

The Angels had won the 2002 World Series but slipped back to third place the following year. In 2004, they won the AL West for the first time since 1986, when they were known as the California Angels and met the Red Sox in the ALCS.

In their nine face-to-face meetings during the regular season, the Red Sox had won five from the Angels and lost four. (Boston might rather have faced the A's, against whom they were 8–1.) Despite the narrow edge, things were trending Boston's way. The Red Sox had won the last four matchups, including a convincing sweep in late August and early September.

Although the Red Sox (98–64) and Angels (92–70) had identical .282 team batting averages, leading the American League, Boston put far more runners on base and had more power in its lineup to bring those runners home. Boston led all major league teams in on-base percentage (.360) and slugging percentage (.472). The Angels were 13th and 17th, respectively. The Red Sox scored more runs (949–836) than Anaheim, a result of walking 209 more times and hitting 101 more doubles and 60 additional home runs.

The Red Sox were well known for their patience at the plate, grinding out at-bats and making opposing pitchers work hard for their outs. They led all teams with 3.93 pitches per plate appearance (the Angels were 27th among the 30 teams). But having discerning batting eyes didn't necessarily mean a Red Sox hitter wouldn't jump on a cookie early in the count.

TERRY FRANCONA:
There's a difference in being patient and wearing down pitchers. Being aggressive in the strike zone can also do the same thing.... We want guys to hit pitches they can do some damage with. If they do that and can keep pitchers in the strike zone, because they are good hitters, they are going to run up their pitch counts. If they start chasing balls out of the zone and make outs on pitchers' pitches, you'll

see quicker innings. But if we hit the way we should, we should make pitchers work hard.[46]

The Angels were led by free-swinging right fielder Vladimir Guerrero, who was voted the league's Most Valuable Player for 2004. He led the league in runs scored (124) and total bases (366); he also finished third in batting average (.337). By just about any statistical measure, Guerrero, Manny Ramirez, and David Ortiz were the best hitters in the American League, all of them finishing in the top four in slugging, home runs, RBIs, total bases, and OPS.

After Guerrero, Anaheim's next best hitter was left fielder Jose Guillen (27 HR, 104 RBIs), but on September 25, Guillen had a run-in with manager Mike Scioscia and was suspended without pay for the remainder of the season and postseason. The absence of Guillen and second baseman Adam Kennedy (who had torn ligaments in his right knee five days earlier) would be a huge loss for Anaheim. The Angels would need every one of their offensive weapons if they were going to beat Boston.

Anaheim matched up with the Red Sox a little better when it came to pitching. Kelvim Escobar led the Angels with a 3.93 ERA, good enough for 11th best in the AL. But no other Angels starter—Jarrod Washburn (4.64), John Lackey (4.67), or Bartolo Colon (5.01)—inspired much fear among the Red Sox. Where Anaheim excelled was the back end of its bullpen. It had three excellent set-up men for closer Troy Percival (33 saves, 2.90 ERA): Francisco "K-Rod" Rodriguez (1.00 WHIP, 123 strikeouts in 84 innings), Brendan Donnelly, and Scot Shields.

With the Angels fighting for a playoff spot to the very end of the season, Scioscia had been unable to set his rotation for the best-of-five Division Series. Although Game 1 fell on Lackey's scheduled day to pitch, Scioscia skipped him, choosing left-hander Washburn for the opening game. Colon and Escobar would follow, with Lackey starting a fourth game, if necessary.

DOUG MIRABELLI, *catcher*:

The Angels have always played us tough and, regardless of whether they're down four or five runs late in the game, it always seems to be a one- or two-run game at the end. They really battle, but they have the capability to crush people. It wasn't a team that I would have picked to play.[47]

TERRY FRANCONA:
You always respect your opponent, but I don't think you fear them. We know how good they have been. We know what kind of run they have been on.[48]

DOUG MIENTKIEWICZ, *first baseman:*
That team is sick in the playoffs. Their pitching and bullpen is solid, and they have a lot of ways they can beat you. And defensively, they make the plays.[49]

JOHNNY DAMON, *center fielder:*
They are definitely going to be very tough. Their bullpen might be the best in the league, and their offense. I mean, they are scrappy, guys who can run, bunt, they hit and run a lot, and then they have the guys who can leave the ballpark, Vladdy, Garrett Anderson, Glaus, Erstad. They are a very scary team.[50]

Francona was able to align his rotation exactly how he wanted it. Curt Schilling would start the series and Pedro Martinez would get the ball in Game 2.

Schilling had beaten the Angels twice during the season with a 2.30 ERA and no walks in 15⅔ innings. He also owned one of the best postseason pitching records of anyone in baseball history. In 11 postseason starts with Philadelphia and Arizona, Schilling had a 5–1 record with a 1.66 ERA. During the 2004 season, the Red Sox were 25–7 in Schilling's starts. Schilling had been charged with only two losses since June 16 and finished with a 13–2 record during his last 18 starts.

Pedro Martinez, the Cy Young Award winner in 1997, 1999, and 2000, understood that he had not finished well. Pedro was 0–4 after September 8, posting a gruesome 7.71 ERA, the first time in his career he had lost four consecutive starts. Two of the defeats had come at the hands of the Yankees during back-to-back outings (September 19 and 24) in which Martinez allowed 13 runs in 12⅓ innings.

PEDRO MARTINEZ, *pitcher:*
I'll pitch in relief. I'll pitch the next day. I'll pitch in all five games.... I actually should pitch fifth or not at all if I continue to pitch the way I am.[51]

CURT SCHILLING:

There are so fewer agendas here than people are led to believe. If anybody had a personal agenda with whether they're starting or playing or this or that, then they're missing the whole point of us being here. Pedro and I both knew whoever got the start, the other guy was going to be perfectly okay with it. We both understand what's at stake here, and it's a lot bigger than either one of our egos.[52]

Teams use a four-man rotation in the playoffs because of numerous travel off-days as opposed to the five-man rotation of the regular season. Francona had to send one of the remaining three starters—Arroyo, Wakefield, or Lowe—to the bullpen.

The Red Sox had grabbed Arroyo off waivers from the Pittsburgh Pirates in February 2003. Working as a starter for the first time, Arroyo, 27, had been solid, posting a 4.03 ERA. The Red Sox had won his last nine starts.

Lowe and Wakefield both had previous experience pitching out of the bullpen. Lowe served as Boston's closer from 1999 through 2001, while Wakefield showed his versatility in shuttling back and forth between the bullpen and starting rotation over roughly the same time frame.

In the end, Lowe's 5.42 season ERA and poor performance in September—18 runs allowed in his last four starts—was the deciding factor. Francona named Arroyo and Wakefield as the starters for Games 3 and 4. Lowe would take the long relief role, ready to start if something unexpected occurred.

Lowe was not happy with being the odd man out. One teammate described him as being "livid" at Francona's decision. When reporters asked about the demotion, Lowe asked for a few minutes of privacy first—and then couldn't be found.

TERRY FRANCONA:

He's disappointed. We told him we understand, but we expect him to be one of our 25 guys and help us win any way he can. I told him, "You've got a day or two to blow off steam and then get ready to go."[53]

DANA LeVANGIE:

Tito let me know what was going on, before Lowe even knew, and he said, "I need your help here." And I walked home with Derek that night and we had a long talk and we talked about moving forward. He was willing to buy in, and I'm glad he did.[54]

The following day, Lowe was saying the right things.

DEREK LOWE, *pitcher*:

If I had pitched better the last two games, maybe the situation would be different. It's their decision, and you go with it. You don't sit around and feel sorry for yourself. There is a difference between being mad and being disappointed. Every pitcher wants to pitch. But we're not called the Derek Red Sox. It's not about me. It's about the 162 games that got us here and got us to the playoffs. You have to put your ego aside because you may pitch all five games out of the bullpen or you may not pitch at all.[55]

Wakefield had struggled in September but ended with a win over the Orioles on October 1 and was pleased he had been designated the Game 4 starter.

TIM WAKEFIELD:

I don't think there was ever a doubt in my mind that I wasn't going to be part of the mix. My last start was a nice tune-up.... Not only me personally but us as a team going into the postseason.[56]

In the pen, lefty Alan Embree and righty Mike Timlin both pitched in more than 70 games, finishing the season with identical 4.13 ERAs. Keith Foulke lived up to all preseason expectations, pitching 83 innings and notching 32 saves with a 2.17 ERA. Foulke allowed an average of less than one base runner per inning (0.94 WHIP). Opposing batters hit only .206 against him.

KEITH FOULKE:

The last couple Octobers I haven't thrown that well. In order for this team to go further, I'm going to have to throw better. I'm going to have to make sure I don't make mistakes. That's what I'm working on right now. I'm trying to make sure I'm ready for this next week, the next two or three weeks.[57]

Francona's other decision was the final spot on the roster—either an extra arm in the bullpen or another player on the bench. Reliever Scott Williamson had a superb 1.26 ERA, but he had pitched in only 28 games, missing more than two months with elbow and forearm injuries. With

Williamson's durability in doubt, Francona went with rookie third baseman Kevin Youkilis, who had filled in admirably after Bill Mueller's knee surgery in May, offering solid defense plus some offensive pop—seven homers and 35 RBIs in 208 at-bats. He had shown some humor, as well. When Youkilis returned to the dugout after hitting his first major league home run, his teammates ignored him, as per baseball tradition. Youkilis didn't miss a beat he began high-fiving imaginary teammates.

TERRY FRANCONA:
We thought having the position player may come in handy. It will allow us to use Dave Roberts in a pinch-running situation a little bit more aggressively and gives us a couple more options.[58]

On the eve of the ALDS, the Red Sox were as confident as a team could be.

JOHNNY DAMON:
We expect to win the whole thing. We definitely got a feel for it last year—the heartache, how we lost it, and how hard it is to get there. We know we have a big job on our hands. We have to be mentally sharp. We've got to make sure we've got our heads in the right spot. We're deeper with our pitching staff. This is a team that can do it.[59]

ALAN EMBREE, *pitcher:*
If I have a chance to win the World Series, I want it to be in Boston. I think it would be the most incredible thing. It takes a certain player to be able to play here. You've got to be able to have a thick skin for the criticism. It's a playoff atmosphere because the fans are great. When the team is playing well, the fans are outstanding. Sometimes you can get too high on that, and when you're not playing well, they get on you a little bit. You've got to be able to have enough confidence in yourself to get through that and just maintain. That's what this group has. Not much fazes us. We don't panic.[60]

DOUG MIRABELLI:
Our team is very confident in what we do. I think this is a team that every guy in baseball would love to play on. I don't know what all of the other clubhouses are like, but I know what this one is. You want to have fun, but when the bell rings, you want to come out ready to play. And this team does.[61]

TERRY FRANCONA:
Within the last couple months we started playing like we wanted to, and you could see that swagger coming back. You can't fake that swagger.[62]

KEVIN MILLAR:
We like being in the clubhouse. We like hanging around each other. Guys get here early every day. It's a family. It's a close-knit group, and that's what you want going into the playoffs. I've been on some teams where guys get there at 4:30. On this team, everybody's here at 2:00, 2:30, 3:00. That tells you a lot.[63]

ORLANDO CABRERA:
These guys have fun here. When I was in Montreal, I was the crazy one. Here, I'm the quiet one![64]

PEDRO MARTINEZ:
I can't wait for these next few weeks. I've been through a lot in seven years with the Red Sox, and I know not to get my hopes up, but, man, we are more balanced and confident than I've ever seen. Everything is how it's supposed to be at the end of the season. Just like you dream. Only now the dream feels real.[65]

3

American League Division
Series Game 1

Tuesday, October 5, 2004, at Angel Stadium

TERRY FRANCONA:

Yeah, I'm nervous! Wouldn't you be?[66]

The day before Curt Schilling faced the Angels in the opening game of the Division Series, he posted to the Sons of Sam Horn, a message board for Red Sox fans that Schilling had frequented since the Thanksgiving trade.

CURT SCHILLING:

Why Not Us? There is no reason the last team standing can't be us. You know it, we know it. Now is the time to go out and prove to ourselves, the fans, the game, how good of a team we are. If 25 guys believe that what we are after is the most important thing in their lives for four weeks, there is *nothing* that can't be done.[67]

TERRY FRANCONA:

I got to Angel Stadium early, and Curt was already in his uniform.[68]

MIKE TIMLIN, *pitcher:*
I like it when I see a 17-year veteran like Schilling being nervous before a game. Because that means it's okay that I'm nervous.[69]

KEVIN MILLAR:
If you're not nervous, you're not ready. Everyone in this locker room is nervous. That's what it's all about. It's a big group of kids in here playing baseball.[70]

CURT SCHILLING:
I firmly believe that from top to bottom, this is the best team I've ever been on.... My expectations are to win a World Series. That's why I'm here. That's why I feel like a kid again.... I love that people are counting on me to be a huge part of winning a world championship. I am caught up in it. I've always felt that the bigger the game, the better I got. I live on adrenaline.[71]

SHONDA SCHILLING, *wife of Curt Schilling:*
Nobody can put more pressure on Curt than he's putting on himself. He knows that this is why he came here. He's here to win a World Series. And he's not going to stop until that's what he does. [Is he superstitious?] He had one of everything on the plate. He leaves five hours before the game starts, no matter where it is.... It's ridiculous. The clothes, he has to have laid out the same things. Who are we to say anything, because it's working.[72]

The Angels lineup that Schilling would face was not the one that brought the Angels 92 wins. In place of Jose Guillen (suspended) and Adam Kennedy (injured), manager Mike Scioscia had second-year outfielder Jeff DaVanon in left field, batting sixth, and Alfredo Amezaga (.161 in 73 games) at second base, batting ninth.

With lefty Jarrod Washburn on the mound for Anaheim, Francona started Gabe Kapler over Trot Nixon in right field. Kapler hit .317 against lefties in 2004, while Nixon batted .133 in only 16 plate appearances.

Tim Salmon, in an Angels uniform, threw out the ceremonial first pitch. Salmon had played his whole career—13 years at that point—for the Angels. He was Rookie of the Year in 1993 and drove in 12 postseason runs for the 2002 World Champion Angels. He'd been hurt in 2004 and had played in only 60 games, but the team hoped that "Mr. Angel" would inspire his teammates.

Washburn fired his first pitch—ball one to Johnny Damon—at 1:09 PM PST. Angels fans were banging their inflatable ThunderStix and holding their stuffed-animal rally monkeys for later in the afternoon, if necessary.

Damon popped to shortstop, and Mark Bellhorn flied out to short right field. Manny Ramirez worked the count full and grounded a ball to third baseman Chone Figgins—a jack-of-all-trades who played six positions in 2004. Figgins hesitated and backed up. The ball glanced off his glove and hopped down the left-field line. Ramirez ran hard and made it to second base.

David Ortiz swung at Washburn's first pitch and he, too, hit the ball hard on the ground—and again the baseball glanced off an Anaheim infielder's glove. This time it was second baseman Amezaga, playing back on the outfield grass. Ramirez scored and the Red Sox had a 1–0 lead.

Before the game, Scioscia had explained that his lineup was intended to counter the vaunted Red Sox offense. It was only one inning, but the Anaheim infield did not look so solid.

GABE KAPLER:
We had a couple of bounces go our way. I don't think anybody expected us to score that way, but scoring first was big.[73]

JOHNNY DAMON:
That helped us get loose. I know I wasn't relaxed. It was definitely a tough one to feel comfortable in early.[74]

CURT SCHILLING:
When we got that run, my thought was, *They cannot tie the game.* I did not want them to have any momentum whatsoever.[75]

Schilling breezed through the first three innings. He allowed a bloop single in the first and a leadoff double in the second, but neither runner advanced. Anaheim put men at the corners in the third, but when Garret Anderson poked a soft dribbler past the mound, Orlando Cabrera sprinted in from shortstop and fired on the run to get the Red Sox out of the jam.

ORLANDO CABRERA:
I thought he hit it harder than he did. When I saw the ball dying on the grass, I tried to charge it fast and get rid of the ball real quick.[76]

CURT SCHILLING:

Orlando is phenomenal, has been since the day he got here. He is a game-changer on the field. That ball goes by me, I'm thinking hit. I see him, he's still got a ways to the ball. I am thinking Garret has got a sore knee, maybe he's got a shot.... That was just a phenomenal play.[77]

DOUG MIENTKIEWICZ:

Those plays to kill a rally are just as important as hitting a ball over the fence.[78]

Speaking of hitting the ball over the fence, the Red Sox used the long ball to take a commanding lead in the fourth inning. Washburn walked Ortiz on four pitches—never a good way to start an inning—and Millar promptly belted a hanging change-up to deep left field for a two-run homer.

KEVIN MILLAR:

He had thrown me a fastball outside on the first pitch then came with a change-up over the middle.[79]

Jason Varitek singled to left, and Cabrera drew a walk. Scot Shields—the workhorse of the Angels relievers, with $105\frac{1}{3}$ innings pitched—started warming up in the bullpen. With no one out, other teams might have asked Bill Mueller to bunt, but the Red Sox had sacrificed only 12 times all season, by far the fewest of any major league team. With Boston's high-octane offense, it made little sense to give the opposing team a free out.

TERRY FRANCONA:

We don't want to waste outs, ever. We don't want to waste anything.[80]

ORLANDO CABRERA:

I remember when I got here, the first night in Minneapolis, Francona said, "What do you need?" I said, "Well, I need to know all the signs." "We have no signs." I said, "Excuse me?" He goes, "We have no signs. You get on first, you look to the coach. He's probably going to give you some shit, but he's not giving you anything. Just do your thing." We didn't bunt. One time we had a tie game with Varitek at second. And I bunted. I was like, "Yeah! I did my job." And everybody said, "Hey, good job." And Tito called me over and said, "We don't bunt here."[81]

Mueller ended up making the first out anyway, striking out looking. Kapler singled sharply to right field. That loaded the bases. Damon hit what looked like a double-play ball to Figgins at third. Figgins decided to throw home, hoping to cut down Varitek. His throw was wild, nowhere near catcher Bengie Molina. Varitek scored, and Cabrera steamed around third and easily crossed the plate behind him.

> **CHONE FIGGINS,** *Angels infielder:*
> It was a weird play. I had to take one step back, and that sped up the play a little more. The ball took a bad bounce on me. When I came up to throw, he was on the inside of the line, and I was thinking, *Okay, where can I throw it now?* My only option was over the top, and it just got away from me.[82]

Boston led 5–0, and Scioscia called for Shields.

Bellhorn fanned for the second out, but Manny Ramirez pounded a pitch to left-center field. It landed beyond the fence in front of the rock pile for a three-run homer. It was Manny's 17th postseason home run.

> **DAVID ORTIZ:**
> Manny makes it easier for everyone, especially me. When I was hitting in front of him, they didn't want to mess with Manny, so they pitched to me. Now that I hit cleanup, they have to deal with him, and you don't want that.[83]

> **MANNY RAMIREZ:**
> I looked for a good pitch that I can drive. That's all I do at the plate. I don't want to put any extra pressure on myself. If it happens, it happens. I've been in the playoffs. I know how it is.[84]

The seven runs in the inning set a Red Sox postseason record.[85]

> **JOHNNY DAMON:**
> Millar's home run was definitely the biggest because we weren't really going too much on offense at the time. But as soon as he hit that, we were able to relax a little bit and we just kept swinging. Manny's, that was the clincher right there. Five runs to the Angels is nothing, but when you can go up eight runs, that's pretty special.[86]

The Angels allowed only 42 unearned runs all year but gave up five in the first four innings of Game 1.

Down 8–0, Anaheim made a little noise in the middle innings as Troy Glaus led off the fourth with a home run and Darin Erstad hit a solo shot in the seventh. Two batters after Erstad's homer, Anderson hit a soft tapper down the first-base line. Schilling dashed off the mound and grabbed the ball but threw wildly past Doug Mientkiewicz, who had replaced Kevin Millar at first base, part of Francona's plan to put in better glovemen in the later innings of each game. Schilling suddenly reached down and grabbed his right ankle as he limped into foul territory.

CURT SCHILLING:
I was at a crossroads with my right ankle at that point. It was painful enough that I was having issues. On the Anderson ground ball, I felt the tendon tear. It popped when I hit the ground after making the throw. I knew something bad had happened.[87]

Boston pitching coach Dave Wallace came out and talked with Schilling. The right-hander stayed in the game but threw only one more pitch. It was a double by Glaus, his third extra-base hit of the day, and it cut Boston's lead to 8–3. Francona called for Alan Embree, who got pinch-hitter Adam Riggs to foul out to Varitek.

The Red Sox scored an insurance run in the eighth when Damon, facing reliever Ramon Ortiz, singled, stole second, advanced on a ground-out, then scored when Mientkiewicz surprised everyone by bunting for a hit.

DOUG MIENTKIEWICZ:
It was my choice. I'd bunted a lot in Minnesota. The third baseman, McPherson, was playing me way back. It was a change-up, up and out.[88]

TERRY FRANCONA:
The last couple of weeks, Doug said, "They're not playing me in enough. I'm going to lay a bunt down on somebody." When it happened, it happened so quick…I thought it was a great piece of baseball but, yeah, he got me, too. And I even had a little advance warning.[89]

DOUG MIENTKIEWICZ:
If the guy is going to give you a hit at third, you take it. It's not how fast you are; it's where you put it. To me, that's a big run. They had

the momentum coming back, and we turned around and scored and took it back.... If I catch some flak, so be it. If they want to drill me, go ahead.[90]

KEVIN MILLAR:
You can never score too many runs. You need to keep piling it on. In the playoffs, you just keep scoring runs.[91]

Anaheim was unable to get another rally started. Mike Timlin pitched the final two innings. He retired all six batters he faced, striking out Figgins, Erstad, and Guerrero in the ninth, capping Boston's 9–3 victory.

JOHNNY DAMON:
It's a huge win, and I'll tell you why. Now we won't go back to Fenway with our backs against the wall. We're definitely not going to be satisfied splitting here. We've got to go for the jugular and go home 2–0.[92]

DAVID ORTIZ:
Schilling gives you the confidence. He's out there inning after inning trying to hold the other team down. When you see a guy like that out there, you have to come with your best and produce for him.[93]

THEO EPSTEIN:
He's really embraced the big stage of Boston. I can't think of a player better suited to embrace all of the passion of the fans and return it. He's made for this town and for this situation.[94]

Schilling was happy for the win but dissatisfied with his own performance. In 6⅔ innings, he allowed 11 base runners on nine hits and two walks. He appeared at the postgame press conference wearing a T-shirt that said, "It's not what you accomplish...it's what you overcome."

CURT SCHILLING:
I did not have real good command. I wasn't as sharp as I have been. This is probably as bad as I have thrown, command-wise, in five, six, seven weeks. I left the ball over the plate a couple of times. Luckily, at that point, solo home runs don't beat you.[95]

Schilling and the Red Sox played down the extent of the pitcher's ankle injury.

CURT SCHILLING:

I got treatment on it after the game. I waited until the game was over. I mean, it's the playoffs. You don't want to leave the bench. And it was the seventh inning. There was no sense of urgency. I had X-rays after the game.... There is a difference between being hurt and being sore, and if you're going to be sore all the time, it's a matter of just dealing with it. As I have gotten older, I have realized that's the way it is. You never wake up feeling perfect anymore, but you don't worry about it because the adrenaline makes you feel all right once the game rolls around.[96]

TERRY FRANCONA:

X-rays came back negative. He's got a problem in a slightly different area in that same ankle. It's higher. I don't know if you'd call it tendonitis. It's a tendon problem. Our trainers and medical staff are confident he can make his next start, whenever that is, without problems.... I don't think it's anything that's going to slow him down.[97]

In the privacy of the locker room, the Red Sox knew it was a serious injury.

DR. WILLIAM MORGAN, *medical director:*

The sheath was fraying. A good analogy is like a rope on a rock. It's kind of going back and forth. It's hanging in there, but it's wearing out. And on that one step that he took heading over to the first-base line, at that point, it let go. So now the tendon is no longer located in the area it's supposed to be. It doesn't stay there because it doesn't have a roof over it. There's no housing for the tendon.

There's that bone on the outside of your ankle called the fibula. The tendon biomechanically goes behind that. The retinaculum keeps it intact. Once that's gone, it will slip over that outside bone and go to the front of the ankle. A ruptured peroneal tendon in baseball is pretty unusual. In 18 years, at that point, I never saw it in a baseball player. You'd see it in dancers but you don't usually see it in a pitcher. We iced it all up and did all the acute things, and tried having him work it the next day. It became apparent that this was a bigger injury than we had thought. We got an MRI on his ankle, and it showed the rupture of the retinaculum and a dislocation of the tendon.[98]

If 2003 was the year of "Cowboy Up", Johnny Damon had a new rallying cry for 2004.

JOHNNY DAMON:

We are not the cowboys anymore. We are the idiots this year. Maybe it's not the greatest thing to say, but for the most part, we are. We've got guys with cornrows—Pokey started it and now Bronson. We've got the long hair, the ponytails. We've got guys with shaved heads. We're doing things that we used to do when we played high school ball and college ball. There's only one person on this team who can say they're not an idiot and that's Dave McCarty because of that Stanford education. But that's all he has going for him.

We had some heartache last year. Now we have something to prove. We want to be known as a team that rewrites the history books. We feel like we can win every game, we feel like we have to have fun, and I think that's why this team is liked by so many people.[99]

TERRY FRANCONA:

I would never call them idiots. I think they are a bit unique in a kind of a lovable way. As a group, they are borderline nuts.... Last year was the Cowboy Up thing, and it took off. The reason it took off is because they played good. The same thing happened this year, second half of the year, we started playing good, and if you want to call it a swagger, they came back and they started with the hair. What matters is we played good. And our ball club formed a personality, and you saw it come together on the field.[100]

THEO EPSTEIN:

That's who we are as a team. It's our personality. We couldn't do it any other way. I mean, let's say we had a policy requiring haircuts and no facial hair. The benefits would be uniformity, discipline, and perhaps a heightened sense of order. But we'd lose individuality, self-expression, and fun. Given our personalities, our players thrive when they're allowed to be themselves. When we've played our best baseball the last two years, we've looked like this. It's a pack of sloppy, fun-loving renegades. Look at us during batting practice. Guys are wearing six different kinds of hats. Four different uniform tops. We're a mess. That's the way we are.[101]

DOUG MIENTKIEWICZ:

We're not the sharpest tools in the shed, that's for sure. When you have a group of 25 guys, there are two ways to handle pressure. You can be quiet and keep a handle on your emotions, or just not let it affect you. Manny's always pointing at people, we're always laughing, but when it comes to playing, we're as intense as can be.[101B]

LYNN JONES, *first-base coach*:

When they were outside the lines, it was chaotic, it was fun. They would joke around, they would get into it with each other, there was chaos sometimes, you know? They reminded me a little of the Oakland A's in the mid-'70s, with Reggie Jackson and Joe Rudi, Blue Moon Odom, Vida Blue, Sal Bando, all those guys. It was chaotic, you always heard about it. You often wondered what was going on. And yet when they were on the field, they were dead serious about winning and they trusted their teammates. And that put a relaxed feeling amongst everybody.[102]

4

American League Division
Series Game 2

Wednesday, October 6, 2004, at Angel Stadium

JASON VARITEK, *catcher:*
A lot of people doubted the man. I don't doubt the man.[103]

DAVID ORTIZ:
Some people were worried about Pedro's confidence because he didn't pitch well down the stretch, but I wasn't. I knew he'd be ready to go. I think Pedro wanted to pitch Game 1—wouldn't anyone? Tito decided to go with Schilling. I knew that would make Pedro pitch even better. Pedro was always at his best when people started to doubt him, when he had something to prove.[104]

Pedro Martinez pitched 217 innings in 2004, the most since 1998, his first season with Boston. Keeping a tighter rein on his pitch counts helped Martinez stay off the disabled list, a problem in previous seasons, but the high number of innings might have tired him in September.

TERRY FRANCONA:
I don't think he looked extremely well the last couple starts, and it cost him. For whatever reason, he went through a little bit of a rough

stretch. But I bet you every manager out there wishes they could start him in Game 2.[105]

Martinez was keeping to himself. He was absent during the pre-game introductions before Game 1, saying he had been working on some things and lost track of time. Then he skipped the Game 2 pregame press conference.

TERRY FRANCONA:
That's his business. However he prepares. I don't need to get in the middle of that. Everybody has a different routine.[106]

JOHNNY DAMON:
I think he's playing coy. He's in great spirits.... He's acting like he doesn't have much left in the tank, but he has been great down there in the clubhouse. He has been talking. He has been having fun.[107]

ORLANDO CABRERA:
I've been telling Pedro the last couple of days that he has a lot to prove. It's going to be interesting. I think he is going to throw a hell of a game.[108]

Angels starter Bartolo Colon excelled in the second half, going 12–4 with a 3.63 ERA after a poor first half (6–8, 6.38). There was one sour note among his recent starts, though—the 10 hits, four walks, and four runs he'd given up to the Red Sox on September 2 at Fenway. Boston had forced the portly right-hander to throw 112 pitches in fewer than five innings.

MIKE SCIOSCIA, *Angels manager:*
Colon is absolutely fearless at challenging hitters. He throws a hard, heavy ball in good locations. He hits spots very well, changes speeds well. He's a throwback power pitcher in the way he goes after it, much like Schilling.[109]

There were minor changes to each team's lineup. Scioscia moved Chone Figgins from third base to second and gave rookie Dallas McPherson the nod at third. For Boston, Francona put right fielder Trot Nixon in the five-spot behind David Ortiz and moved the next four hitters down a notch.

TERRY FRANCONA:

In August, I don't think anybody thought Trot would be back playing. The thought was if he came back, we might have him as a pinch-hitter. We were trying to figure out how to give him enough at-bats where he could be a good pinch-hitter. For him to be doing what he is doing is pretty amazing. First of all, he is a good left-hand hitter, and the harder you throw, sometimes the better hitter he is, but he also brings some fire in the dugout and he has got a little edge to him at times during a game.[110]

TROT NIXON, *right fielder*:

My quad was pretty close to rupturing completely. That would have probably cost me my career. Every doctor told me there was a really good chance—well over 80 percent—that I wouldn't be healthy enough for the postseason. That was frustrating to hear, but I put my nose to the grindstone. The team provided me with my own personal therapist, and I did some hard work, and I was able to play in September.[111]

Fans on the East Coast settled in at 10:00 PM to watch Game 2, the first of many late nights over the next three weeks. Johnny Damon began the night with a clean single to right field.

TERRY FRANCONA:

The surprising thing to me this year is all the talk about good players and impact seasons. But I haven't heard people mention Johnny Damon's name as much as I think is deserved. He ended up with 94 RBIs out of the leadoff spot. He had an incredible year.[112]

RON JACKSON:

People don't realize that he's the guy who makes it all happen here. If Johnny's not rolling, then we don't. David and Manny get all the attention, but offensively, we're only as good as Johnny Damon.[113]

JOHNNY DAMON:

People always take notice of the home runs and the runs driven in. I'm just one of the sleeper guys.... But for the team, I feel there's a lot of pressure on me. I think if I can get on base this series, it will go fine for us. When I'm getting on, the team does well.[114]

Mark Bellhorn followed Damon with a hit of his own, and after Manny Ramirez struck out, Ortiz walked to load the bases. Nixon swung at the first pitch—a good one—but broke his bat and flied out to shallow left field. Kevin Millar grounded to shortstop, and the Red Sox left three men on base. But they had been successful in one respect—they forced Colon to throw 24 pitches.

Colon threw 32 more pitches in the second inning. Boston loaded the bases again, as Bill Mueller and Damon singled and Bellhorn walked. With two outs, Ramirez jumped on a fastball and hit it foul down the right-field line, missing a grand slam by only a few feet. He ended up drawing a walk, bringing in Mueller with the game's first run.

More runs might have scored, but as Ortiz took ball three, making the count 3–1, Angels catcher Jose Molina (the younger brother of Game 1 catcher Bengie Molina) snapped off a throw to second base. Shortstop David Eckstein, who had been shaded toward right field and was almost directly behind the bag, darted in and picked off Bellhorn, who had wandered too far off the base.

The Angels tied the game in their half of the second. Troy Glaus walked, and Jeff DaVanon and McPherson followed with singles.

In the fifth, Pedro ran into further trouble. Jose Molina's popup dropped between Orlando Cabrera and Ramirez in short left field for a hit. After Figgins popped up a bunt attempt, Martinez plunked Darin Erstad, loading the bases. Vlad Guerrero stroked a clean single to right-center, driving in two runs and giving the Angels a 3–1 lead. Martinez escaped further damage when Garret Anderson smoked a line drive right at Millar. The first baseman speared it and took two easy steps to the base, doubling off Guerrero for an unassisted double play.

Colon recovered from his rough beginning and retired the Red Sox in order in the third, fourth, and fifth innings. But with two outs in the top of the sixth, Millar grounded a single up the middle. Jason Varitek, who had struck out swinging in both the second and fourth innings, swung at Colon's first pitch and hit it hard into the seats in right-center. Home run. Tie game, 3–3.

JASON VARITEK:
I got myself out on those first two at-bats. Bartolo battles. He moves the ball around. I wanted to get my legs under me and drive the ball to center. But I got a pitch to pull.[115]

Martinez put down the Angels in order in the bottom of the sixth, and Scioscia brought in Francisco Rodriguez for the seventh. Mueller singled on a ball that Figgins bobbled at second.

DAVID ECKSTEIN, *Angels shortstop*:
No way can you give them extra outs. They get you down, and they go for the throat.[116]

DARIN ERSTAD, *Angels first baseman*:
They smelled blood and got after it.[117]

Dave Roberts ran for Mueller and was forced at second on Damon's grounder. Damon stole second before Bellhorn walked. A wild pitch put runners at second and third. With the Angels' infield in, Ramirez lifted a fly ball to center field. Anderson made the catch, but Damon scored easily, giving the Red Sox a 4–3 lead. Ortiz was walked intentionally, and Nixon grounded out to first. The sacrifice fly was the only ball the Red Sox hit out of the infield in the inning.

The Angels were retired in order in the bottom of the seventh, but they did not go easily. After Casey Kotchman lined back to Martinez, Pedro needed 12 pitches to dispose of Eckstein on a fly to left field and 10 pitches to strike out Figgins.

The Angels' rally monkey made an appearance on the scoreboard in the eighth when Mike Timlin took over for Martinez. Erstad began the inning with a single. Guerrero put on a tough at-bat before striking out on the same outside slider Timlin had struck him out on to end Game 1. Francona called on Mike Myers to face Anderson, who was 1-for-14 against the lefty specialist.

MIKE MYERS, *pitcher*:
Erstad was on first base and he was in the prime of his career, stealing bases and all that. Anderson put on a great at-bat, fouled off a couple of pitches. Erstad tried to steal a couple of different times, playing the cat-and-mouse game while Anderson fouled a few pitches off. I got Anderson swinging at a fastball on the inside part of the plate.[118]

Francona then brought in his third pitcher of the inning, Keith Foulke, who caught Troy Glaus looking on a questionable outside strike. Three pitchers, three strikeouts.

CURTIS LESKANIC, *pitcher:*
Just the perfect guys in the perfect spot.[119]

Anaheim's Brendan Donnelly was tasked with keeping the score at 4–3 in the ninth. He failed. With one out, Ramirez doubled down the left-field line. Ortiz was walked intentionally. Nixon fouled off four pitches before lining the ball back through the box into center field for a single, scoring Ramirez. It was a critical insurance run.

TROT NIXON:
We know people are always going to pitch around Manny and Ortiz. You have to be able to make them pay...I get geared up, sometimes too much. There's no way not to be too amped for the playoffs. The key is to get out in the field and get in the flow of the game and settle down.[120]

Donnelly recorded the second out, and then the Angels decided to walk Varitek intentionally and pitch to Cabrera with the bases loaded.

ORLANDO CABRERA:
They walked the guy in front of me. I was pumped! Donnelly threw me a splitter for a strike. I remembered, wait a second, this guy, he loves the splitter. So I said, *Just stay back and swing if it's high. If it's too high, just let it go because if I walk, we can get a run.* I waited on him. I saw his hand when he threw it. It was high. I said, *Yeah, this one. Let it come down.* When it came down, I put a good swing on it. It was a line drive over the shortstop. Eckstein, he's like—what—5'3"? He jumped and I was like, *No way he's going to get it.*[121]

Eckstein was listed as 5'6", but he still couldn't reach Cabrera's line drive. It rolled almost all the way to the wall in left-center. All three base runners scored. What had been a tight game for eight innings was now 8–3 Red Sox.

BRENDAN DONNELLY, *Angels pitcher:*
I made a bad pitch to Cabrera. I left a split-finger over the plate, and he belted it. But I think anyone in a Red Sox uniform could have

hit that pitch. It was awful. Heck, I think I might have been able to hit it, and I suck. I've faced them enough to know that they're good hitters all the way through the lineup. Every one of them has a certain pitch they're looking for, and if they don't see that pitch, they're not going for it. They're smart. They get the count their way, and then they're going to get the pitches they want to hit. That was really true tonight—especially on me.[122]

For the ninth, Francona continued his pattern of swapping in defensive replacements in the late innings. The Sox put Pokey Reese at second and Gabe Kapler—who had pinch-run for Nixon—in right field. Doug Mientkiewicz was already at first base.

GABE KAPLER:

Francona was as predictable as any manager I've ever played for. And that predictability is the right way to manage a game. Because you know the moves you're going to make before the game starts, you know who you're going to use and when you're going to use them. Tito managed the playoffs and World Series just like he managed the regular season. Management of the bullpen was a little different because you don't have everybody available all the time, and you're playing with off-days that you don't have during the season, and you set your rotation differently. But a bench is used almost identical to the way it's used during the regular season.[123]

DOUG MIENTKIEWICZ:

We all knew our roles. Before every series, Tito and his staff did a phenomenal job of breaking it down for every single guy. "These are the three guys you might face from the bullpen. This is your situation." He told me, "As soon as I get a lead...Kevin might get two at-bats, Kevin might get three, but as soon as we get the lead, you're in the game." We could follow the game, and we all knew when to get ready. The importance of that was often overlooked, but I think that's why our bench was so successful. Nothing surprised us.[124]

Keith Foulke had no trouble in the ninth. DaVanon grounded back to the mound, McPherson grounded to second, and pinch-hitter Curtis Pride struck out.

Boston was heading home up 2–0, having scored 17 runs on 23 hits. The Angels' pen—supposedly their area of clear superiority—had allowed five runs in Game 2. The Red Sox held a huge advantage, but they were not banking on anything. After all, they had come back from 0–2 only one year earlier [2003 ALDS against Oakland].

DOUG MIENTKIEWICZ:
The hardest game to win is the last one. Nothing is over yet. We realize that. But we're going home and we're looking forward to that because we play well at home.[125]

Pedro Martinez had pitched seven innings and allowed six hits, two walks, and three runs while striking out six. He threw 116 pitches, and according to the Angel Stadium radar gun, each of Martinez's final 20 fastballs registered between 90–95 mph. If it wasn't vintage Pedro, that's because Martinez had set the bar so high in previous seasons.

PEDRO MARTINEZ:
I was number one today. That's all that matters to me. I don't believe in what the experts from out here have to say. I am just here to do my job, anywhere they choose to put me. I actually shut my mouth—I ate my ego—because I wanted to let go on some of these experts around here talking trash. It doesn't matter how many days I have to wait. It was an honor to see Curt Schilling win. He pitched better than me. I am admitting it, so enough with the trash talking. We get along really well. I have never been mad because he pitches any game. He has been outstanding not only against the Angels but any team we played. We get along great. Please don't make up stuff that's not true.[126]

5

Travel Day

Thursday, October 7, 2004

TROT NIXON:
When you got a guy hanging over the cliff holding on with one hand, you don't want him to get his other hand up there. You want to go ahead and stomp on it.[127]

In both 1999 and 2003, the Red Sox had been down 0–2 in the ALDS and battled back, winning three consecutive games to clinch the best-of-five series.

MIKE TIMLIN:
Going into Game 3 last year, we were in the Angels' shoes. We were fighting for our lives at that point. We were up against the wall, and we played like it. We had nothing to do but come out and give it our all in every game.[128]

KEVIN MILLAR:
We know they won't give up. We'll have to fight them all the way to the end.[129]

The Angels faced long odds. Games 3 and—if necessary—4 would be played at Fenway Park, and the Red Sox's 55–26 home record was the best in baseball. In the regular season, they had lost consecutive home games only four times. They had never lost three in a row.

MIKE SCIOSCIA:
We don't need to be hit in the head with a brick to know that we're down 0–2 and we've got to win three in a row. It's a challenge, and we're ready for it.[130]

Kelvim Escobar would pitch Game 3.

MIKE SCIOSCIA:
Guys who have seen him day in and day out know he has been our most consistent pitcher, particularly down the stretch. He very easily could be sitting right now as a candidate for the Cy Young Award if he had the support we should have given him.[131]

Escobar finished with the team's best ERA (3.93, tenth in the AL) but an 11–12 record. He had received paltry run support all season long (3.78 runs per 27 outs). By comparison, Curt Schilling received 7.18 runs per 27 outs. Twice in September, Escobar had pitched eight innings and allowed only one run but had been saddled with a loss.

Johnny Damon had two hits in each of the first two games—all while suffering from migraines that had plagued him since his violent collision with teammate Damian Jackson in the 2003 ALDS.

JOHNNY DAMON:
I need to see a chiropractor. If I get that done, then hopefully I'll feel better. Physically, I'm all right. I'm just having headaches again. I can tell when it's coming on because it comes up through the neck. I had migraines every day the first months of last off-season. I felt them coming so I went and got adjusted, and I was good for a month, then they started coming back. Over the course of the season I have to get my neck adjusted. It's been about 12 days now, and I need it once every week. A nice swift "pop" and it will be gone.[132]

On the recommendation of the Red Sox, Curt Schilling met with orthopaedic surgeon Dr. George Theodore, an ankle and foot specialist at Massachusetts General Hospital, to get another opinion on his right ankle.

A few players commented on the camaraderie in the Red Sox clubhouse.

GABE KAPLER:
The importance of our clubhouse should not be underestimated. We have a lot of superstars on this team, and it's important that those guys are selfless and human. Manny makes sure to involve everybody in everybody else's business. Millar will rip anyone in here when they need to be ripped, and they give a boost of confidence when they need that.[133]

KEVIN MILLAR:
We will not allow cliques on this team. Some clubs have black guys over here, whites over there, Latinos over there. I won't allow it. We play together, we shower together, and we eat together. We're a family. There is no reason to be segregated.[134]

MANNY RAMIREZ:
The biggest thing here is that we all get along so well, no matter what differences we have on the outside. Everybody gets along with everybody. No one here eats dinner alone.[135]

DAVID ORTIZ:
We definitely faced that once. We called a meeting to talk about it, and we never had any problems again. When we see something wrong now, we'll call a meeting to get it out in the open. Everyone here has the same attitude. All that stuff about differences—we don't play that here.[136]

TERRY ADAMS, *pitcher:*
We did a lot of things together, things I didn't do on other teams. We had team dinners with not only the players but some of the families—wives, girlfriends—both at home and on the road. Even with the new faces that came in, we were pretty tight-knit. It was an even-keeled team. It was very relaxed—not too relaxed where people weren't doing their job, but it was just relaxed enough to where you weren't playing tight.[137]

CURT SCHILLING:
There's a huge ego in here, and it's a collective ego. No one is bigger that what we're trying to do, no one person, no one player, no group of guys, and everybody understands that. You've got to believe. You're playing great teams, you're facing great pitchers every night, you're facing great lineups, you have to believe in your ability to beat the best in the world.[138]

CHRIS CORRENTI, *trainer:*

The starting pitchers were a tight-knit group. They all believed in the programs I set up. They believed in each other, supported each other. Everybody watched everybody's bullpen session. When someone threw a bullpen session, the pitching coach, the rest of the starters, and I would watch. I was the organizer. We had two future Hall of Fame guys on the staff. Who is going to help Derek Lowe or Bronson Arroyo better than Curt Schilling or Pedro? I felt it was important for these guys to communicate and to support each other.[139]

JOHNNY DAMON:

My first day in the Red Sox clubhouse in 2002, it was weird. No one was playing cards, no one was playing video games. No one was really talking to each other. Everyone was on their own. Then it got better last year when we brought Kevin Millar here, and Gabe Kapler was great to bring along. And it's getting better and better. More guys are comfortable, and they are not afraid to speak up and be a leader. Our team, we have 25 players, and we have about 25 leaders, too.[140]

TERRY FRANCONA:

For the longest time this year, I wanted our team to latch onto their personality. Last year they did the Cowboy Up thing. And finally we started kicking it in gear, and people were commenting on their hair, their clothes. I was glad that we had something to latch on to, and they seemed to come together with it. If this was Cub Scout Troop 14, I'd ask them to cut their hair. It's not. We're trying to play the best baseball we can, and I think these guys really have come together as a ballclub.[141]

6

American League Division Series Game 3

Friday, October 8, 2004, at Fenway Park

CURT SCHILLING:

Friday is going to be a legit struggle, got a team fighting for its life against a kid making his first ever postseason start. FWIW I take the kid Friday night. He's got nuts the size of Saturn.[142]

GO YANKS! WE WANT TO KICK YOUR BUTT ON THE WAY TO THE WORLD SERIES.

The Red Sox were still one win away from clinching the Division Series, but the *Boston Herald*'s front-page headline was busy cheering on the hated Yankees. It was an audacious and potentially embarrassing decision, but it also echoed what a lot of Red Sox fans were feeling: *Let's send the Angels home as soon as we can and get to the* real *playoffs!* At the time, the series between the Yankees and Twins was tied 1–1.

TERRY FRANCONA:

When I walked to the food room, I had a good feeling. Most teams, they're watching *Hoosiers*. I was in the food room, and there's John Belushi smashing the guitar over somebody's head in *Animal House*. They're right where they need to be.[143]

DOUG MIENTKIEWICZ:

It's a carefree atmosphere. I think in situations like these, that's why we're so successful. There's not a lot of pressure on each other. I hate the word *pressure*. There's no pressure in the game of baseball. It's just fun. This is what the game is supposed to be. The only pressure out there is the pressure you put on yourself.[144]

BRONSON ARROYO, *pitcher:*

In spring training, Curt [Schilling] used to get on me about being so loose in the clubhouse on the day I pitch. I try to act like every day is the same when I come to the ballpark. The day I'm pitching I like to mingle and talk to the guys. Curt is just the opposite. He likes to be quiet and go over his notes. Everybody has got their own personalities. You have to figure out what works for you. I'm going to treat it like just another game, which in my case means I'm going to be nervous going in but okay once I throw the first pitch. That's how I am all the time, even in a spring training game.... Being up 2–0 will allow me to be aggressive early in the game and establish the strike zone.[145]

For the third consecutive game, the Red Sox made the opposing pitcher work hard for his outs. Escobar gave up a walk and a single in each of the first two frames, throwing 24 and 21 pitches, respectively. Boston broke through in the third. Mark Bellhorn began with a walk—the third consecutive inning Escobar had walked the leadoff batter. Manny Ramirez flied to straightaway center, but David Ortiz doubled off the left-field wall. Bellhorn scored when Trot Nixon slashed a sharp, hard single to right field. It was the 64th pitch for Escobar, and there was only one out in the third inning. In a repeat of Game 1, Scot Shields was warming up in the bullpen.

Kevin Millar grounded out to second base, and Ortiz scored from third. Boston led 2–0. With Nixon on second, Escobar intentionally walked Jason Varitek—who was 7-for-17 against him—and succeeded in getting Orlando Cabrera for the third out.

Meanwhile, it was smooth sailing for Arroyo. Through the first three innings, he allowed only a single and a hit batsman. Troy Glaus continued to torment the Red Sox by hitting a two-out solo home run, but the Red Sox responded with three runs in their half of the fourth as the Angels' defense faltered once again. The rally began when Bill Mueller's leadoff grounder went under Chone Figgins' glove. Johnny Damon blooped a single to the opposite field, and Bellhorn—again—walked. Mueller scored on Ramirez's sacrifice fly to left. Boston led 3–0.

Mike Scioscia called in Shields. Ortiz doubled to deep right, driving in Damon. But—respecting Vlad Guerrero's arm in right and with only one out—Bellhorn held at third. After Shields missed with his first three pitches to Nixon, Scioscia called for an intentional walk. It was the sixth Red Sox walk of the game. Millar sent a tailor-made three-hopper directly to David Eckstein at short, but the ball bounced off the heel of his glove. Eckstein picked it up and tried to shovel the ball to third for a force play, but that didn't work, either. Bellhorn scored, and it was 5–1 in favor of the Red Sox.

Three singles in the fifth inning—from Mueller, Damon, and Ramirez—brought Boston another run. They held the 6–1 lead through six innings with only nine outs standing between them and a return to the League Championship Series.

In the seventh, Doug Mientkiewicz came in to play first base. When Arroyo walked leadoff batter Jeff DaVanon, Francona brought in Mike Myers. Arroyo had thrown 91 pitches.

TERRY FRANCONA:
The way he approached DaVanon, he didn't look like the Bronson of the inning before.... He looked like he was out of bullets.[146]

BRONSON ARROYO:
I definitely wasn't out of bullets. I felt strong. I just didn't command the strike zone on that hitter. I think he wanted to go lefty-lefty matchup regardless, so even if I was 0-2 and had given up a base hit, I think I was coming out anyway.[147]

Arroyo left to a loud standing ovation from the Fenway faithful.

BRONSON ARROYO:
Unbelievable. You can't describe it. Walking off the field, knowing you've earned the respect of the fans and your teammates.[148]

Arroyo had pitched the best game of the three Red Sox starters, allowing only three hits and two walks in six innings, striking out seven.

Casey Kotchman had been announced as a pinch-hitter for Bengie Molina, but with Myers coming in, Scioscia pulled him and put in Jose Molina. Myers walked Molina. Another pinch-hitter was announced—Adam Riggs—and Francona countered with righty Mike Timlin, who had now pitched in all three games. Timlin was riding a run of 13⅔ scoreless playoff innings dating back to 2000. Scioscia burned another bench player, having Curtis Pride bat for Riggs.

Pride hit a soft liner to shortstop for the first out. Eckstein flared a single to right field to load the bases. Timlin struck out Figgins on three pitches and got ahead of Darin Erstad 0–2, but after a tense seven-pitch battle, Erstad walked, forcing in a run. Guerrero, 1-for-11 in the series, swung and missed Timlin's first pitch before driving an outside fastball into the right-center field bleachers. It was the first postseason grand slam in Angels history, and it tied the game at 6–6. Fenway, which had been rocking with appreciation for Arroyo's performance only moments ago, was now pin-drop quiet.

JOHNNY DAMON:
Oh, shit. That team is a pain in the butt, but we couldn't let them win this game. If they won, the momentum would have shifted. We would have to wake up early and play again, and we're not morning people.[149]

TROT NIXON:
Unless it's five feet in front of the plate, Guerrero's going to hit it.[150]

MIKE TIMLIN:
I made a bad pitch to a very good hitter. It put us a little bit out of the game, but it didn't take us all the way out…. I was very down. I was very down for a long time. I don't like to let my teammates down like that. That's not my job. I let them down, and that wears on me.[151]

TERRY FRANCONA:
Any time they keep the series alive, something can happen. We weren't losing, we weren't going to quit, but we saw the mood shift. We gave a good team a chance to get back in the game.[152]

DOUG MIENTKIEWICZ:

We very easily could have folded right there. It took us one inning to regroup. A bunch of us came up here into the clubhouse and reminded each other, "We knew it wasn't going to be easy. Now let's go out and get it."[153]

KEVIN MILLAR:

The thing with the Angels, for some reason, we played them well. They were a good ballclub; they were a little scary. And the Guerrero grand slam—you know, it was like, ahhh, whatever—because at that point we were already up two games. It wasn't that big of a thing, it wasn't a game-winning grand slam. We weren't in panic mode, we had that series pretty well in hand.[154]

Alan Embree relieved Timlin and got the final out of the inning. Things stayed quiet—until the Red Sox batted in the bottom of the eighth.

After Francisco Rodriguez struck out Bellhorn and Ramirez, Ortiz singled. Now Terry Francona had a decision to make. Should he pinch-run Dave Roberts and add speed on the basepaths? With two outs and wanting to keep Ortiz's bat in the game, he decided against it. Nixon walked. Now Ortiz was on second, but again, Francona left in the slower man. Mientkiewicz grounded out to second.

The Angels threatened in the ninth against Keith Foulke. With one out, Figgins singled. Erstad doubled off the left-field wall, and Figgins, who was having a rough series in the field, now committed a base-running error. Uncertain whether or not Ramirez was going to catch the ball, Figgins held up while running around second base. Ramirez had no chance at the ball. Instead of scoring the go-ahead run, Figgins was standing on third.

CHONE FIGGINS:

I haven't played here enough to know that ball was going to go off the wall. I didn't want him to catch it and get doubled off with the big boys coming up. The ball was not that high. I thought he had a chance to catch it.[155]

Guerrero was next, and to no one's surprise, he was walked intentionally. Then Foulke bore down and struck out both Garret Anderson and Troy Glaus to deafening cheers.

MIKE TIMLIN:

For Keith to do what he did gave the entire team a lift. That's clutch pitching. That's the kind of pitching that gets the whole team going. It put the momentum right back to us.[156]

Derek Lowe came out of the bullpen for the top of the 10th, relieving Foulke.

TERRY FRANCONA:

Our players were excited that he was in the game. For all his ups and downs this year, his teammates score runs when he pitches, laugh at his antics, and love him to death.[157]

JOHNNY DAMON:

You can talk about New York all you want, but we have something special here. I mean, when you hear the fans chanting "D-Lowe! D-Lowe!" after all he's been through. Oh, man, we knew we had to win that game.[158]

EUKY ROJAS:

A starting pitcher and a reliever have different warm-up routines, and what impressed me about D-Lowe was that he was able to jump into a reliever's warm-up routine right away. Starting pitchers need around 35 or 40 pitches to warm up before the game. A reliever has to do it in about 15 pitches, and D-Lowe was able to do that right away.[159]

DaVanon led off for Anaheim and hit a deep fly ball that looked like it might go over Damon's head, but the center fielder raced back and hauled it in.

JOHNNY DAMON:

That scared me. I didn't expect it because Derek is a sinkerball pitcher, and I was playing in a little. The ball kept going and going. I was lucky I got a good jump.[160]

Jose Molina walked—although he lost track of the count and had to be reminded it was ball four. Alfredo Amezaga bunted, and Mueller raced in on the grass, barehanded the ball, and threw in time to first. Molina took second.

Eckstein, swinging at Lowe's first pitch, hit a high chopper into the shortstop hole. Cabrera's strong throw was late, and the Angels had runners at first and third with two outs. Figgins showed bunt on the first pitch and took a strike. Then he also hit a chopper to shortstop. Cabrera fielded it perfectly and fired to first to end the inning.

In the bottom of the 10th, Boston would have the top of its order up as Rodriguez—one of the heroes of the Angels' 2002 postseason—began his third inning of work. He was at 29 pitches after throwing 44 in Game 2.

MIKE SCIOSCIA:
Between innings, we talked to him and he felt a bit tired but thought he could go back out.[161]

FRANCISCO RODRIGUEZ, *Angels pitcher:*
I told him I was fine, but to be honest, I had nothing.[162]

Damon began with a single up the middle, the tenth time he had reached base in the series. With none out and the potential winning run at first, the Red Sox bunted. Bellhorn pushed the ball toward third. Figgins, who had moved over from second base, grabbed it and threw wildly to second. Eckstein dove for the ball, his body pointed toward left field, and somehow managed to both catch the ball and keep one foot on the bag for the force. With one out and Ramirez and Ortiz coming up, Pokey Reese ran for Bellhorn at first base.

POKEY REESE:
I knew around the sixth or seventh inning they might need a pinch-runner. Tito always made sure we stayed loose. All the extra guys, we'd go up in the locker room and stretch out, drink our coffee, and get ready, knowing it might be our time. That's what we did every game—myself, Kapler, Dave Roberts. We knew we were probably going to go in as defensive players or pinch-runners. They had a treadmill. We had the weight room up there. The bike. They had all the stuff. Most of what we did was stretch and get our legs loose.[163]

Rodriguez fooled Ramirez on a 1–2 pitch, striking him out looking on a fastball down the middle. Rodriguez was now at 38 pitches. Scioscia had a few decisions to make. He could have K-Rod face Ortiz, or he could go to his bullpen where Jarrod Washburn and veteran closer Troy Percival were waiting.

MIKE SCIOSCIA:

Frankie had really stretched himself to the limit. He was really on the verge. Did he have three, four, five pitches left in him? We'll never know.[164]

Scioscia brought in the left-hander Washburn to face Ortiz. Washburn had started Game 1, though he'd lasted only 3⅓ innings and 79 pitches. Percival was available, but Scioscia went lefty-against-lefty for Ortiz, saving Percival for a possible pinch-hitter for Nixon or perhaps the 11th inning.

MIKE SCIOSCIA:

If Ortiz happened to get on, we'd see what they wanted to do with Nixon on deck. If they were going to counter, we were ready with Perci.[165]

In Game 1, Ortiz faced Washburn twice and had a first-pitch single and a four-pitch walk.

POKEY REESE:

I knew if he hit a gapper to right-center I was going to score. Lynn Jones told me to get my rear end around the bases and score if he hit one to left.[166]

TROT NIXON:

I was on deck. While he was getting ready, I said, "This is your time, brother."[167]

JOHNNY DAMON:

When he came up, we knew he was going to have a good at-bat. We didn't know it would be that good.[168]

TERRY FRANCONA:

I wasn't sitting there thinking. I was *begging*. I looked at Millar and said, "Can he hit one here?" No sooner were the words out of my mouth than it left the bat. The players seemed to know before me that it was going out.[169]

MIKE TIMLIN:

I was sitting next to Manny and I joked, "Nice of you to leave the RBI out there for him."[170]

MANNY RAMIREZ:

I told Timlin that David had not hit a home run in four days and it was time for it. The pitch. Boom![171]

Ortiz hammered Washburn's first offering into the Green Monster seats.

MIKE TIMLIN:

Manny just looked at me. "I told you so." I couldn't believe it.[172]

MIKE MYERS:

I was standing on the top step. It was one of those times where I very rarely say, "I got a good feeling Ortiz is going the opposite way" and he ends up hitting that thing and we just went absolutely berserk.[173]

TROT NIXON:

Washburn's the kind of guy that will come right at you. He'll try to get ahead of you early, but you couldn't sneak a cheese past Big Papi! When he hit it, my hands went up in the air because I knew David had gotten it. The way he reacted...he looked back toward us, and we knew that he had gotten it.[174]

BRONSON ARROYO:

I took off running from the clubhouse. I didn't even wait for it to go over the fence. I got down there in about three seconds.[175]

POKEY REESE:

Did you see how high I jumped when I got to the plate? Man, that was awesome. That was a great feeling. I have that photo up at my mom's house.[176]

DAVID ORTIZ:

Washburn is a guy I've faced a lot. Pretty much the last couple of games, he's trying a lot of sliders because I'm driving his fastball pretty good. As soon as I saw him coming out of the bullpen I thought, *Here comes my slider. First pitch, he's going to throw me this, and I'm going to look for it. Give it to me.* It was a slider, up, kind of high.... I wasn't really thinking about hitting a home run. I want to get on base. I want to make sure somebody else steps to the plate. If I had been thinking about hitting a home run, that's when you get in trouble. I would have hit a ground ball to second because that's pretty much what you do.[177]

KEVIN MILLAR:
When Ortiz crossed home, it was an amazing feeling. You're trying to protect your toes. There's a lot of guys jumping up and down, and there's some spikes out there. You're trying to stay careful with each other, but it was an amazing feeling.[178]

DAVID ORTIZ:
I said, "They better score [in the top of the tenth], because if they don't, I'm coming up, and I'm going to do something." That's not talking trash. That's how you stay positive. I say stuff like that a lot. It doesn't always work out like this.[179]

Doug Mientkiewicz had played with Ortiz on the Minnesota Twins and remembered when Ortiz's mother, Angela Rosa Arias, died in a car crash in January 2002.

DOUG MIENTKIEWICZ:
I got to meet his mom a few times. What a wonderful woman. For what that man has gone through in the last three or four years, my gosh. The one thing I told him when he crossed that plate was, "Momma would be proud." And he said, "You know it." She was a big part of his life and the first thing I thought of when he hit it was, *Come on, Momma. Blow it out of here!*[180]

DAVID ORTIZ:
I told Timlin, "I got your back." I hit the home run, I came back in, and he gave me a kiss.[181]

Ortiz's blast meant that Tim Wakefield would not start Game 4.

TIM WAKEFIELD:
Pitching tomorrow or celebrating today, I don't care. But this is better.[182]

While the raucous celebration continued in the Red Sox clubhouse, some of it spilled onto the field. Millar, Lowe, and Dave McCarty were among the players spraying the crowd in the lower boxes with beer and champagne. Kevin Youkilis and Ellis Burks threw baseballs into the crowd.

ELLIS BURKS, *designated hitter:*

That was the excitement of it all. We wanted to show the fans that we were definitely excited and to help them share it with us.[183]

ORLANDO CABRERA:

There was a reporter with me from Colombia. He was staying with me. I got him a media pass, and he was inside. Remember how small that clubhouse was? We destroyed that place! Everybody was incredibly happy. And I didn't know. I was like, "Is this the way you guys party?"[184]

JOHN HENRY:

I was talking with Alan Embree. As we were talking, he was slowly pouring beer over my head. Very slowly. It was a sign of respect.[185]

ALAN EMBREE:

Nobody else would do it. They were scared. He deserved to celebrate and experience that moment. I'd been in a lot of celebrations. I knew what this meant. I looked at him and I thought, *I'm going to ruin a $500 shirt right here!* I didn't dump it or get crazy. I wanted him to realize what he'd done with a group he'd put together, and how special it really was.... Plus, I was already signed for 2005.[186]

JOHNNY DAMON:

We could not be happier for Derek, and the fans really appreciate him and what he's given to this ballclub over the past years. You know, to hear them chant "D-Lowe," that was special.[187]

TERRY FRANCONA:

Here is a guy we send to the bullpen. He's not, I don't want to say, somewhat broken-hearted, but I understand that. I think it's kind of fitting. Comes out, gets an out, gets a win. We've used a lot of people this year, and we've never been afraid to go to anybody, and I think it was very fitting that he got the win.[188]

DAVID ORTIZ:

I don't think people should ever give up on D-Lowe. He's the kind of guy who, when you really need him, he steps up.[189]

DEREK LOWE:

My relationship with this city is a lot like a marriage. We have good times and we have bad times, but at the end of the day we respect each other. All kidding aside, I hope they understand it really helps to hear the cheers.[190]

KEVIN MILLAR:
This is the way it's going to be for us. Nothing's going to come easy.[191]

JASON VARITEK:
It's actually better this way. This is a building block. That's the way this team wins. When we're faced with adversity, we seem to come through.[192]

The Red Sox were the first of the eight playoff teams to clinch a series. Their reward? A few days of rest.

TERRY FRANCONA:
Now we can sit back, watch games, get our rotation together, and prepare.[193]

The Red Sox outscored the Angels 25–12, scoring at least eight runs in each of the three games. They collected 35 hits and 20 walks in 28 innings. Throw in three Angels errors and a hit batsman, and that's an average of two base runners per inning.

Boston's relentless offense got the leadoff man on base in five of the 10 innings in Game 3, and three of those runners scored. For the series, the Red Sox's leadoff man reached base 12 times and scored eight times. Boston also excelled at two-out RBIs—13 of its 17 runs in the first two games, and 16 of the 25 runs, came with two outs.

Ten different Red Sox players scored in the three games, and eight players scored at least two runs, showing a remarkably balanced lineup.

The Red Sox exercised superb plate discipline throughout the series, averaging 4.33 pitches per plate appearance against the three Angels starters. That number was almost identical to that of Bobby Abreu of the Phillies, who led all players in pitches per plate appearance in 2004.

Part of that plate discipline meant getting on base by any means necessary. No one showed that more than Mark Bellhorn. During the regular season, Bellhorn had set a Red Sox record with 177 strikeouts, but he also led the team with 88 walks. It was much the same in the ALDS. Bellhorn went 1-for-11, but he drew five walks, giving him an excellent .375 on-base percentage. In Game 3, Bellhorn struck out three times but walked twice and scored two runs.

RON JACKSON:

I didn't mind the strikeouts. He had a good on-base. That's the key. And he didn't hit into a lot of double plays—because he'd strike out! It's hard to explain his approach, but when you look around, if you go to sleep on him—BAM!—he's going to bust you. You have a lot of guys hitting for a higher average, but they're not driving in runs. He's got 82 runs batted in and 93 runs scored.[194]

MARK BELLHORN, *second baseman*:

I always struck out throughout my career. I know a lot of people think of that as negative, but that was part of my game. I always worked the count deep, so I wasn't a guy who swung at the first pitch. I don't think I struck out a lot in the clutch.[195]

In 2004, Bellhorn batted .225 with the bases empty, .309 (with much more power) with men on base, and .304 with runners in scoring position. Bellhorn struck out in 35 percent of his plate appearances with the bases empty but only 21 percent of his plate appearances with men on base.

The Red Sox defense allowed only one unearned run, while Anaheim— the superior fielding team on paper—allowed six.

ORLANDO CABRERA:

We take a lot of pride in our defense here. It's not something we talk about too much except when we think there's something to get better at. We spend a lot of time trying to make sure we can hold runners on base better, but guys just come up with the big plays when we need them.[196]

MIKE TIMLIN:

When you know the guys behind you are going to catch the ball, it does wonders for a pitcher's psyche.[197]

There was no MVP trophy awarded in the Division Series, but had it existed, it would have belonged to David Ortiz. Big Papi went 6-for-11 with two doubles, one home run, five walks, four RBIs, and four runs scored. His gaudy batting line: .545/.688/1.000. Johnny Damon was 7-for-15 (.467), and Manny Ramirez was 5-for-13 (.385) with seven RBIs.

For the Angels, Guerrero drove in half of his team's 12 runs in the series.

DAVID ORTIZ:
[Guerrero's grand slam was] about the only good thing that happened for Anaheim in the series. Vladi had a great September and he basically got the Angels into the playoffs all by himself, but he was just one man. We were a whole team.[198]

KEVIN MILLAR:
We've won three, but the goal is to get to 11. Tonight we celebrate. Tomorrow it's back to work.[199]

PEDRO MARTINEZ:
Winning a World Series is a big job for any team. This is only the beginning.[200]

Newsday called Boston's sweep of the Angels "a dress rehearsal for destiny."[201]

DARIN ERSTAD:
Those boys are winning the World Series. That's the deepest team I've ever seen. They have every piece of the puzzle. I don't see anybody beating them.[202]

Who would the Red Sox face in the LCS? It hadn't been determined. The Yankees and Twins were tied at one game apiece. Fans at Fenway chanted, "We want the Yankees! We want the Yankees!" Most of the Red Sox players professed not to care.

CURT SCHILLING:
I know the angle of it works for the media, but for us it doesn't. We're trying to win a world championship. I don't care how we get there.[203]

KEVIN MILLAR:
You don't get an extra ring by going through Yankee Stadium. All we need is an opponent. We're not worried about who it is.[204]

BRONSON ARROYO:
It doesn't make a difference. But New York would obviously be sweeter because you're always going to hear it if we don't beat those guys.[205]

DEREK LOWE:

Politically, you can't say the right thing. You can't come out and say, "New York." It can't matter to us who we play.[206]

JOHNNY DAMON:

Why not? Isn't that the way it should be? If we have to do that dance again, we will.[207]

JOHN HENRY:

I prefer the Twins. Then it will be the American League Championship Series instead of the Red Sox and the Yankees. But I really don't care. I just want to play a National League team.[208]

7

American League Championship Series Preview

IT HAD TO BE THIS WAY.

After the drama and heartache of 2003, Red Sox fans—ever resolute, ever hopeful—were ready to take another shot. They yearned to get back in the ring for another (possible) seven-round heavyweight bout with their longtime rivals, the New York Yankees. And once the Yankees had beaten the Minnesota Twins in the other American League Division Series, some Red Sox players admitted that they also wanted the rematch.

GABE KAPLER:
Before the playoffs started, everyone asked us, "Does it have to go through New York? Do you have to play the Yankees?" At the time, we said "No." But we probably should have said, "Yes."[209]

THEO EPSTEIN:
Now that it's here, we can admit that if we're able to win a World Series and go through New York along the way, it'll probably mean that much more.[210]

JOHNNY DAMON:

If we didn't, we would hear all the time, "Well, they didn't have to face the Yankees." It's got to go through New York. They don't want to be the Yankee team that loses the year the Red Sox win the whole thing, so there's pressure on them.[211]

KEVIN MILLAR:

There was no other team we wanted to play. Obviously, your goal is to win a ring and win a World Series for the city of Boston, but it seems like all the cards were dealt the way the baseball gods were going to have it.... Last year we were a real giddy group. We had a lot of fun. It's the same group this year, but we're a prepared group. We are much more relaxed, and it's a controlled swagger we have. Last year, we walked off the field after Game 7. It was gut-wrenching. But that makes you stronger and tougher, and here we are.[212]

DAVID ORTIZ:

This is the World Series. Everyone said we would handle our business against the Angels and that the Yankees would crush Minnesota and we'd do it again. But this is the first time people have told me that they feel good against the Yankees.[213]

CURTIS LESKANIC:

When we played in Anaheim, that was a playoff game. When we played in Yankee Stadium, or they played against us, that was a playoff game and the Super Bowl mixed into one. The Red Sox and Yankees is one of the biggest rivalries in sports, and then on top of that, whoever wins this is going to go to the World Series.... We had the beards, they had the straight-shaved faces. We had the long hair, they had the short haircuts. That was the coolest thing about it. We were just so different. We had respect for them, and they had respect for us. But you still want to punch them in the mouth, you know what I mean?[214]

POKEY REESE:

That was another thing about me choosing the Red Sox. The Yankees, you had to be clean-shaven. Hair, collar length. I had no problem with that, but sometimes you just want to be yourself and have fun.[215]

It was inevitable that the media would focus on the obvious contrasts between the Red Sox's raucous, unkempt crew and the serious, buttoned-down Yankees. Michael Silverman of the *Boston Herald* wondered, "Can a roster full of Alfred E. Neumans, the Red Sox idiots, beat a roster full of Cary Grants, the pinstriped and proper Yankees?"[216] Filip Bondy, *New York Daily News* columnist, described the ALCS showdown as, "the world's most one-sided and overheated archrivalry" with "the whale taking another run at the plankton."[217]

The Yankees won 101 games in 2004—the third consecutive year that they had won more than 100 games—and finished in first place in the American League East for the seventh consecutive year. In all seven of those seasons, the Red Sox ended up in second place. Boston's saving grace was the wild card. Since its inception, the Red Sox had clinched the final playoff spot four times and advanced to the ALCS twice, in 1999 and 2003, only to be turned back by the Yankees. Once again, New York stood directly in front of the Red Sox on the road to the World Series.

The Yankees had been in the playoffs each year since 1995 and had played in five of the last six World Series—and six of the last eight, winning four of them.

The Red Sox and Yankees were considered the two best teams in the American League, finishing 1–2 in several offensive categories, including runs scored (Red Sox 949, Yankees 897), on-base percentage (Red Sox .360, Yankees .353), and slugging percentage (Red Sox .472, Yankees .458). The Yankees belted 242 homers, tied with the Chicago White Sox for the most in the AL. The Red Sox were fourth with 222.

The Yankees had a lineup nearly as powerful as Boston's, with four batters whose OPS topped .880: right fielder Gary Sheffield (.927), left fielder Hideki Matsui (.912), third baseman Alex Rodriguez (.888), and catcher Jorge Posada (.881). Rodriguez and Sheffield led the team with 36 home runs. Sheffield knocked in 121 runs, with Matsui (108) and Rodriguez (106) also over the century mark. The Yankees could also run a little—A-Rod stole 28 bases, while shortstop Derek Jeter had 23. The entire Red Sox team had only 68 steals.

The question mark for the Yankees was starting pitching. The team had lost four-fifths of its rotation from 2003; Mike Mussina was the sole holdover. After being unable to acquire Curt Schilling, GM Brian Cashman signed Javier Vazquez as a free agent and traded for Kevin Brown. Mussina and Vazquez had slumped badly in the second half. The Yankees were also counting on two starters who had missed all of 2003: Orlando Hernandez and Jon Lieber. No Yankee pitcher who made more than 15 starts had an ERA less than 4.00: Brown (4.09), Lieber (4.33), Mussina (4.59), Vazquez (4.91), and Jose Contreras (5.64). The strength of New York's bullpen lay solely in the arms of Tom Gordon and Mariano Rivera.

In their Division Series against Minnesota, the Yankees lost the first game before coming back to win three straight: 7–6 in 12 innings, 8–4, and 6–5 in 11 innings. In Game 2, Mariano Rivera blew a two-run lead in the eighth inning before the Yankees rallied after falling behind again in extras to salvage a split at home before heading to the Metrodome. New York staged a remarkable comeback to win Game 4. Trailing 5–1 in the eighth inning, they scored four times, three runs coming on a home run by Ruben Sierra. In the 11th inning, Alex Rodriguez doubled, stole third, and scored on a wild pitch.

And the Yankees might be starting the ALCS without one of their most important players. Rivera, who had a 0.71 ERA in 65 postseason games, had flown to Panama on Sunday, after two of his relatives were accidentally electrocuted by a fence at Rivera's home. The funeral was scheduled for Monday morning, the day of Game 1. Yankee officials told Rivera to stay in Panama for as long as he needed.

Tom "Flash" Gordon, who saved 46 games for the Red Sox back in 1998, would take Rivera's place, if necessary. However, Gordon had been struck in the left eye by a champagne cork during New York's ALDS celebration. Gordon reported that his vision was "still a little blurry" and clouded with "black dots."[218]

Boston's rotation of Curt Schilling, Pedro Martinez, Bronson Arroyo, and Tim Wakefield remained unchanged. The Red Sox did make one roster switch, dropping backup third baseman Kevin Youkilis and adding right-handed relief pitcher (and former Yankee) Ramiro Mendoza.

The Red Sox were 11–8 against the Yankees in 2004, outscoring New York by a single run, 106–105. There was no shortage of drama, as the winning runs in eight of those 19 games were scored in one of the teams' final at-bats. The Yankees were confident in their ability to win games late, having put together three comeback victories in the ALDS on top of a major league record 61 come-from-behind regular season wins.

DEREK JETER:
This is what everyone expected. It doesn't get any tighter than it did last year, going to Game 7. There are always going to be stories, and I'm sure this series will have its own.[219]

ALEX RODRIGUEZ, *Yankees third baseman:*
Any log you throw onto the fire is going to add to the rivalry, and with me almost going there and now being here, it adds intensity.... I was watching very closely last year as a fan. I'm going to enjoy playing in it a lot more.[220]

BRIAN CASHMAN, *Yankees general manager:*
All year long, I've had private conversations with Theo, which is, "We're the two best teams in our league." Everybody knows it. I don't know how much of a higher level it can get with Boston, but I'm sure it will reach new levels.[221]

Curt Schilling threw 35–40 pitches during a bullpen session on Sunday at Fenway Park—a "test run" for his start Tuesday evening in Game 1. Seeking to mimic game conditions as much as possible, Schilling's troublesome right ankle was taped, he wore a brace, and he received a shot of the painkiller Marcaine.

Schilling was suffering from a tear in the sheath that held one of the two tendons on the outside of his right ankle. The displaced tendon was sliding across the outside of the bone during his pitching motion, causing pain and a distracting clicking sound. The Red Sox had not disclosed the true extent of Schilling's injury to the media. Before the ALCS began, it was reported as only a high ankle sprain[222] or inflammation of the tendon.[223]

Francona considered flip-flopping Schilling and Pedro Martinez against the Yankees, but the team's medical staff said an extra day or two of rest for Schilling wouldn't make any difference with this type of injury.

CURT SCHILLING:

I thought I had an idea of what it was going to be like when I signed last winter. I got a feel for it the first time I was in Boston, but I had no idea that it was going to be at the level it was right from the get-go. As much as the people in the stands dislike each other in both cities, they are exactly alike. In Boston it's "Yankees suck," and in New York it's "1918." I don't know that I've ever pitched in a game that will have the atmosphere that tomorrow's game will have. In Arizona during the 2001 World Series, it was electric. But the Yankees and the Red Sox is a step above everything else. I want to be a part of something that hasn't been done in nearly a century.... In the 1993 NLCS we went to Atlanta and I was talking to Terry Mulholland, and he said the awesome thing about being a starting pitcher on the road is you have the ability to make 55,000 people shut up. I'm not sure I can think of any scenario more enjoyable than making 55,000 people from New York shut up.[224]

In the fall of 2003, the Arizona Diamondbacks were looking to get rid of Schilling's contract. The right-handed pitcher said that he would agree to a trade to either the Yankees or the Phillies. When asked about Boston, Schilling specifically said he would not consider the Red Sox.

CURT SCHILLING:

I had pitched in Fenway once before, in interleague play. I threw like seven innings and gave up seven or eight runs one night [June 22, 1998] and [we] ended up getting the win. I remember the park feeling incredibly small. Being a fly ball pitcher, that's generally not a good mix.[225]

But when Schilling heard that Terry Francona—his manager for part of his time in Philadelphia and someone Schilling respected—was being interviewed for the job of Red Sox manager for 2004, he reconsidered.

BRIAN CASHMAN:

The initial asking price was extremely high [Alfonso Soriano and Nick Johnson]. In terms of our discussions with Arizona, they didn't go very far ultimately because Boston swooped in and made a deal to convince Curt to go to Boston. That was something that was unanticipated, at least by me. When a player comes out publicly and says he won't go somewhere, I never expected Boston to come out and try to make a play and convince him otherwise. [226]

THEO EPSTEIN:

We went out on a limb. I think that got his attention. When we were out there [in Arizona], we told him that we really wanted him. After the first day, it was clear he wanted to be a Red Sox. It just became a contract issue.[227]

CURT SCHILLING:

Theo Epstein and Jed Hoyer came to the house the night before the meeting and dropped off a note from Bill James with a statistical breakdown on how I would have fared in Fenway given my spray charts and hitting charts from the year before. And Fenway was actually better than Bank One. That was clearly part of the sales pitch.[228]

BILL JAMES, *senior baseball operations advisor:*

Fenway actually is a very good park for a right-handed fly ball pitcher. I wrote a letter to Schilling, pointing out that in the previous 20 years, right-handed fly ball pitchers had won five Cy Young Awards in Fenway Park [Roger Clemens (3) and Pedro Martinez (2)], and also that we had many other very successful right-handed fly ball pitchers over the years.[229]

CURT SCHILLING:

We started off the discussions on Wednesday with Larry Lucchino, Theo Epstein, and Jed Hoyer. We discussed potential salary and things like that. They made a couple of offers, and they were not even remotely doable. We kept talking into the evening. In the background, at the same time, I got a call from a person locally who was well connected with the Yankees. That person informed me that their general manager, Brian Cashman, was going to call in the near future and that they were very interested. I ended up having a couple of conversations along those lines. I was told if I let a certain window run out, I could basically fill out a blank check. Which was obviously interesting. That was a nice fallback, if it didn't work out with the Red Sox.

The problem was that at this point, I had sat with Theo and Jed long enough to really like both of them, and so I started to kind of want to go to Boston. Larry had left. We found out Theo and Jed had nowhere to go for Thanksgiving, so we invited them over. They politely declined, but I said, "These contract discussions are completely off if you guys don't show up." So they came over.

Jed was really sick that day, and we spent most of the day watching football, just talking. I could see that, from an analytical standpoint, Theo and I were birds of a feather. He believed in the things I believed in to be a good pitcher. We believed in data and stats the same way. There was a lot of common ground, but we parted ways on Thursday feeling like this was not going to happen. At the same time, I was talking to the other party, and we were setting up a potential Saturday get-together as soon as the Red Sox window of opportunity ran out.

But then, as I understand it, Theo made a call to John Henry and got him to change his mind on the finances. At one point, we were in the room where my World Series trophy was sitting. It was actually sitting in the background between Larry and Theo, and I said, "What you have to figure out is what kind of value you place on that"—and I pointed to the World Series trophy. "You're bringing me there to win one of those. And I've done it against the team you can't get past. I know there's some value there. You guys are going to have to decide if it's worth it." And ultimately they did.[230]

Schilling and the Red Sox agreed on a $37.5 million contract for three years (2004–06), which included a provision for a $2 million bonus if the Red Sox won the World Series in any of those years.

There may have been something else that aided Boston's acquisition of Schilling. After the 2001 season, free agent pitcher David Wells reached an oral agreement with the Diamondbacks only to sign a contract with the Yankees a short time later, after talking with Yankees principal owner George Steinbrenner. Perhaps Diamondbacks owner Jerry Colangelo remembered that incident when dealing with the Yankees and had been unwilling to cut New York any breaks. Perhaps it was Steinbrenner's hubris that guided Schilling toward the Red Sox.

8

American League Championship Series Game 1

Tuesday, October 12, 2004, at Yankee Stadium

CURT SCHILLING:
Didn't we all know it would come to this to get to a World Series? This will hopefully be a series for the ages.... But again I ask, "Why not us?"[231]

The Red Sox had suffered a devastating defeat in 2003—the first true heartbreak for a new generation of Red Sox fans, and a sadly familiar (but no less painful) one for older fans. The media seemed to revel in the tired notion of a curse. But this particular group of Red Sox players appeared unburdened by the franchise's history of near-misses.

KEVIN YOUKILIS, *third baseman*:
I didn't know about Boston sports until I got there. Guys are from all over the country. As a kid, I read all about the Cincinnati Reds. We get to Boston and we're expected to know about Carl Yastrzemski and Ted Williams.... There are some guys who don't know anything about the history of baseball. They play baseball, and they love it. Some guys are historians, and then there's guys in between. The

2004 team had the attitude—we don't believe in the curse, some higher being that doesn't want the Red Sox to win. We refused to buy in to the negativity.[232]

In response to what Youkilis called "a cloud of negativity" that often surrounds coverage of the Red Sox, Curt Schilling had T-shirts made for his teammates saying, *"Why Not Us?"*[233]

CURT SCHILLING:

It happened in August some time. I was hearing all these reasons we couldn't win and all the reasons why it wasn't going to happen. I didn't believe in all the bullshit. This team hadn't won a World Series for 86 years for no other reason than a lack of talent. The best teams always find a way to win in October. I don't care what it says on paper. And so—I don't remember where I was when I said it, but I said, "Why not us?" Really, you couldn't honestly answer the question. If you looked in that clubhouse and you looked at that roster, if you looked at that staff and that lineup, there was no way that we couldn't win it. The only reason we were not going to win it all was going to be for some internal reason. Something we did to ourselves.[234]

After all the pre-series hype—the Red Sox were favored, but not by much—it was finally time to play ball. It was a pleasant Tuesday night in the Bronx, with a game-time temperature of 59 degrees. After Mike Mussina set down the Red Sox in the top of the first, Schilling walked to the mound, and while he was ready and willing, his ankle was not able.

CURT SCHILLING:

I knew it before the game when I hit the top step to head to the bullpen. I felt the tendon roll over the bone. I was like, *Aw, this is not going to be good.* It wasn't the pain as much as it was the awkwardness of the feeling. I could hear it pop and feel it roll over. With every pitch I was anticipating hearing it and feeling it. It was throwing a wrench into the middle of my mechanics. I was adjusting physically to pitching with it, but I was afraid of blowing my arm out.... I knew five pitches in that I was in trouble.[235]

Derek Jeter and Alex Rodriguez both flew out to right field, but doubles by Gary Sheffield and Hideki Matsui and a single from Bernie Williams gave

New York two runs. Several times during the inning, Schilling had to re-tie his right shoe—he was not wearing his normal cleats and had trouble with the knots—and once he was back in the dugout, he changed the tape on his ankle and adjusted the brace.

In the second, Schilling retired the Yankees without incident, but his fastball velocity had dropped to 88–90 mph. He had nearly abandoned his split-fingered fastball and was relying mostly on his curveball and slider, but even those pitches lacked bite and were ineffective. To be successful, Schilling needed to work low in the zone, but because he could not properly drive off his right foot, most of his pitches stayed up.

CURT SCHILLING:
I couldn't accelerate off the rubber. The tendon was popping. My stride foot was landing about a foot shorter than usual. My arm felt phenomenal, but I couldn't push off. I was trying as hard as I could to make adjustments, but it just wasn't working.[236]

Jeter led off the bottom of the third with a single to center. Rodriguez beat out an infield single to shortstop. Sheffield walked, loading the bases. After Schilling re-tied his right shoe yet again, Matsui smoked a double off the wall in right field. All three runners scored, and New York led 5–0.

Pitching coach Dave Wallace went out to talk to Schilling and catcher Jason Varitek, although there wasn't much to say. Mike Myers and Curtis Leskanic began warming up for the Red Sox. Matsui went to third base on Williams' groundout and scored on Jorge Posada's fly ball to center. Schilling walked John Olerud on four pitches. Myers was ready in the pen, waiting for the call, but Miguel Cairo flied out to center for the third out. Far from making 55,000 New Yorkers shut up, Schilling's ineffectiveness prompted jeers and taunts as he walked off the mound. One huge handmade sign hanging from the upper deck read: "CURT SHELLING."

Schilling's night was over after only three innings and 58 pitches; he allowed six runs on six hits and two walks. It was only the second time in 13 postseason starts that he had allowed more than two earned runs.

CURT SCHILLING:
I can't argue with the manager taking me out right there. The bell rang, and I couldn't answer it. I'd been looking forward to this for

a year, and it's incredibly disappointing. I went in thinking I could do what I needed to do. I failed at that. Once I realized the velocity wasn't there, I tried to work on location. I couldn't do that, either.[237]

TERRY FRANCONA:
We talked when he came out. He didn't complain about any pain. He just wasn't right. He couldn't feel anything. They'd injected him, but he could hear the tendon snapping. It made it hard to focus on what he was doing.[238]

After Schilling's departure, Francona gave most of his relievers some work, using Leskanic in the fourth, Ramiro Mendoza in the fifth, Tim Wakefield in the sixth, Alan Embree in the seventh, and Mike Timlin and Keith Foulke in the eighth.

TERRY FRANCONA:
We were trying to match up a little bit and not overuse anybody. And also pick innings where we thought we could get them to go out there and get a zero.[239]

Kenny Lofton greeted Wakefield with a solo home run to right field. Two outs later, Sheffield doubled and Matsui singled him in; it was Matsui's fifth RBI of the night, which tied an LCS record. The Yankees led 8–0. The largest deficit the Red Sox had overcome in the regular season was five runs. They had done that twice, the last time coming on July 24, the day of the Rodriguez-Varitek brawl.

Meanwhile, Mussina was methodically setting down the Red Sox batters one after the next. With seemingly little effort, he retired the first 19 hitters. At one point, he struck out five consecutive batters, tying an ALCS record set by Schilling in 1993 and by Mussina himself in 1997. In his last five postseason starts, Mussina had received only five runs of support in 33⅓ innings. Tonight, he was pitching with the unexpected riches of a comfortable lead.

After six innings with no Red Sox batter having reached base, many fans might have been thinking about Yankees pitcher Don Larsen and his perfect game against the Brooklyn Dodgers in Game 5 of the 1956 World Series. Mussina's performance was also reminiscent of a gem he pitched against the Red Sox on September 2, 2001, in which he retired the first 26 batters before giving up a single to Carl Everett.

DOUG MIENTKIEWICZ:
Mussina, he was like our Kryptonite.[240]

In the first six innings of Game 1, the Red Sox hit only four balls out of the infield, and only one of them was hit hard. Mussina exploited the Red Sox's tendency to forego swinging at the first pitch, as seven of the first nine Red Sox batters took a first-pitch strike. Mussina was moving his fastball around effectively and generating weak swings against his slider and knucklecurve.

MIKE MUSSINA, *Yankees pitcher:*
I had command of everything. That's the best six innings I've had all year. The curve was in a good location, and I had good velocity on my fastball so I stayed with it. I knew what was going on. Of course you think about it. I knew I hadn't pitched out of the stretch.[241]

TERRY FRANCONA:
The vibe in the dugout was actually pretty good even when we were down 6–0, 8–0. They kept saying we'd peck away.[242]

JASON VARITEK:
We didn't panic on the bench. There was a lot of game left.[243]

In the top of the seventh with one out, Mussina got two quick strikes on Mark Bellhorn, but the Boston second baseman was able to whack an opposite-field double, a high fly that landed at the base of the fence in left center. The chance for a perfect game or no-hitter was gone.[244]

Mussina got the second out, but then things started to unravel. David Ortiz lined a 1–1 curve to right for a single, and Bellhorn stopped at third. Millar drove a ball to left-center. Matsui leapt, but the ball hit off his glove, and he staggered after it as it rolled to the wall. Bellhorn and Ortiz both scored easily on the double. Mussina's first pitch to Trot Nixon bounced away from catcher Jorge Posada for a passed ball; Millar took third. Nixon singled to center two pitches later, bringing in Millar. New York manager Joe Torre came out to make a pitching change. The Yankee infielders gathered at the mound, and Mussina left the game to a standing ovation.

RON JACKSON:
Sometimes when you haven't pitched with guys on base, you've been
in the windup the whole time and all of a sudden you get guys on base,
you lose that rhythm. We probably broke up that rhythm, and he just
couldn't find it again.[245]

Jason Varitek greeted reliever Tanyon Sturtze with a two-run home run.
In the span of 14 pitches, Boston had gone from being eight outs away from
losing a perfect game to trailing by only three runs, 8–5. The home run was
Varitek's first hit at Yankee Stadium all year; he had been 0-for-34 (with 19
strikeouts) during the regular season.

JOHNNY DAMON:
We were relaxed; we weren't down. Maybe we didn't think we'd come
all the way back at first, but then we were in it.[246]

The Red Sox continued their comeback in the eighth inning against
Tom Gordon. Mueller lined a single off Cairo's glove at second base. After
Damon struck out (for the fourth time in the game) and Bellhorn popped to
left, Ramirez blooped a single into short left field and Mueller raced to third.

Mariano Rivera had been warming up in the pen, having arrived at the
park from Panama during the third inning, but Torre stayed with Gordon.
Ortiz crushed a long drive to left-center. Matsui leapt at the wall but this
time he had overrun the ball and it glanced off his glove. Ortiz legged out
a triple, making it an 8–7 game.

DAVID ORTIZ:
I almost got him. He threw me a backdoor slider, and in this ballpark,
it's hard to get it out.[247]

What was once a rout was now a nail-biter. With the potential tying
run on third base, Torre summoned Rivera to face Millar. Rivera threw two
balls before Millar popped out to shortstop for the third out.

In the eighth, the Yankees added two insurance runs off Mike Timlin.
Rodriguez and Sheffield both singled and scored on Williams' opposite-field
double over Ramirez's head in left.

JOHNNY DAMON:
Bernie struck it well. Manny had to be playing a little shallow because Alex Rodriguez was on second and he had to have a chance to throw him out at the plate.[248]

What could have been a Red Sox comeback for the ages fell short in the ninth. Facing Rivera, Varitek lined a one-out single to right and Cabrera grounded a single to left. Mueller represented the potential tying run. He worked the count to 2–2 before chopping the ball back to the mound. Rivera gloved it, quickly turned around, and started a double play that ended the game. Rivera notched his 31st postseason save.

Despite the 10–7 defeat, and the questions surrounding Curt Schilling's ankle, the Red Sox were upbeat.

DAVID ORTIZ:
I like it, man. I like it. They've got their ace on the mound, throwing a perfect game in the seventh inning. We're down 8–0 with eight outs to go, and they had to use all their pitchers to keep us from coming back. We almost got this one, and they know we're here.[249]

JOHNNY DAMON:
The Yankees must be shaking their heads. Damn, it got close pretty quick. It was great to hear the fans out there get quiet a little bit. We definitely gave them a scare.[250]

CURT SCHILLING:
Bummed out would be the understatement of the year. The whole night was just a nightmare. If we'd sent anybody else out there but me tonight, we would have won the game. If I can't do more than I did tonight, I won't take the ball again. That would be the peak of selfishness in my mind. This is not about me braving through something. This is about us and winning the world championship, and if I can't give them better than I had today, I won't take the ball again.[251]

9

American League Championship Series Game 2

Wednesday, October 13, 2004, at Yankee Stadium

JOHNNY DAMON:

There's no way we can get back to Boston down 0–2. That's a tough road to climb.[252]

After the Yankees defeated Pedro Martinez and the Red Sox at Fenway Park back on September 24, the Boston ace appeared hollow-eyed and tired.

PEDRO MARTINEZ:

I can't find a way to beat them at this point. I wish they would fucking disappear and never come back. I'd like to face any other team right now. To pitch a good game, make good pitches, and still can't beat them it's frustrating.... How many times am I going to have the lead and let it go? It was all me. I wanted to bury myself on the mound.... What can I say? I just tip my hat and call the Yankees my daddy.[253]

It was a shocking statement from someone as proud as Martinez, a raw honesty that professional athletes almost never reveal in public. "Who's your daddy?" became a rallying cry for Yankees fans for the entire series.

The New York media couldn't get enough of it. The cover of the *Daily News'* ALCS preview section featured a cartoon of Martinez wearing a diaper and holding a rattle. "Come To Daddy," the headline read. "Pedro, Sox Pop In For Annual Spanking."

Surprisingly, even Major League Baseball got in on the act, selling an officially licensed T-shirt with the message "Hey Red Sox…Who's Your Daddy?" above the Yankees' logo and a picture of a red pacifier with the Boston "B" on it. The shirt was available for five days before it was pulled out of stores and off MLB's website.[254]

For Game 2, the question of Martinez's paternity hung on any number of fans' signs. Stan's Sports Bar, a grungy tavern on River Avenue across the street from Yankee Stadium, had a huge banner: DA BAMBINO IS YOUR DADDY. One fan came to the game dressed as Darth Vader holding a sign: "Pedro, I'm Your Father," referencing both Martinez's quote and Larry Lucchino's description of the Yankees organization as the "Evil Empire." At the start of Game 2, a huge sign hung in the upper deck proclaiming, "It's Father's Day."

Martinez skipped the pregame press conference, as he had before his ALDS start. Other members of the Red Sox were asked about Martinez's "Daddy" comment.

THEO EPSTEIN:
Have you ever had a bad day at work? And have you ever had someone ask you about your bad day at work five minutes after you're done?[255]

TERRY FRANCONA:
I put more credence in his pitching the last 10 years than I do one sentence when he was a little frustrated.[256]

One constant refrain in the media was Martinez's struggles against the Yankees. When you looked beyond his win-loss record—10–11 in 30 starts—the numbers told a different story. For example, while Martinez was 1–2 against the Yankees in both 2000 and 2001, his ERAs were excellent: 2.10 and 2.37, respectively. Pedro's overall ERA against the talented Yankees lineups was 3.35—something any pitcher would be proud of.

Before Game 2, the Red Sox revealed the full extent of Schilling's injury.

DR. WILLIAM MORGAN:
When he grabbed his ankle during the game in Anaheim, it became apparent that he had more than tendonitis. He had dislocated a tendon. It was snapping over the side of the bone itself. We worked on ways of bracing and keeping it in position. Going into the game yesterday, we felt very confident. But once he began pitching, it started subluxing, or snapping, out of position, and even though it wasn't painful because he had Marcaine, it was causing some instability and interfering with his ability to pitch. If we were not where we are right now, he would have the surgery done.... The other question: are we causing injury, allowing him to play? The answer is no.[257]

There was the distinct possibility that Schilling would miss his next start in a possible Game 5 or perhaps be lost to the Red Sox for the rest of the postseason.

DEREK LOWE:
They're saying Schilling may not be able to bounce back. The next guy in line could be me. But who even knows if they'd pick me, you know? You'd love to get an opportunity to start a game, but I don't have my hopes too high. He's had an ankle problem for the majority of the year. At some points, there was talk like he was going to have surgery the next week. He's dealt with it a long time, and he's never missed a start. In my eyes, he's going to pitch.[258]

Lowe also expressed surprise that when Schilling exited Game 1 after three innings, he did not get the call.

DEREK LOWE:
I was live last night, and they held me out. I've always been under the impression that when the fifth guy is sent to the bullpen and the starter has trouble, that's when he comes in to take pressure off and take innings from the other guys. You're the starter's caddy, so to speak. But then the situation presents itself and you still don't get into the game. As far as what my role is right now, I don't really have any idea.[259]

If Schilling was unable to make his next start, they would need Lowe fresh for Game 5. The first roar of "Who's your daddy?" erupted from the bleachers a little before 8:00 PM. The chant rang in Martinez's ears all night long. It echoed from the upper decks after he walked leadoff hitter Derek Jeter on four pitches. Jeter was aggressive and stole second base on the first pitch to Alex Rodriguez. Then Martinez grazed Rodriguez's left wrist with a pitch, and the Yankees had two base runners. Gary Sheffield followed with a hard single to center, and Jeter scored. Martinez rebounded, however, striking out Hideki Matsui and Bernie Williams—both looking—and getting Jorge Posada on a ground ball to second.

For the second night in a row, Boston's offense was virtually nonexistent in the early innings. The Red Sox managed only two runners in the first six innings against Jon Lieber—David Ortiz's second-inning walk and a leadoff single from Orlando Cabrera in the third.

Meanwhile, the Yankees were doing what they always did against Martinez: making him throw a lot of pitches, knowing that after 100 pitches, he lost his effectiveness. Martinez threw 26 pitches in the first inning and 20 more in the second. By contrast, Lieber threw only 45 pitches over his first five innings.

With one out in the sixth, after Posada had walked, Jason Varitek set up away on a 1–2 pitch to John Olerud, but Martinez's 106th pitch of the night stayed inside, just above the belt. Olerud lined it to right field, and it just cleared the fence, landing in the first row of seats near a fan holding a "1918" sign. The "Daddy" chants began again as New York led 3–0.

PEDRO MARTINEZ:
I did not feel tired. It was a fastball. I wanted it away, but it cut inside. I didn't release it well, and he took full advantage of it. Give him credit. My mistake.[260]

JOHN OLERUD, *Yankees first baseman*:
A 1–2 count against Pedro—that's a bad position to be in because he can do so many different things to get you out. I was protecting the plate and tried to take a short stroke and get the barrel of the bat to the ball.[261]

After Cabrera's third-inning single, Lieber retired 13 batters in a row—working steadily, methodically. Contrary to their usual approach at the plate, the Red Sox were more aggressive. Lieber was around the strike zone all night, and the Red Sox had to swing early in counts to avoid falling behind.

As Lieber mowed them down in the middle innings, the Red Sox did nothing to disrupt his rhythm. Lieber's only battle came in the sixth inning when he needed 16 pitches to retire Johnny Damon, who fouled off 10 of them.

Boston had a golden opportunity in the eighth. After Trot Nixon knocked a hard grounder into right field for a single, Joe Torre pulled Lieber (after only 82 pitches) and brought in Tom Gordon. Varitek ripped a high slider into the gap in right-center for a double, and Nixon, bothered by a troublesome quad muscle, was held at third with no outs. Cabrera grounded out to shortstop, and Nixon scored. Varitek held at second on that play but went to third when Bill Mueller grounded to second. With Damon coming up and a runner on third base and two outs, Torre went to Rivera, who struck out Damon to end the rally.

In the ninth, Rivera got Bellhorn to ground to first. It was an important out with Boston's big bats coming up. As if to emphasize that point, Manny Ramirez doubled to left-center. Ortiz (7-for-13 against Rivera) came up as the potential tying run. After swinging and missing the first pitch, Ortiz pulled Rivera's second offering down the right-field line, but foul. Ortiz then struck out on the next pitch. Millar also fanned as Rivera hit 96 mph with his final pitch of the game. It was Rivera's second four-out save in two nights.

Lieber kept the Red Sox off-balance all night by varying his speeds and exhibiting pinpoint control. In the first two games, Mike Mussina and Lieber had walked only one batter, neutralizing a big weapon in Boston's on-base arsenal. Fifteen of Lieber's 24 batters saw three or fewer pitches.

RON JACKSON:
We didn't have much patience, like we normally do. The guy's around the plate a lot. And even when he's 3–1, 2–0, he's not going to give you anything over the middle.[262]

JASON VARITEK:
He was strike one with all his pitches. Not to take anything away from Lieber, but we got ourselves out. We tried to be overly aggressive, overanxious early in the game, tried to do too much. Pedro pitched well, but we didn't do our job.[263]

JOHNNY DAMON:
We had a lot of two- and three-pitch at-bats.... It's very frustrating. That's why I can say I'm not going to be a Yankee ever. I've been on so many teams that looked at them as rivals. That's my goal in life, to knock them off.... I'm 0-for-8 with five strikeouts. I'm better than that. I take full responsibility for these two games. They know that one way to beat our team is to stop me, and that's exactly what they've been doing. It starts with me. When I'm not doing my job, it makes it even tougher for my teammates. The minute I start swinging the bat better, it's going to be a different story. The unbelievable thing about our team is we're upbeat all the time. We know we're in a hole, but even idiots know how to dig themselves out of a hole.[264]

The two losses were hardly all Damon's fault. In the first six innings of the two games, the Red Sox batted .027 (1-for-37). No one was hitting.

PEDRO MARTINEZ:
I did everything possible to keep my team in the fight. I can't say I'm disappointed, but it's not the result I wanted. I can't do anything if we don't score runs. I can only pitch, do whatever possible to keep my team in the game, and from there on, it's up to them.[265]

TERRY FRANCONA:
He was in line for an outstanding outing. We just didn't put anything up on the board. If we had put up five or six runs and won the game, we'd all be talking about how well he pitched.[266]

Martinez was finally forced to address the inevitable questions about the "Who's your daddy?" chants, though it was hard to tell if he was being honest or sarcastic. Was Martinez toying with the media or artfully deflecting questions he'd rather not answer? Perhaps a bit of both.

PEDRO MARTINEZ:
You know what, the chanting actually made me feel really, really good. I realized that I was somebody important because I caught the attention of 60,000 people, plus the media, plus the whole world watching a guy that if you go back 15 years ago, I was sitting under a mango tree without 50 cents to pay for the bus. And today, I was the center of attention of the whole city of New York. I thank God for that, and you know what? I don't regret one bit what they do out there. I

respect them, and I actually kind of like it because I don't like to brag about myself. I don't like to talk about myself, but they did make me feel important.[267]

ALAN EMBREE:

The chanting was pretty funny. I enjoyed it. Everyone had a little grin. It was good clean fun. You just had to say, "You've got us there." Pedro opened a can of worms with that. I think we would have done it if the situation was reversed.[268]

KEVIN MILLAR:

We never make it easy on ourselves. But this team's not gonna quit. We're gonna make this a great series. It's the first team to four wins, not the first to two wins.[269]

TERRY FRANCONA:

The only way I'd be disappointed was if this was a best-of-three. There's too much baseball left to play. I still think we're capable of winning this series. We'll regroup tomorrow, go home for three, and see if we can get back in this.[270]

ALAN EMBREE:

We came into this favored, for crying out loud. We didn't like that. We play better with our backs against the wall. It's something we feed off.[271]

Several Red Sox were asked if Game 3 was a must-win.

CURT SCHILLING:

Great [expletive] question. You [expletive] me?[272]

JOHNNY DAMON:

It definitely is, yeah, because the Yankees really don't lose four in a row. Every game is a must-win right now.[273]

10
Travel Day

Thursday, October 14, 2004

KEVIN MILLAR:
We're in our park, and we're playing in front of the nation. This isn't over.[274]

Alan Embree walked into the Fenway clubhouse on Thursday, whistling the sing-song chant he had heard at Yankee Stadium so many times— "Nine-teen eight-een."[275] The team was confident of coming back in the series. On the chalkboard in the clubhouse was written, "We can change history. Believe it."[276]

KEVIN MILLAR:
This is our house. The way we feel about this place is an indescribable thing. Right down to the batter's box. I personally like our batter's box here better than the one at Yankee Stadium. It's dirt. The batter's box at Yankee Stadium is clay. If one guy digs in down there, that's where the hole is going to stay. At least here, this is dirt. And I love it. I love dirt. I don't like clay. Plus, we got our fans and our own music playing. You're eating your home cooking. This is where you want to be.[277]

TERRY FRANCONA:
Any team that plays at home, I think, enjoys advantages. You're at home, you sleep in your own bed, you get to hit last, you're in your home clubhouse, things like that, all of the things that you're used to. And when you have a place like Fenway, it makes it even better for us. Our left-handed hitters know they can hit that wall, and there are a lot of nooks and crannies we're very comfortable with here. I have a feeling when you're in the batter's box, center field is not exactly straight. That can mess with some hitters, and our guys are used to it.[278]

At Fenway, the Red Sox hit .304 with a .378 on-base percentage, .504 slugging percentage, and an average of 6.4 runs per game. On the road, they hit .260/.342/.441 and scored 5.3 runs per game. Eight of the nine regulars had higher batting averages at Fenway.

The Red Sox had solicited advice and suggestions from just about anyone and everyone, leaving no stone unturned in their attempt to find a solution to Schilling's ankle injury.

DR. WILLIAM MORGAN:
We opened Fenway for a day for people to come in—and it was a dog and pony show. I got about a thousand emails from people who had the solution. I had people sending me modified cowboy boots. I had an Army guy send me boots that had a bladder system that was sewn into it that could expand and hopefully hold the tendon in place. I had therapists, trainers—everybody had an answer. But nothing was working.[279]

THEO EPSTEIN:
I was sitting in the training room with Curt, Dr. Morgan, and Dr. George Theodore, a foot specialist at Mass General. We were talking about the different possibilities. Curt had his ankle up, and Dr. Morgan was trying to explain to me what had happened and what we could possibly do. He took out a pen and started drawing on Curt's ankle, showing us where the tendon was likely split and where it was scraping or slapping back and forth over the top of the bone. We started, almost jokingly, to wonder if there was some way to simply staple the tendon down so it didn't flap over the ankle. We didn't need to repair the tendon so much as keep it in place. If we could do that, it would be a temporary but potentially effective solution. It seemed like that

was the only thing that would give us a chance and not risk any more damage than had already occurred.[280]

Schilling was too sore to throw his normal side session on Thursday. The team announced that Schilling would not start Game 5 on Sunday; Derek Lowe would get the ball in his place. Schilling left Fenway Park with his family without speaking to the media.

THEO EPSTEIN:
This is the same bunch of guys who lost their starting shortstop and starting right fielder in spring training and had a great April, and then overcame more adversity in the middle of the season. We can win this series with Curt or without Curt. It will be a greater challenge without him.[281]

TERRY FRANCONA:
If we're not able to overcome some adversity, we're not a good enough team. We've cleared some hurdles this year already, and I think we'll do it again if we have to. If you don't believe that, how can you compete?[282]

DEREK LOWE:
I look forward to starting Game 5 instead of carrying the candy bucket out to the bullpen. But all the talk should be about tomorrow's game and Game 4. In a perfect world, the series will be tied and I'll get a chance to give us the lead. We're losing sight of the fact we're down 0–2. We're putting all this emphasis on who's going to pitch Game 5 and Game 6. But before we can talk about Game 5, we have to get to Game 5.[283]

Pedro Martinez volunteered to pitch on three days rest in place of Schilling, but the Red Sox said they had no plans to move up Martinez.

Francona bristled when asked if he had considered altering his lineup since the top of the order—Johnny Damon and Mark Bellhorn—were a combined 1-for-16 in the two losses in New York.

TERRY FRANCONA:
How about the other 162 games? To me, that would show a lack of confidence in a team that won 98 games. I'm not going to do that. I'm confident in what these guys can do. The way you win is when your players are in their spot and they play good. Damon has hit leadoff since March 2. We may flip-flop a guy or two, but nothing drastic.[284]

11

Postponed

Friday, October 15, 2004, at Fenway Park

Some of the Red Sox arrived at Fenway Park on the overcast Friday afternoon looking somewhat more professional, though no one would have mistaken them for the Yankees. Kevin Millar had cut back the Brillo-esque tuft of hair on his chin, and Johnny Damon's flowing locks had been trimmed to near shoulder length.

> **JOHNNY DAMON:**
> I didn't realize how long my hair was. I went to my friend's salon last night, and they took good care of me. They made me a better-looking guy.[285]

After being too sore to throw on Thursday, Curt Schilling played long toss on Fenway Park's outfield on Friday, testing his ankle in a 20-minute session amid steady rain under the watchful eyes of Terry Francona, Theo Epstein, pitching coach Dave Wallace, and assistant trainer Chris Correnti.

Schilling wore a high-top shoe, a specially designed version of Reebok's Vero baseball cleat, with two extra inches of supportive foam padding for ankle stabilization and a wider base through the heel to allow room for a brace. However, the shoe turned out to be the wrong size and Schilling eventually changed back to his regular shoe. He appeared more comfortable with his delivery than during Game 1, and the team was cautiously optimistic that he could pitch again in the series.

> **TERRY FRANCONA:**
> He was comfortable with that high top, as long as he gets the right size. He still experienced some clicking, but not to the point where he couldn't manage it. He threw with more of a normal stride than we saw in New York, which by itself was encouraging. The next step is to see how he shows up tomorrow. The door hasn't been closed. It's way too early to rule him out for the entire series.[286]

Rain fell steadily in Boston throughout the afternoon and early evening, growing heavier as the night went on. Game 3 was postponed at 8:06 PM, roughly 20 minutes before the scheduled first pitch. In addition to having another day to work with Schilling, the Red Sox now had the option of using Pedro Martinez on his regular rest instead of Derek Lowe in Game 5.

> **JOHNNY DAMON:**
> A lot of people are saying we've got nothing to lose right now. So the Yankees can wait it out and keep thinking about the games. We're carefree and loose.[287]

12

American League Championship Series Game 3

Saturday, October 16, 2004, at Fenway Park

THEO EPSTEIN:

They didn't want me to be alone, they were worried about what I might do.[288]

Friday's postponement removed the scheduled off-day between the potential fifth and sixth games. If the series somehow went the distance, the Yankees and Red Sox would play on five consecutive days. However, to get to that point, the Red Sox would need to start winning.

BRONSON ARROYO:

I don't feel the weight of the entire season, but I obviously feel a lot of pressure from this series. We're not down 0–3, but we're backed into a corner and it's going to be a huge, huge game.[289]

KEITH FOULKE:

I've never seen anybody be able to throw a breaking ball with the command he does. That's his gig. That's what makes him tough. He can feature three or four different breaking balls, inside, outside. That's one thing that keeps hitters off balance.[290]

TERRY FRANCONA:
He has such a great feel for his breaking ball and drops down on different angles, and he's using his change-up to left-handers. He's going to get better the more he learns to pitch inside with his fastball to right-handers.[291]

BRONSON ARROYO:
The first three guys in the order—Sheffield, A-Rod, and Jeter—I've got to get inside on them. If I don't, they're just going to look away and they're going to hit good breaking balls and put them in play. I probably throw inside less than 75 percent of the starters in the American League, but when I do, it's for a purpose.[292]

Arroyo hit 20 opposing batters during the regular season, leading the American League and tying for the MLB lead. In fact, the Red Sox held the top three spots in AL HBPs, with Pedro Martinez and Tim Wakefield each plunking 16 hitters.

BRONSON ARROYO:
I learned so much from Schilling. Nobody studies hitters more thoroughly. Nobody prepares better than him. And he's perfectly willing to share all of his information with you. All you have to do is ask—actually, you don't even have to ask, because he's going to tell you anyway.[293]

Come game time, anything the burly right-hander might have passed on to Arroyo had little positive effect. Derek Jeter walked to start the game and scored when Alex Rodriguez smoked a breaking ball into the left-field corner for a double. After Gary Sheffield flied out, Hideki Matsui cranked a two-run homer into the visitors' bullpen and New York had a 3–0 lead. New York had scored in the first inning in all three ALCS games.

In the bottom of the first, Manny Ramirez singled with two outs. David Ortiz followed with a hit to right, but Ramirez was gunned down at third base by Sheffield after being waved around second by third-base coach Dale Sveum. Rodriguez had applied a high tag, and Ramirez might have gotten in safely.

The Red Sox continued hitting in the second inning, batting around against Kevin Brown. Jason Varitek walked, and Trot Nixon golfed a home run to right field. One out later, Bill Mueller doubled. The Fenway fans loudly serenaded Brown with derisive chants of, "*Kev*-in! *Kev*-in!" Orlando Cabrera grounded out, but Johnny Damon singled to right. Sheffield's throw to the plate was late. Varitek scored, tying the game at 3–3, and Damon alertly took second on the throw.

Brown uncorked a wild pitch on his first offering to Mark Bellhorn and Damon raced to third. Bellhorn eventually walked—and the Yankees' pen got busy. The fans' chant morphed into, "Punch the wall! Punch the wall!" a reference to Brown breaking his left (non-throwing) hand when he punched a clubhouse wall on September 3.

Ramirez's hard grounder to shortstop hit off Jeter's glove for an error; Jeter recovered and flipped to second, but his throw was late. Damon scored. Boston led 4–3, their first lead in 20 innings of play. While Ortiz was batting, TV viewers saw Damon on the top step of the dugout, shoe and sock off, hair dangling in his face, clipping his toenails. Ortiz ended the inning by grounding to second.

A one-run lead was cause for optimism, but Arroyo gave it back in only four pitches, as Alex Rodriguez blasted a home run over the Green Monster and out of the park. Sheffield walked and Matsui doubled—and that was the end of Arroyo's night. The corn-rowed right-hander threw a total of 60 pitches in two-plus innings, walking two and allowing six hits. He was eventually charged with six runs.

BRONSON ARROYO:
It was one of those days when I went out in the first inning and I couldn't believe I gave up the three-spot, but then we came back and took the lead. You're hoping you find a groove, but it never happened.... When I'm missing with my fastball, with a team as good as they are, it's impossible to get by with one pitch. They were spitting on my fastball and sitting on my breaking ball. They basically knew what I was going to throw in certain counts.[294]

TIM WAKEFIELD:
I was sitting down at the far end of the bench with some guys, I think Mirabelli was one of them. When Bronson got into trouble in the second, I wondered, "Should I go ask Tito if he needs help?" And everybody said, "Yeah." We were talking about if we used Embree and Timlin, we'd have no chance tomorrow. So I got up and went over and said, "What do you want me to do? You need help?" and he said, "Go

ask Derek [Lowe] if he can pitch tomorrow." I asked Derek and he said, "Yeah." They told me, "Go get your spikes on." So I went inside and got my spikes on and went down to the bullpen.[295]

DOUG MIRABELLI:
A couple of players were encouraging Wakefield to go talk to the manager about it. At the end of the day, you don't want your bullpen to get blown out because we've still got four games we need to play. Hopefully. For him to be able to go out there and suck up some innings for us, that was a huge help. He loses his start the next night, but Derek Lowe is not a bad fall-back plan.[296]

Ramiro Mendoza—the former Yankee—was the first man out of the bullpen. Bernie Williams greeted him with an RBI single. Although Mendoza retired the next three batters, he allowed another run to score on a balk. New York led 6–4.

Javier Vazquez took over for Kevin Brown at the start of the third inning. The Red Sox jumped on Vazquez, loading the bases with one out on a walk to Varitek, Kevin Millar's double, and a walk to Mueller. With Cabrera at the plate, Sheffield played a bit shallow in right, hoping to guard against a slap hit to the opposite field. Eight pitches later, Cabrera's line drive sailed over Sheffield's head for a double. Two runs scored, tying the game 6–6, but Mueller, running about 15 feet behind Millar, was tagged out.

DALE SVEUM, *third-base coach*:
I had in my mind to get Millar home, and Billy was right on his butt. I wanted to stop him, but I couldn't just wave and stop—they were just too close. Millar is not fleet of foot, and he got a bad break. If I try to hold Mueller, then maybe Millar is going to hold and I've got two guys on third base. They were so close. It was a cluster.[297]

Mueller's out was costly. Now instead of runners at second and third with one out in a tie game, the Red Sox had two outs and Cabrera at third. Damon ended the inning by grounding hard to first base.

The Yankees struck for five runs in the top of the fourth. After Mendoza hit Miguel Cairo with his first pitch, Francona made a pitching change and Curtis Leskanic came in. He faced four batters—Jeter lined out to right, Rodriguez walked, Sheffield hit a three-run missile into the Monster seats, and Matsui doubled to left.

TERRY FRANCONA:
We had Lesky face the guys he's gotten out in the past. We tried to get guys in a position where they could succeed, but it didn't happen.[298]

Wakefield relieved Leskanic. After a pop-up and an intentional walk, Ruben Sierra tripled to the wall in right-center for two more runs. In the fifth, Rodriguez and Sheffield each had RBI doubles, and the Yankees scored four more times in the seventh. Wakefield lasted 3⅓ innings, throwing 64 pitches and allowing five runs.

TIM WAKEFIELD:
I did what I could. It wasn't very good, but I tried to stop the bleeding as much as I could.[299]

TERRY FRANCONA:
Because Wake did what he did, we were able to stay away from Timlin and Foulke. They can throw multiple innings tomorrow and give us a chance to win. We got into a position we didn't want to get in. Wake really picked us up. And he would have stayed out there and pitched more. When we win tomorrow, we'll have Wake to thank for that.[300]

To save the rest of the bullpen, Francona asked Mike Myers to pitch the final two innings. Myers, who often came in to face only one batter, threw 42 pitches and allowed another home run to Matsui.

MIKE MYERS:
I knew what my role was—don't let another pitcher come in. Whether I go six up, six down or whether I give up 10 runs. My job was to finish it, suck up whatever happens out there for the eighth and ninth innings. That way, the guys who were used quite frequently, Foulke and Timlin, they could rest their arms for the next day.[301]

The final score was 19–8. With all the scoring and pitching changes, it was also the longest nine-inning game in postseason history at 4:20.

CHRISTIAN ELIAS, *Fenway Park scoreboard operator*:
There were a lot of number changes and it was a little bit surreal, what was happening. 19–8, that's like a football score. To have a 19–8 game with the Yankees in the playoffs was almost mind-blowing. I

remember being completely drained. There was a definite feeling that this series was over.[302]

In Game 3, the Yankees established League Championship Series game records for the most runs scored (19) and extra-base hits (13), and they tied LCS records for most hits (22) and home runs (4). They also tied a postseason record with eight doubles. The Yankees batted .468 in the game and collected 44 total bases.

The Red Sox had been battered and beaten in every facet of the game. They had lost two tough games in New York only to be blown out on their home field. They were in a deep hole. No team in baseball history that was down 0–3 had ever even *tied* a best-of-seven series. It seemed an impossibly high mountain to climb.

BRONSON ARROYO:
It was an ass-kicking all around. To get destroyed like this when it's crunch time and have a football score up there at the end of the game, it's definitely embarrassing.[303]

JASON VARITEK:
Sometimes a closer loss, depending on how you look at it, grabs you a little bit more because there's usually one play or one incident that changes the game. But they just annihilated us.[304]

TOM WERNER, *chairman*:
I can still hear all those balls hitting off the metal scoreboard—a dead sound because there was nobody left in the park cheering. It was the most painful game. I'm not much of a drinker, but that night I opened up a 20-year-old bottle of Scotch and had a few shots. A tough game. It was horrible.[305]

BEN CHERINGTON, *director of player development*:
After Game 3, we were already starting to think about 2005. "Well, okay, we've got a little more work to do." But in the clubhouse, they were feeling something.[306]

JOHNNY DAMON:
We're very upset. And we're definitely stunned.... They're doing exactly what we thought we'd be doing in this series. Those guys found another switch.... [But] unless I'm mistaken, we've won four straight before.[307]

In fact, the Red Sox had six streaks of at least four consecutive wins, including two streaks of six straight wins and a 10-game winning streak. The Yankees had lost four games in a row only once during the 2004 regular season (April 22–25). After that skid, they lost as many as three in a row only three times. The 2004 Yankees were uncommonly good at avoiding losing streaks of any length.

CURTIS LESKANIC:

I remember thinking that we had wasted an opportunity. We got our asses beat about as bad as you can in a playoff game. I honestly thought I could be home in two days. But some people believed we were still in it. We were going to win this thing. My locker was outside of Terry Francona's office. We came in, it was kind of quiet, players mulled around a little bit. We always played the same song after every victory, Eminem's "Lose Yourself." All of a sudden, the music's on. This is like 20 minutes after the loss. And the mood totally changed. Francona walked out of his office and he looked around. It was like he wanted to give us a little pep talk, saying don't worry about it, we're going to come back. I was thinking, *If I were a manager, what would I say to a bunch of guys right now? What kind of pep talk could you give?* He looked around and the music was playing, there was a couple of guys drinking some beers, relaxing and talking—and he just walked back into his office. Maybe he thought, *These guys will be all right.*[308]

DOUG MIENTKIEWICZ:

I looked over at Trot right after that game in the clubhouse. Someone from MLB came over with a camera, and Trot snapped. That was a very light-hearted group, but the frustration had set in a little bit. It was short-lived. It was quick. It was about five minutes, but it was quiet in there, and that team was never quiet. We all had that same feeling—*I can't believe this is happening.*[309]

CURT SCHILLING:

We were down 0–3, and we'd just got beaten like a Little League team. In our park. But there were times in my career where you're in a situation that you know is not supposed to be this way—and this was one of them. I kept thinking, *This is not how this is supposed to happen.* Everything seemed out of place.[310]

DR. WILLIAM MORGAN:

I was talking to David Ortiz and Kevin Millar in the clubhouse, and there was no doubt that they were going to win. Still. There wasn't a question. It was remarkable to me, as both a physician and a fan, standing back and seeing the assuredness all these guys still had in their eyes. *Yeah, now we'll come back.* These guys are intrinsically remarkable players, but the assuredness and motivation that they had just pushed them over the top. They were so sure they were going to win. They were calm. And it was palpable. It was incredible.[311]

DOUG MIRABELLI:

We realized it wasn't a perfect situation for us, but there was a lot of hope and positive feelings that with our pitching we could see ourselves right back in this thing again. I think we always had a feeling that if it got to Game 7, the pressure would be so high on the Yankees that we would win. We just had to get to Game 7.[312]

DAVID ORTIZ:

I was driving from my house to the stadium on the work-out day, and I saw a big sign on the street that said, "Keep the faith." It was a photo of Manny with the big smile. I parked in front of the photo, and I sat there for a minute, and I thought about what we had been through the whole year. Then I went to the field, and I expressed myself to my teammates about what the Boston Nation has been waiting for and what they expect from us. I said it doesn't matter if we are down 0–3. We have got to keep the faith.[313]

TERRY FRANCONA:

I sat in that dugout for a lot of wins this year and took the smiles and the laughs and everything. You have to sit through a night like this. I won't bail on these guys. It was disappointing for everybody, but we're not done. I fully expect we'll come out tomorrow and play our asses off.[314]

After the reporters left to write the Red Sox's obituary, Theo Epstein sat by himself in Francona's office, trying to reconcile the high hopes he had for the 2004 team with the grim reality staring him in the face. The Thanksgiving Day trade for Curt Schilling, signing relief ace Keith Foulke, hiring a new manager who was receptive to the front office's ideas, sending Nomar Garciaparra away at the trade deadline—it was all intended to carry the club deep into October. To erase—as much as possible—the nightmare of 2003.

THEO EPSTEIN:

I was pissed. That was probably our worst game of the year, including spring training. You hate to play your worst game of the year at the most important time. I was thinking, *God, is this the way this team is going to be remembered? This team should have won it all.*[315]

Eventually, Epstein left the ballpark and ended up at an apartment on Boylston Street, drinking vodka tonics with four friends from the front office.

THEO EPSTEIN:

We were obviously pretty down—Jonathan Gilula, Adam Grossman, Jed Hoyer, Peter Woodfork, all of us who worked in baseball operations. That was a brutal beatdown we had suffered, and it seemed like we were going to get swept and lose a great opportunity. We had all previously lived in the same apartment building near Fenway, so we went back there and started drinking vodka tonics and beers. We were talking, and we turned the TV on and we were flipping channels and we came across, of all things, Game 7 of the 2003 ALCS on ESPN Classic, which we had suffered through and I had not previously been able to bring myself to watch. We were howling at how perfect this was. "Kick us while we're down," and, "The only thing that can make tonight worse is having to watch fuckin' Aaron Boone do that again." They wanted to turn the channel, but I was playing the role of masochist. "No, bring it on, let's watch every fuckin' pitch." We kept drinking. At some point, someone ran out to a gas station to get Ring Dings or something. But the game ended—I think we made it to the end—and we were wasted and struggling to stay awake, half passed out in our easy chairs.[316]

Epstein awoke at dawn, still wearing his sports jacket.

13

After Game 3

DAN SHAUGHNESSY, *Boston Globe*:
The Yankees stripped the Red Sox of all dignity last night, pummeling six Boston pitchers en route to a hideous 19–8 victory, which gives them a 3–0 lead.

So there. For the 86th consecutive autumn, the Red Sox are not going to win the World Series.

ERIC WILBUR, *Boston Globe*:
This series is over. Baseball in Boston is over for another season. If you headed [*sic*] to the game this evening [for Game 4], you're forgiven for leaving in the seventh. Not to avoid traffic. To avoid watching the Yankees celebrate on your team's home turf.

This Red Sox team, the vanilla Red Sox for nearly half a season, choked at the wrong moment. The Yankees are their daddy for reasons unknown.... [E]njoy your last chance this year to watch what was admittedly a fun Boston team.

TONY MASSAROTTI, *Boston Herald*:
They are doing more than just losing now. They are disgracing the game and embarrassing themselves, and they are doing a disservice to the paying customers who blindly and faithfully stream through their doors.

Shame, shame, shame on the Red Sox.... What a joke.

SEAN McADAM, *Providence Journal*:
Let the record show that, for the second straight season, the beginning of the end of the Red Sox season came on October 16.

BOB RYAN, *Boston Globe*:
Soon it will be over, and we will spend another dreary winter lamenting this and lamenting that. Sure, you can root for the National League team to defeat the Yankees, but just exactly how satisfying is that going to be?

August seems a long time ago. The Anaheim series seems a long time ago. The idea that the Red Sox accomplished anything good at all this season seems inconceivable.

JACKIE MacMULLAN, *Boston Globe*:
So now the Sox are down, 3–0, and it's over, and everyone knows it, even the resilient Boston players who have never said die all season.

JIM DONALDSON, *Providence Journal*:
Johnny Damon may look like a prophet, but his words have proven false.

It is not, as he said, the Red Sox who are a bunch of idiots. What they are is a bunch of chokes.

The idiots are all those fools who truly believed this would be the year.... Only a bunch of idiots would continue to put their faith in this chronically overpaid and underachieving aggregation of ill-kempt characters.... Sure, they're loose. They're also losers.

JEFF JACOBS, *Hartford Courant*:
Never did the Yankees look more professional. Never did the Red Sox look more amateurish. Never did the Yankees' hitting machine look more relentless. Never did the Red Sox's pitching staff look sillier.... This baby is over. It was supposed to be the best series in history. Instead it was just another cheap Fox sitcom.

SELENA ROBERTS, *New York Times*:
Torre emanates calm; Francona reflects desperation. Torre manages against the reservoir of his own greatness; Francona manages against the ghost of Grady Little.

Perception is fluid. If the Red Sox fight their way back against the Yankees in this series—though no team has come back from an 0–3 deficit—Francona could go from being a pushover for his rebellious team of latent teenagers to a man who understood the value of a carefree clubhouse for a franchise miserable since 1918. He could, but he won't.

JOHN HARPER, *New York Daily News:*
So much for another epic series between these teams. The Sox are done, not only because no team has ever come back from a 3–0 deficit but because Derek Lowe is all they have left to throw at a Yankee lineup that is salivating at the sight of fastballs, curveballs, knuckleballs, you name it.

"I believe we can do it," Damon said. "I do." He sounded like, what else? An idiot.

GEORGE KING, *New York Post:*
The victory gives the Yankees a 3–0 lead in the best-of-seven series going into tonight's Game 4. No team in baseball has flushed such a bulge. That means the Yankees are a lock for their 40th flag and their second straight World Series appearance.

IAN O'CONNOR, *USAToday:*
This had nothing to do with a curse and plenty to do with a hoax. The Boston Red Sox, the 2004 edition, had everyone good and duped. They will go down as an Enron-sized monument to consumer fraud.... April Fool's Day came to a mid-October night, when the Red Sox exposed themselves as counterfeit postseason goods.

PETER SCHMUCK, *Baltimore Sun:*
The Yankees squashed the Sox like so many bugs around a drain, leaving little doubt who would be the eventual American League participant in the World Series. The only thing haunting the Red Sox were those horrible hairdos, which don't look quite so rakish and charming when somebody's smacking you across the face. The Red Sox were so over-matched that fans were waxing nostalgic for Bill Buckner and Grady Little. At least they provided some drama.

STEVE POLITI, *Newark Star-Ledger:*
Eighty-five years from now, when the Red Sox fans are sitting around in their spaceships and discussing the missed opportunities during the 17 decades without a world championship, they will certainly remember the collapse of 2004.

The Curse lives. Long live The Curse!

14

American League Championship Series Game 4

Sunday, October 17, 2004, at Fenway Park

KEVIN MILLAR:
Just put us to bed tonight.... This is the game that they've got to win.[317]

The task was both improbable and unprecedented. In Major League Baseball history, 25 teams had lost the first three games of a best-of-seven series, either in the World Series or the League Championship Series. Twenty of those 25 teams lost Game 4 and were swept. Three teams won the fourth game, but lost Game 5. The remaining two—the 1998 Atlanta Braves and the 1999 New York Mets—had won two games (both in the National League Championship Series) but lost Game 6. No team had ever battled back to play a Game 7.[318]

In the National Basketball Association, teams in an 0–3 hole were 0-for-73.

In 140 opportunities in the National Hockey League, it had happened twice: the 1941–42 Toronto Maple Leafs and the 1974–75 New York Islanders.

For those three major U.S. sports, that was a combined 2-for-238.

JOHN HENRY:

I quantified the odds of coming back, and it was pretty darn bad: 6¼ percent. Then *Baseball Prospectus* took it further and said our chance of winning the series was 1.8 percent.[319]

THEO EPSTEIN:

Walking to the ball park the next day, there was a sense of doom. It was pretty dark. Because no team had ever come back from 0–3. We had just been humiliated. There was a sense of how bad can this get? Once we got in the clubhouse, I was encouraged by how light the mood was with the players. Millar and a few others were optimistic and energetic and a little out of control. Their refrain was, "Don't let us win. Don't let us win tonight," and Millar rattled through the whole pitching rotation. Win tonight, then we got Pedro, then we got Schilling, and he was getting pretty into it.

My own personal turning point, as far as my outlook on it, came when I was on the field for batting practice. I was walking back from the bullpen across the field. At first it was just Dan Shaughnessy, then a couple of other writers, and soon the whole gaggle of reporters was waiting for me in foul territory on the first-base line. It looked like the firing squad assembling. And the line of questioning, especially from Shaughnessy, really pissed me off. He asked something along the lines of, "Does the result of this series thus far indicate anything about the Yankees' class and professionalism and your group's lack thereof?" You know, calling themselves idiots and so forth and the way both organizations approached the game, respectively. It was such a condescending, cynical question.

I said, first of all, the outcome of the series hasn't been determined yet. There's a long way to go. And second of all, it doesn't say anything about our approach to the game or our professionalism. We are who we are, and our personality has gotten us to this point and we've accomplished quite a bit because of it. I answered defiantly because I felt defiant. It was such an easy question to ask, but also a lazy and irresponsible question. I don't hold that against Dan, that's the character he plays. He was going to write that column anyway, about how the idiots got swept and we were doing it the wrong way and we crumbled when it mattered most. But it offended me because I was proud of who we were as a team.

That team had unbelievable character, great personality. It was all genuine and organic, and we all enjoyed each other's company. The players really cared about one another and were motivated by making each other happy, and that's why I think we wanted to win so badly. And that's one of the reasons why I was so pissed that we were potentially going to lose to the Yankees—because I felt like we were extremely talented. We'd gone 40–15 down the stretch against the best teams in baseball after making those trades. And I noticed my own personal mood going from troubled and worried about which shoe was going to drop next to being excited about the opportunity to come back and a little defiant in the face of a lot of people who expected us to fail.[320]

DAVID ORTIZ:
Everybody was a little down when we left the ballpark, but we were ready to go when we showed up for Game 4. We felt like we could win. We felt that way every day. Going back to the start of 2003, we won so many times when it looked like we were going to lose. All we needed was to get a little momentum, get our confidence back, and we knew we could beat the Yankees. If we won one game, we could win two. If we won two, we could win three. If we could win three, we could win four.[321]

DOUG MIENTKIEWICZ:
On the way to David's house after Game 3, I saw a group of five 40- to 50-year-old men and they were crying, walking to their car. We were disappointed, obviously, but when you see that much anguish on a man's face.... We care that much because it's our job. It is our game, and we want to win. Players do want to win the World Series. But these weren't eight-year-old kids. These were grown men. David said, "Well, we can make them smile tomorrow." Let's start with that. Let's turn those tears into joy tomorrow. And then worry about the next day, the next day.[322]

BILL MUELLER, *third baseman*:
I think everybody felt like we had a better team in 2004 than the year before. It just wasn't showing. We truly believed that we needed just a crack, some kind of hope, in a sense. And as soon as we could crack the code on getting that first win, the floodgates would open for us.[323]

DOUG MIRABELLI:

There was always a sense of what we knew we were capable of doing. We knew this wasn't an accurate showing of what our offense was all about. All we needed was one positive feeling that we could get something done. If the Yankees were going to come out and crush the ball like they did that third game, well, we could do the same.[324]

MIKE TIMLIN:

We didn't have a meeting. But to a man, in our clubhouse, we all said, this is not how we want to go out. We're going to fight you tooth and nail. If you knock us out, that's fine. But we're going to give you all we have.[325]

JOHNNY DAMON:

We began packing our bags, hoping to get some good mojo going, because when you don't pack, you get clobbered. So before Game 4, a bunch of us started packing to go home in the hopes we wouldn't.[326]

TERRY FRANCONA:

They didn't need me to drop a Knute Rockne on them. They call themselves idiots, but they are smart enough to know if they lose, we go home. This entire season, we've had—I'm not exaggerating—about one minute worth of meetings. The mood in our clubhouse has been the same all year. I don't ever remember seeing guys down or quiet. It's just not the way they operate.[327]

On the day of Game 4, Curt Schilling threw a 15-minute afternoon bullpen session while wearing a special boot designed to support the displaced tendon in his right ankle. Schilling threw harder and less gingerly than he had on Friday. Afterward, he took no questions from the media.

Around the same time, Dr. William Morgan was at the University of Massachusetts Medical Center. During the off-day, he had thought of a possible way to solve the issue with Schilling's ankle.

DR. WILLIAM MORGAN:

I was very familiar with the anatomy lab because I did a lot of research down there. I do a lot of arm and shoulder work and lower extremity work. They had put aside multiple frozen limbs for me. So I had an ankle—a man's leg, it wasn't a little kid and it wasn't an elderly person—and I wanted to see what kind of pressure it might be able to stand. Get an idea how strong a recommendation this could be—get some science behind it. We had a leg that was amputated at the knee, and I set it up in an apparatus. Through a very small incision, I recreated the injury by incising that retinaculum. Then the muscle for that peroneus longus tendon was sitting in the calf. I isolated that muscle. I put some sutures through it so I could pull on it. Really hard. And indeed, when the retinaculum was cut, that's what it would do. It slipped in front of the ankle.

Then I did the type of surgery that I was considering. I made a row of about six or seven sutures through the skin after putting the tendon in the front, where it did not belong but where it seemed to want to go. I made a wall of sutures, sewing through the thickness of the skin, through the subcutaneous tissue, down and into the periosteum, which is the lining of the bone, and then came up through the skin again and really tacked down the whole wall of tissue so that the tendon couldn't snap back.[328]

Morgan felt confident enough about the radical procedure—he found no record of it ever having been performed before—to recommend it to the Red Sox front office, and to Curt Schilling.

Back at Fenway, Derek Lowe, who had pitched so badly in September that he had been banished to the bullpen, was getting the ball in Boston's most important game of the year. Lowe's only appearance since the end of the regular season on October 3 had been throwing 10 pitches in the top of the tenth inning of ALDS Game 3. Lowe got credit for the win when David Ortiz cracked his game-winning, series-winning home run.

DEREK LOWE:
I told my wife this was going to be the hardest game I've ever pitched. We're down 0–3, and it could be my last game for the Red Sox. And I've pitched once in 16 days.[329]

For Game 4, Terry Francona changed his lineup slightly, something he had adamantly opposed two days earlier. He dropped Mark Bellhorn to ninth and moved Orlando Cabrera to the second spot in the order.

ORLANDO CABRERA:
Bellhorn was struggling. And Johnny was struggling. So with the first two guys not getting on base, Manny and David were coming up to hit without people on base.[330]

Francona also considered starting Doug Mientkiewicz at first base because Lowe's sinker led to a lot of ground balls and Mientkiewicz was the better fielder, but in the end he decided to stay with Kevin Millar.

TERRY FRANCONA:
I wrestled with Mientkiewicz a lot. I talked to the staff a lot. We've gone with these guys the whole way. I'm not sure I have all the correct answers. So far I haven't.[331]

For the Yankees, Tony Clark replaced John Olerud at first base. Olerud had hurt his left foot in Game 3, either hitting himself in the foot with the bat or stepping on the bat while leaving the batter's box.

During batting practice, Kevin Millar was wearing a microphone at the request of MLB and Fox Sports. Millar had already called out *Globe* columnist Dan Shaughnessy in the Red Sox clubhouse for his description of the team as a "pack of frauds." Now Millar had another message, and it was caught on camera: "Don't let us win tonight!"

KEVIN MILLAR:
It wasn't premeditated. It came from me really believing in our team and wanting fans to still believe in us, despite having the odds stacked against us. Looking at it realistically, I knew it was hard enough to win four games in a row against the Royals, let alone the mighty Yankees, you know? How do you beat that team four games in a row? We were down three games, got crushed in Game 3, and I didn't really like our pitching match up in Game 4 because the Yankees had a knack for hitting Lowe's sinker since they'd seen him so much. But if he could come through...we'd have Pedro in Game 5 and Schilling in Game 6 and then anything is possible in a Game 7 because even the Yankees have that human factor. They'd be so tight and scared if we could just put them in that situation. So I knew if we could win that game, the entire pressure went to them. We didn't have any pressure. We were supposed to lose. Now we're just having fun. Now we're going to watch them choke.[332]

Millar's brash confidence was in sync with his teammates.

GABE KAPLER:
We had done everything that we could to compete in the series, and we would do everything we could to win Game 4. It was a

one-game-at-a-time approach. I believe that anything is possible. I don't ever give up that faith. But the way to accomplish that is to win one game. In fact, it's to win one at-bat. You have to break it down into tiny little steps. Otherwise, it becomes too big a task, whether you're down 0–3 to a Little League team or you're down 0–3 to a devastating Yankees team. Because it's never happened in the history of baseball, if you are responsible, you're thinking, *Okay, it is very unlikely to happen*. The only way is if you break it down into its smallest parts and take it piece by piece. But Kevin was definitely a rally-the-troops guy. He's definitely a showman. He's a great *convincer*—one with the ability to bridge gaps between players, and he had the capability to sort of bounce around that day. And that became the central theme—*Don't let us win tonight!*—which was beautiful. It couldn't have happened any better.[333]

LYNN JONES:

Kevin was always trying to rally the troops. Was Kevin the team leader? No. But there were team leaders all over the place. And they led the team in different ways. And everybody accepted those players and those roles as being a part of leadership. I knew Kevin—I was his first manager when he signed with the Marlins' organization [1994]—and he likes to be in the middle of things. He's going to say whatever he wants to say, and he was going to be heard. He'll convince you that he knows what he's talking about. And a lot of what he said made sense.[334]

CURTIS LESKANIC:

I don't know if Millar was convincing or if he was just a used-car salesman selling to a bunch of dumb guys who wanted to buy a car. Because the thing was, a lot of people wanted it so bad that we were willing to believe it. And coming down to it, you couldn't help but think, *You know what? He's right! If we can win this, we still have Pedro to pitch another game, we still have Schilling to pitch another game.... Shit, what if we win one? You never know!* It was reality. If we do win one, you never know what can happen.[335]

DOUG MIENTKIEWICZ:

I had spent almost the entire night at David Ortiz's house, my family and his family. We came to the park the next day and we just felt like, "Guys, it can't get any worse." Kevin was saying it—"Don't let us win today"—but we all felt that way. [336]

TROT NIXON:

Jason Varitek simplified the situation. "We know we have to win four games, but let's break this down into one game. And once you get to that game, you've got a top half and a bottom half of every inning. Let's try to win the top half of the inning. And then when we go to the bottom half, let's try to win that one." We broke up the game into 18 games.[337]

DAVE MELLOR, *Fenway Park director of grounds*:

They were definitely a close-knit group that was very positive. I got the impression they weren't going to let things get them down. They were going to give their best efforts. I'm a big believer that adversity makes you stronger and challenges give you opportunity, and I felt like they viewed it the same way. I never felt like the guys were grumpy or pissed off or mucking about. I never heard anybody say, "Hey, I'm going duck hunting," or "I'm going on vacation next week." They were concentrating on one day at a time. Let's get going.[338]

DOUG MIRABELLI:

You know you have to play seven games now. You've lost three and, I guess when I look at it, my feeling was we need to win three games—because we're winning Game 7.[339]

ORLANDO CABRERA:

Pedro said, "We need a *chivo*." A goat. "I'm going to have my sister make a goat for us." I said, "Go ahead! Go ahead!" So he called and she made the *chivo* and they brought it before the game. It was delicious! I remember going out to shortstop with a bone in my teeth. That was the first game we won. After the game, he said, "Gotta get another *chivo*!" So he would make his sister cook a new goat every day. Dominican style. Oh! The best! They put beer on it.... Unbelievable.[340]

Theo Epstein was in Terry Francona's office as the Boston manager prepared his pregame glass of Metamucil. Francona had been drinking the orange laxative for more than 10 years to settle his stomach. In a show of solidarity—and not above thinking a change of routine might bring the Red Sox some good luck—Epstein asked Francona to mix up a second glass.

THEO EPSTEIN:

He has a nervous stomach, and I teased him about it all year. It looked like something a 70-year-old grandma would drink. But before Game 4 I decided, what the hell, and I had a glass of it, too.[341]

TERRY FRANCONA:

Theo would do anything for luck. If he thought we could win, he'd have drank that stuff until he wasted away.[342]

THEO EPSTEIN:

We used to do some pretty interesting things to try to break losing streaks in Boston. There was this one Thai food place that will remain nameless. One day somebody from our office got some food and there was a little rat in the fried rice. So when we were down 0–3 to the Yankees, we made everybody in the office order from that place, including me.... Whenever the Red Sox had a losing streak, we'd always suck it up and go get that food.[343]

The Red Sox also changed batboys. Chris Cundiff replaced Andrew Crosby.

CHRIS CUNDIFF, *batboy*:

I'd been batboy back in the 1990s, took a couple seasons off, then came back in 2000. I was the backup in 2004 whenever Andrew didn't do it. When we went down 0–3 to the Yankees, we said, "We might as well do something to mix it up." I don't know if Andrew had had enough of it. It's hard when you sit through a long game and you're just getting killed. Especially when you're on the home side, He might have just been frustrated, not wanting to do it after sitting through that. It's not like it's on TV and you can turn it off or leave the room for a while. Even if you're at the park, you can go get something to drink or whatever. Here, you're forced to watch and pay attention because you've still got to make the game function. You still have to bring balls to the umpires and keep the field cleaned up and everything. It's not always easy to sit there when the game means something. It's one thing in the regular season, but now it's the one thing you've been rooting for forever.[344]

There was also a prayer meeting before the fourth game. Several Christians on the team got together and prayed for the strength to compete.

CURT SCHILLING:

It was Wake, Timlin, Mirabelli, Mueller, myself, and maybe one or two others. Walt Day, our chapel leader, and this group prayed, hard. Not for a win, not for anything tangible, but for the strength and will to compete. The Big Man listened.[345]

WALT DAY, *chapel leader:*

There's a lot of misunderstanding about chapel. It's not that we got together and prayed for wins. I would put the emphasis on glorifying God, to reflect well on Him by the way you played. I think what the Lord expects of you is to play hard and get the most of what He's blessed you with, regardless if you're down 0–3 or if you're up 3–0. What I tried to help guys understand is if you see that your love from God is not conditional, that your self-image is not based on performance, it can free you up from that fear of failure.[346]

When Derek Lowe walked out to the bullpen to warm up before the game, the fans at Fenway gave him a standing ovation and chanted, "D-Lowe! D-Lowe!"

DEREK LOWE:

It occurred to me as I was driving to the park that this could be my last game here. I thought about it all day long. You're down in the series 0–3. You're pitching. You think of these things. And then when you get to the park, and you hear them cheering for you—even when some of the cheers haven't always been warranted—you want to give something back.[347]

Lowe had finished the 2004 season with a 5.42 ERA and the worst WHIP of his career. In five regular-season starts against the Yankees, he had an abysmal 9.28 ERA. One month earlier, on September 18, Lowe had lasted only one inning at Yankee Stadium, allowing seven runs.

As Lowe walked back to the dugout, he was still hearing the loud, sustained cheering—the unconditional support. Tonight, no one cared about Lowe's inconsistent work during the season. This was the only game that mattered.

CURT SCHILLING:

For all I know, the fans felt the same way we did. We win one and everything changes. If there was anything we came to hate about the series, it was all the media bullshit hype around it. But it could actually turn around and work 100 percent in our favor. Nobody outside of Boston would expect us to win—but you knew that somebody in both of those cities was going to write a "Oh, my God, what would happen if..." And they did.[348]

DEREK LOWE:
Varitek came up to me before the game and, with Gary Sheffield, who was killing us, he said, "This is what we're going to do." He wasn't asking me what I thought, he just said, "This is what we're going to do. We're going to throw curveballs right at him that are going to end up right down the middle. Trust me, if you throw it right at him, he will flinch and take it." And I'm like, "Oh, man." And he said, "We're going to throw a lot of change-ups to right-handers"—I threw my change-up pretty hard—and he said, "It's going to look like a sinker. I think that's going to work." So the way I pitched was completely different than what I normally did. And I think his plan had to do with what he had seen in the first three games—and how I had done in my last game against them. He came up with a totally different game plan.[349]

Lowe delivered his first pitch at 8:21 PM. Derek Jeter hit it hard on one hop right back to the mound. It smacked off the side of Lowe's right thigh and caromed towards third base. Bill Mueller barehanded the ball and threw Jeter out. Lowe waved the trainer off, saying his leg felt fine.

DEREK LOWE:
There was no way I was coming out of that game unless something had broken. I had to stay in there. Not necessarily for bravado reasons, but for the team, too, because if I had to leave the game, I don't even know who—we might have had a position player pitching.[350]

He set down the next two Yankees on eight pitches, striking out Alex Rodriguez and getting Gary Sheffield to fly out to Trot Nixon in right field. Things were looking up already—for the first time in the ALCS, New York had not scored in the first inning.

Hideki Matsui continued his torrid hitting, doubling to left field to start the second inning and then going to third on a groundout. Terry Francona brought his infielders in, not wanting to concede an early run and hoping to have a play at the plate on a ground ball. Jorge Posada lined the ball on one hop to shortstop, and Matsui sprinted for the plate. Orlando Cabrera backhanded the grounder, took a split-second to set himself, and fired the ball home. Jason Varitek caught the ball at shoulder height on his left side, in perfect position to tag Matsui out.

Lowe continued his aggressive approach, pounding the strike zone with his sinker, not shying away from going after the hitters. The Yankees were trying to pull Lowe's sinker, which was 5–6 mph slower than his fastball. Hitters were out in front of it.

DEREK LOWE:

It was weird how the Yankees played, because you would think that a team that had just scored 19 runs on 22 hits would have all the confidence. And in that game, actually, they chased more pitches than they normally chased. They were doing stuff that they didn't do the first three games. And that gave me a little bit of an advantage because they weren't as patient. We tried to take advantage of it by throwing breaking balls out of the zone and, again, they were swinging at those pitches where they hadn't earlier.[351]

With two outs in the third, Jeter lined a hot shot that skipped past Mueller's glove into left field for a single. Lowe tried to come inside to Rodriguez, but his pitch drifted back over the middle of the plate. Rodriguez crushed it as if it were batting practice. It sailed over everything in left for a home run. New York led 2–0.

Lowe got ahead of Sheffield 0–2, and before he could throw his next pitch, the crowd roared as a baseball landed in left-center field. Someone in the parking garage on the other side of Lansdowne Street had thrown back Rodriguez's home run ball. Johnny Damon walked over, picked up the ball, and fired it back over the Monster seats, out of the park. The crowd cheered. A moment later, the ball came flying back into the park again. This time, second-base umpire Joe West went out and confiscated the ball. He put it in his pocket, and the game continued. Sheffield struck out on the next pitch.

Orlando Hernandez was going on 16 days rest and had pitched only three innings in 24 days. "El Duque" allowed only one hit in the first four innings and retired the Red Sox in order in the third and fourth on a total of 20 pitches.

The fans had been following the game intently, cheering at various points, but for the most part they were quiet, just watching...but waiting. In the bottom of the fifth, Kevin Millar led off with a four-pitch walk, and the fans suddenly came alive. Mueller forced Millar at second, but there was no relay back to first. When Hernandez walked Bellhorn, the fans were on their feet. They would not sit down for the next four hours.

Damon worked a full count and hit what looked like a sure double-play ball to shortstop. Jeter threw to Miguel Cairo at second, but Cairo was late getting to the bag, and they only got the force. Cabrera followed with a hard single to right field, and Mueller scored. Manny Ramirez walked, and then Ortiz hammered a change-up to right-center for a single. Damon and Cabrera scored easily, and Boston led 3–2.

Before the game, Francona had indicated that both Mike Timlin and Keith Foulke were rested and that he planned to use them a lot if the situation warranted. As soon as Boston took a 3–2 lead, Timlin began warming up. In the top of the sixth, after Lowe gave up a one-out triple to Matsui, Timlin came in to face a string of switch-hitters: Bernie Williams, Jorge Posada, and Ruben Sierra. Francona's quick hook raised a few eyebrows.

DEREK LOWE:
I didn't even know anyone was warming up! There was no talk about this being your last guy. I was a little shocked and upset, to say the least. Anybody in my situation would have wanted to stay in the game. We had just gotten the lead. I thought I had good enough stuff to keep us in the game.[352]

Williams and Timlin battled for eight pitches before Williams tapped the ball to the right side. Cabrera ran in on the infield grass and tried to barehand the ball, but it didn't bounce as high as he expected. The ball glanced off his fingertips for a hit. Matsui scored the tying run.

A wild pitch put Williams on second, and then Timlin walked Posada on four pitches, prompting a visit from pitching coach Dave Wallace. Facing Sierra, Timlin threw a pitch that got away from Varitek. Williams broke for third. Varitek pounced on the ball and made a perfect throw to Mueller, who blocked the bag and tagged Williams out. Posada advanced to second base, but there were now two outs. Sierra hit a ground ball up the middle. Bellhorn ranged far to his right behind the second-base bag to glove it, but his throw to first was late and off target. Posada moved to third. Tony Clark hit Timlin's next pitch to Bellhorn's left. The second baseman raced the other way, knocked the ball down, but could not make a play. Posada scored, and the Yankees were back on top 4–3.

Timlin had been touched for three hits—but none of them had left the infield. A quick chant of "Po-key! Po-key!" sped around Fenway. Frustration with Bellhorn's performance in the series was boiling over, and many fans were convinced that the sure-handed Reese would have handled one or both grounders.

POKEY REESE:
Personally, I didn't like it. He's out there trying to win. He's playing great. I want to see him continue to do that.[353]

After Cairo walked to load the bases, Jeter grounded out meekly to second. The inning was finally over. New York led 4–3.

Dave Roberts left the Red Sox bench after the sixth inning and went to the team's video station. He hadn't played since the second game of the Division Series, 11 days ago. If Roberts was going to have any role tonight, it likely would be as a pinch-runner. And if the score stayed the same, it would probably be against either Tom Gordon or Mariano Rivera.

The Red Sox had acquired the speedy Roberts from the Los Angeles Dodgers at the July 31 trade deadline. In the final two months of the regular season, Roberts played sporadically and had stolen only five bases—but one of them had come against Rivera, back on September 17.

During the playoffs, Roberts had been working with first-base coach Lynn Jones on his breaks from first.

LYNN JONES:
I would act as if I was a pitcher, and Dave would work on keys. We would do this during batting practice. We would be out in the field, or there were times when you go down the sideline and practice there, down in the corner and work off of one of the foul lines. But the key is to try to stay sharp. Dave has a high degree of skill in that area,

so it really didn't take much to keep him sharp. He just needed an opportunity.[354]

BILLY BROADBENT, *video/advance scouting coordinator*:
He knew that there would be a pretty good chance that he'd be pinch-running. At that point, Tom Gordon was in the game, so Roberts said, "Show me all his throws to first base, and show me him pitching with men on base." In between batters, I set it up on the computer. He sat there and he watched it, almost in a running position, so that he would get a better idea of what to look for. He didn't get in that inning, and then I saw that the next inning, they were likely going to put in Mariano Rivera. So I called up Rivera's clips on the screen and he came back and he watched the same thing the same way.[355]

Roberts was looking for a telltale sign in the pitchers' motions, something different they did when they were going to the plate, as opposed to throwing to first. If Roberts could detect even the slightest tip-off—a leg angle, the position of the glove—it would give him a huge advantage.

GALEN CARR, *advance scouting coordinator*:
We had a whole sheet with pick-off tendencies and release tendencies and whether or not these guys used their slide step. For Mariano, we said, "Rare use of abbreviated leg kick in path. Not a true slide step." All the release times we had for him, they were kind of average at best. With all the information that was provided, there was a good chance that somebody with good speed, getting a good jump, was going to make it.[356]

Timlin walked Rodriguez on four pitches to begin the seventh. After Sheffield fouled out to Varitek, Francona made another pitching change. Timlin stomped off the field, furious at his own lackluster performance and the cheap infield hits he allowed in the sixth. He continued scowling, fuming, and pacing back and forth in the dugout.

The Red Sox, already trailing by one run, could not let the Yankees score again. The game was on the line—*the entire season* was on the line. Francona treated the seventh inning as if it was the ninth, because now every inning was the ninth. He brought in his closer, Keith Foulke.

Foulke's first batter was Matsui, who had eight hits in his last 10 at-bats. With men on base in the series, he was 8-for-12.

KEITH FOULKE:

There comes a point for any manager or any team, when you know it's nut-crunching time. You want your best players out there. I always had a hard time calling myself a closer. I was a bullpen guy. Sometimes, with the tough part of the lineup, the key moment in the game is in the sixth or seventh inning. And if you don't get through a key moment right there, what's the point of having good back-end guys if you can't keep a lead or keep it close? I think I had better numbers against left-handers like Matsui than I did against right-handers. The ability to control the inside part of the plate against a left-hander and also having a change-up that went down and away. So I had stuff that ran up and in on him and stuff that ran down and away.[357]

Foulke got Matsui to ground out sharply along the first-base line to Millar, and Rodriguez went to second. Bernie Williams, batting left-handed, put on another tough at-bat. Foulke needed nine pitches before finally striking him out with a high fastball.

Tanyon Sturtze breezed through the seventh, striking out Bellhorn, who had now failed to put the ball in play in his last eight trips to the plate, then getting Damon on a grounder back to the mound, and retiring Cabrera thanks to Williams' sliding catch in right-center.

Meanwhile, Roberts was doing everything he could to get ready. It had been a cool night—temperatures were now in the high 40s—and he was a little stiff from sitting on the bench.

DAVE ROBERTS:

I was up in the clubhouse, down in the tunnel, kind of running around, trying to get my legs loose. I was jumping up to the ceiling. I did high knees up and down those wood planks in the tunnel. The area wasn't very conducive to a pinch-runner getting loose, but you got to make do.[358]

Foulke faced the Yankees in the top of the eighth. Posada walked— the third time in four innings in which New York put its leadoff man on base—but Foulke easily retired the next three hitters. Sierra grounded into a fielder's choice, Clark struck out, and Cairo popped to shortstop.

During the regular season, Yankees manager Joe Torre had used Mariano Rivera almost exclusively in the ninth inning. But in the playoffs, with each victory so crucial, Torre often had no qualms about occasionally stretching out Rivera. Tonight, even though the Yankees held a three-game lead, Torre asked Rivera for six outs.

JOE TORRE, *Yankees manager*:
We were facing their 3–4–5 guys. That's like a save situation going through the heart of the lineup. He was the only one available. He had not pitched in three days.[359]

Manny Ramirez led off against Rivera by singling through the shortstop hole into left. Boston had the potential tying run on first base, but with the meat of the order coming up and not wanting to lose Ramirez's bat later on, Francona chose not to use a pinch-runner.

Ortiz struck out, unable to check his swing on a high fastball. Varitek grounded to first with Ramirez advancing to second. Nixon grounded out weakly to first as Rivera darted over to take the throw. After eight innings, the Red Sox still trailed by one run.

Up in the owners' suite, Red Sox president and CEO Larry Lucchino began scribbling notes on a yellow pad for the postgame media conference: "deeply disappointed," "bitter taste of defeat," "after the acute pain of this wound subsides." Charles Steinberg, executive VP for public affairs, was nearby, typing similar sentiments.[360]

LARRY LUCCHINO, *president/chief executive officer*:
We were concerned we might say something inappropriate or intemperate. I didn't trust my instincts to say the right thing.[361]

JOHN HENRY:
[I was] utterly distressed. We thought we had done everything we could to get back to the point we were at last year when it didn't happen. You always ask, "What went wrong?"[362]

TOM WERNER:
The idea that we [would] have the American League trophy handed to them in this clubhouse was a little more than I could stomach.[363]

In the top of the ninth, Foulke walked the leadoff man but got the next three hitters. Now if the greatest closer in baseball history could get three outs before the Red Sox scored one run, the Yankees would be on their way to another World Series.

During the middle of the inning, with Boston on the verge of being swept, Eminem's "Lose Yourself"—the team's locker room victory song—played over the Fenway loud speakers:

If you had one shot, one opportunity

To seize everything you ever wanted

Would you capture it or just let it slip? . . .

You only get one shot, do not miss your chance

This opportunity comes once in a lifetime.[364]

Rivera would face the bottom three hitters in Boston's lineup: Millar, Mueller, and Bellhorn.

JOE TORRE:
If there's one thing I can second-guess myself about, it's Mo going out in the ninth inning.... I was going to go to him and tell him, "Don't get too fancy. Go after him. Don't worry about trying to make too good of a pitch." The only reason I didn't say anything is I remembered the last time he had faced [Millar], in Game 2.... Because of how easy that at-bat was, I said, "Fuck it." Because I didn't want to plant a seed that wasn't there. It was so easy the last time.[365]

TERRY FRANCONA:
You try to set up the inning in advance. If this happens, this is what we're going to do. I was down in the tunnel with Dave Roberts and I said, "Millar is going to get on and you're going to steal."[366]

KEVIN MILLAR:
There was never a panic because at that point, we had nothing to lose. But if you sit back and look at the big picture, you're going, *"Holy shit."* You're down three games, you're down in Game 4, you got Mariano Rivera trotting in with the greatest postseason ERA of any closer—holy shit, right? That's the big picture. The small picture is, I got to get on base. People ask me, "What were you thinking?" and, honest to God, I was thinking homer. That was it. Fenway Park. I

loved hitting there, it's a short porch, Mariano throws fastballs, I'm a pull hitter, I'm trying to pull a homer.[367]

Millar had been 4-for-16 against Rivera during his career. In 2004, he was 1-for-3 with an RBI.

KEVIN MILLAR:

I actually enjoyed facing Rivera. I was probably the only one, but I'm a little crazy. I had a pretty good idea what they were going to try to do—come up and in and get me to chase one out of the strike zone. It was a pretty good approach because I couldn't resist those high heaters sometimes.[368]

Rivera had retired Millar in a tight spot in Game 1 and had struck him out swinging to end Game 2. In the stands, everyone was standing. Fans were hoping, praying, pleading for the Red Sox to score. Fans in the front rows pounded on the padding in foul territory, trying to make as much noise as possible.

Rivera's first pitch to Millar missed inside.

CHRIS CUNDIFF:

I looked over at the batboy the Yankees brought up from New York and thought, *This is so unfair. They enjoy this every year. In 10 minutes, he's probably going to be so happy and we're going to be all sad again.* But as soon as Rivera threw ball one, I thought, *Well, you know what? If he can walk here, you never know.*[369]

Rivera's second pitch was out over the plate, and Millar lined it foul into the third-base grandstand.

KEVIN MILLAR:

I was looking for something middle in I could pull. Mariano made mistakes to right-handed batters. I was pretty confident that if he made one, I could get it. At 1–0, I tried to hone in on a pitch, and I lined it near their dugout.[370]

The clock above the Fenway center-field bleachers clicked from 11:59 PM to 12:00 AM. It was Monday morning. A new day had begun.

Rivera's infamous cut-fastball usually ran down and away from right-handed hitters. But his next three pitches were all inside, each one a little further up and in, well out of the strike zone. Millar found none of them enticing. He backed away from ball four, ducked his head, and trotted to first.

KEVIN MILLAR:
Ball four really wasn't that close, which sort of surprised me because once it got to three balls I thought they'd come after me a little more. It's not like I was Manny or Papi and needed to be pitched around. I'm proud that it was a disciplined at-bat, though, because what we needed was a base runner. Though a homer would have been pretty cool, too![371]

JOE TORRE:
Even though he's the best doesn't mean bad things don't happen. I think he was trying to be too careful with Millar. And that's what happens in a one-run game in this ballpark. I can't fault him for it. You certainly don't want him to throw one down the middle.[372]

Rivera's pass to Millar was the first unintentional walk he had issued in his last 35⅔ postseason innings, a total of 134 batters dating back to 2001.

THEO EPSTEIN:
As soon as Millar dropped his bat on the plate, I think everyone knew what would be coming next. We just needed the visuals. And then Roberts came out of the dugout.[373]

Larry Lucchino stopped writing, put down his pad, and walked over to the suite's window overlooking the field.

DAVE ROBERTS:
Terry told me at the top of the ninth that I'd be running for whoever got on. Right before I was going to take the field, he looked at me and gave me a wink. And I knew what that meant.[374]

TERRY FRANCONA:
That was my way of saying, "Go get 'em, big boy."[375]

KEVIN MILLAR:
I couldn't get off the bag quick enough, knowing they're going to pinch-run Roberts—get my slow butt off the bases. No words were necessary. It's not like I was about to give him base-running advice. So I gave him the knuckles, got off the field, and tried to get some elbow room by the railing to watch him go off to the races. We knew

he was going. The Yankees knew he was going. Are they going to pitch out? Are they going to slide step?[376]

DAVE ROBERTS:

I was scared and excited. I can't tell you how many emotions went through me. To be honest, the fear of being the goat definitely went through my mind because I hadn't played in 10 days and didn't feel fresh. I knew in my mind what I wanted to do, and I had to hope my body followed. I remembered being on a back field in Vero Beach in 2002. Maury Wills told me that at some point in my career there will be an opportunity for me to steal a base, a big base, and everyone in the ballpark knows I'm going to steal, and I can't be afraid to steal that base. Did I think it was going to be in the ALCS against the Yankees while I was playing for the Red Sox? Absolutely not. But when I was jogging out there, I realized, *This is what Maury was talking about. This is my opportunity. Don't be afraid to take this chance.*[377]

When Roberts got to the bag, first-base coach Lynn Jones told him Mueller would be bunting.

DAVE ROBERTS:

Third-base coach Dale Sveum initially flashed the bunt sign for Bill, assuming we'd sacrifice. Terry hadn't sent it. I told Jones, "No, no, no, I'm going to steal."[378]

Jones had a flash of panic. He quickly got the attention of the Boston dugout. Roberts made a rolling motion with his left hand across the diamond at Sveum: *Go through the signs again!* It took a few seconds to get the strategy straightened out. There would be no bunt.

LYNN JONES:

I told Dave, "Do what you do."[379]

Roberts took a huge 3½-step lead, daring Rivera to throw over. If Rivera could get Roberts to shorten his lead by even a few inches, it could mean the difference in a close play at second base.

DAVE ROBERTS:

From running against Rivera in that series in September in New York, I knew what he would do to try to defense me, and that's the way it played out. They held the ball on me, trying to catch me jumping, so I made sure not to be too eager. If he had gone to the plate right away, I don't think I would have made it because my legs weren't under me yet. As a base runner, it's important to know that the pitcher is not going to quick-pitch you once he gets set. It gives you a couple tenths of a second to calm your nerves and stay relaxed and then be ready to steal. That's what I was banking on right there. If Mariano had come set and went right to the plate, I wouldn't have been ready to go because I was waiting for that hold—that 2/10 of a second hold—that extra-long hold. And so Mariano picks over one time. And the emotions start to dissipate a little bit. And he picks over a second time. And then the nerves really calmed and I was at peace.[380]

ALAN EMBREE:
When he almost got caught, you're going, "Oh no, oh no, not that way. Come on, stay close now. We know you're going, but don't get picked off."[381]

DAVE ROBERTS:
That second time, I felt like I was a part of the game. And the third time, I felt like I had played the whole nine innings.[382]

LYNN JONES:
There was no doubt the pickoff throws heightened his senses. It allowed his muscles to start reacting. It was perfect. It couldn't have worked any better. The throwovers were exactly what he needed. They helped take those jitters away. He kept moving out there a little bit further, and we're talking about inches, but when you're out there that far, holy smokes. He's *way out there*.[383]

DOUG MIRABELLI:
That guy got the biggest lead I've seen from any stealer. And he was still able to get back to first base. He needed every inch of that lead, that's for sure.[384]

DAVE ROBERTS:
After the third throw, I was ready to go. I was thinking there's no way somebody throws over four times. Just instinct, I guess. A base-stealing instinct. I was waiting for that move of his going to the plate. As far as a key, whether it be a knee or hip or shoulder,

it was nothing like that. As soon as I saw movement, I was gone. If he had thrown over one more time, he would have picked me off.[385]

Rivera did not throw over a fourth time. On his move to the plate, Roberts took off. Rivera's pitch to Mueller was outside, at the letters. It wasn't a pitchout, but it functioned like one for catcher Jorge Posada.

BILL MUELLER:

I was hoping I would get enough pitches so that Roberts could pick one and steal. That was my main concern once the bunt came off—either moving him over to second or making sure that I allowed him a chance to steal. And making sure that I don't go after the ball if he takes off. At that moment when your eye catches movement from the base runner, you don't want to move a muscle. I'm going to let this play out and then we'll deal with the situation after that.[386]

Posada caught the ball in his left hand while simultaneously coming up out of his crouch and cocking his right arm. His throw was strong but slightly off-line to the left, tailing away from the base and the runner. With a left-handed batter at the plate, Derek Jeter was covering second. He reached forward for the ball, trying to speed up the play, then quickly brought his glove back for a tag. Roberts went in head first. As his left hand hit the base, Jeter's glove was perhaps six inches away from Roberts' left arm.

BILL MUELLER:

It was darn close. You hold your breath and wait for the umpire's call. Then it's, "Oooh, he's safe."[387]

TERRY ADAMS:

It was a bang-bang play. He was clearly safe, but it could have gone either way. It was one of those plays where you see guys get called out who were more safe than that. We were also fortunate enough to go into the clubhouse and watch things like people at home would. We saw it in slow motion over and over and over again.[388]

DAVE ROBERTS:

I thought I was in there pretty good, but then you go back and look at footage and you realize how close a play it was. I always make a joke that the more I watch the play, the closer I am to being called out. Hopefully down the road, Joe West doesn't change his call! The crowd was buzzing, but once I got out there to run, there was a peace—a calm. Then when I got into that sequence with Mariano, it was dead silent. Lynn told me, "Do what you do." After that, the next thing I heard was Derek Jeter putting the tag on me and me brushing the dirt off and him saying, "How the heck did you do that?"[389]

CURT SCHILLING:
The whole thing was surreal. Everything he'd ever been taught about stealing bases was on display there. The lead. Knowing the pitcher. The jump. The slide. Everything. And he had to do every single one of those things perfectly, or he would have been out. At the most crucial moment in his career, to be asked to do the one thing he was extremely good at, when everybody knew he was going to try to do it—and he still did it.[390]

MIKE TIMLIN:
It seemed to not just give us a spark. It seemed to happen as a flashfire.[391]

KEVIN MILLAR:
That throw by Posada was probably the greatest throw he ever made to second base. He was like a 1.8, 1.9 to second, the perfect tag by Jeter, and literally, you're talking about a wrist length of winning it. We're like, yeah, he stole a base. I mean, everything went right.[392]

Red Sox bench coach Brad Mills checked his stop-watch after the play: Posada caught the ball and threw to second base in 1.79 seconds. Mills couldn't believe it. It was the fastest time he had ever seen. When the inning was over, Mills went into the clubhouse and ran a video of the play a few times. The slowest time he could clock was 1.81 seconds.[393]

Now the Red Sox had the potential tying run at second base with no one out. Mueller set himself to bunt before Rivera even began his motion. But it was merely for show, and he pulled back the bat and took a strike. The count was 1–1.

THEO EPSTEIN:
The crowd's murmuring, "Bunt—you don't have anyone out." But the bunt is not the right play there. With Rivera throwing 94-mph cutters in on Mueller's hands, the most likely outcome is a ground ball to

second base, which gets him over to third anyway. Without the bunt, you have a shot at getting a base hit.[394]

DAVE ROBERTS:

Billy Mueller had success and a good history against Mariano. Tito was going to let him swing that bat and hit a ball to the right side of the infield to get me over. There was definitely no thought of a bunt. And bunting a 94-mph cutter is not easy.[395]

BILL MUELLER:

I had a special bat I used only for Rivera. Instead of my usual 31.5- or 31.7-ounce bat, I used one that weighed 30.9 or 31. And I choked up a little, which I didn't do against anyone else. In order to get at that cutter, I needed to cheat a little. I probably started using it in 2003, as soon as my first bat blew up in my hands. I realized there was no way I could make solid contact or get to his stuff with my other bat. On occasion, if someone was throwing 98, I might go up there with a lighter bat, but I never thought, *I have to use this bat in order to face this guy*, like I did with Rivera.[396]

ORLANDO CABRERA:

Ricky Gutierrez was with me in the dugout. He wasn't on the roster, but he didn't want to leave. He said, "I'm having too much fun here. I'm staying." And he said, "I say this"—that's the way Cubans talk—he said, "I say this. If they let Billy face this guy with people on second base, we win this game." I said, "Why?" He said, "Look up the numbers of this guy [Mueller] against this guy [Rivera]. He's like the only lefty that can hit this guy."[397]

Rivera's 1–1 pitch was on the outside edge of plate; Posada had set up inside, but Rivera missed his spot. Mueller swung and hooked it up the middle, a hard ground ball right back through the box. Rivera stuck out his left leg and glove hand, like a hockey goalie trying to make a kick save.

BILL MUELLER:

Once he stole, my mindset changed to getting him in. Mariano left the pitch out over the plate, and I was able to Charlie Brown it right up the middle. Might have gone through his legs. It had enough topspin to get past Rivera. But then you've got Jeter back there, and I'm hoping he isn't going to make another great play. I don't need to see Derek Jeter that night on ESPN.[398]

DAVE ROBERTS:
I was thinking he would yank something to the right side, but when the ball got through, I said, "I'm gonna score." I wasn't stopping at third, even if there was a stop sign.[399]

Rivera fell to the ground and lay on his stomach, watching Jeter, who had no chance. The ball went into center field. There was no stop sign. Bernie Williams charged the ball, but his throw never reached the plate.

Roberts sprinted home and slid in safely with the tying run. He popped up out of his slide, did a little spin, and pumped his fist. Rivera caught Williams' throw in front of the mound. It looked like he wanted to spike the ball into the infield grass in frustration, but he composed himself.

The game was tied 4–4.

The immediate pressure was off. At the very least, there would be a tenth inning. But the Red Sox wanted to end this game *now*. Doug Mientkiewicz, batting for Mark Bellhorn, bunted Rivera's first pitch to the third-base side of the mound. Rivera grabbed it and looked at the runner, then threw to Miguel Cairo covering first base for the sure out. Mueller was now at second with one down.

DOUG MIENTKIEWICZ:
Pinch-bunting in my first at-bat of the series against Mariano Rivera, who's cutting balls right at you. You know you've got to go to third with it. I was thinking, *Just get it over with the first pitch*. Please. Please. I actually bunted that ball off my finger, but I wasn't going to say anything because that would have been a foul ball. I was running to first base saying, *Please don't say anybody saw that*.[400]

Johnny Damon's high chopper to first was bobbled for an error by Tony Clark, and Mueller raced to third. In the dugout, Roberts was excited, pounding on one of the water coolers and tossing cups of water in the air. The Yankees brought in their infield. Orlando Cabrera was overanxious and struck out, flailing at three unhittable pitches. Two outs.

ORLANDO CABRERA:
I was so mad! I wanted to hit a fly ball. Hit something. The thing with Rivera—he'd always try to throw me inside. So I was like, *Don't get jammed. Don't get jammed. You either strike out here or hit a fly ball. Don't hit a ground ball because that's a double play*. Then he threw

me those high pitches every time, and I swung at them. Three times. I'd never been in that position before. I had won games before, but the problem is you do repetition so that when times come like that, the brain shuts down and it's muscle memory. You react. And I didn't react that well.[401]

Manny Ramirez, who had yet to drive in a run in the series, worked a seven-pitch walk to load the bases and keep the rally alive. With the Fenway crowd in a frenzy, David Ortiz pulled a foul down to the tarp, then he missed a pitch that was a bit up. He took a pitch away before getting jammed and popping up to Cairo at second. Ortiz was devastated as he walked back to the bench.

JASON VARITEK:

I told him you can't do it every time. It's not humanly possible to get a hit every single time in these situations.[402]

DAVID ORTIZ:

That's my mentality. Every time I go to the plate, I feel it's my responsibility to get it done. And I carry that over with me as long as I've played baseball. It's my priority. That's what I feel like. I missed my pitch...I couldn't believe it. I guess that helped me out for my next at-bat. My next at-bat, I was more confident.[403]

After 2⅔ innings and 50 pitches, Foulke's night was over. It was his longest outing of the season. He had walked a tightrope, putting the leadoff man on in both the eighth and ninth innings, but he had not permitted either runner to advance.

Alan Embree, who had allowed two runs in one-third of an inning the previous night, was in for the 10th with Mientkiewicz at first and Pokey Reese at second. The inning passed without incident. Embree allowed only a two-out single to Ruben Sierra. Tom Gordon, in relief of Rivera, retired the Red Sox in order on only eight pitches.

Embree came out for the top of the 11th with Mike Myers and Curtis Leskanic up in the bullpen. Cairo singled to right; the Yankees had put a man on base in 32 of the 36 innings in the series. Jeter bunted him over to second. Rodriguez lined a ball toward the shortstop hole. Cabrera, who may have been cheating slightly toward the bag to keep Jeter close, dove to his right and snagged the line drive just as it was about to hit the dirt. Two outs.

ORLANDO CABRERA:

I was playing him to pull. Always, to pull. A-Rod was a guy that they were going to throw inside. No fastballs away. Every fastball was at his belt. They wanted him to think the whole time that they were going to come inside. That's where Varitek was so smart. He'd make people believe that he was going to come inside the whole time, and then here comes a splitter, here comes a curveball, so I always played him in the hole. I stole a lot of hits from A-Rod. A lot. And Sheffield, too.[404]

After falling behind 3–0 to Sheffield, Embree put him on intentionally. Myers came in to pitch to Matsui and walked him on four pitches, loading the bases for Bernie Williams. Francona made another pitching change, bringing in his third arm of the inning: Leskanic. Like Embree, Leskanic had been pummeled in Game 3, giving up three runs in one-third of an inning. Behind him, Tim Wakefield, who had thrown 64 pitches the night before, was getting loose in the bullpen.

CURTIS LESKANIC:

As a guy who pitches at the back end of the games, there's a lot of hero and a lot of goat. There's not much in between. And the one thing I've learned over my years of playing is you really do have to forget what you did yesterday. If you struck out three to save the game or you gave up three to lose the game, you had to forget. Because every day was a different day.... I was sore. This was toward the end of my career. I knew that I was pitching on fumes. I was getting cortisone shots every other day and doing whatever I had to do to get in there. I came in thinking, *My slider is good, let's concentrate on that.* My fastball was flat. When I came in to the game, Tek said, "What do you got tonight?" and I said, "Well, the slider is good, I can throw it for strikes. It's got some good tilt to it." I wasn't nervous. I was thinking this might be the last time I pitch. But I'm okay, I'm good with it. I threw a first-pitch slider for a strike. And I ended up popping him up to center to get out of the inning. It was all adrenaline; my arm was pretty much done.[405]

The Red Sox went quietly in their half of the 11th. Damon drew a two-out walk and stole second, but Cabrera grounded out to Jeter.

Leskanic pitched the 12th. He allowed a bloop single to Jorge Posada. Sierra hit a hard grounder off Leskanic's leg. The ball rolled a short distance toward first base, and Leskanic quickly grabbed it and made an easy toss for the out. The Boston trainers came out to check on Leskanic, but after one practice pitch, he insisted he was fine. Tony Clark flew out to left, and Cairo chased a breaking pitch out of the zone for strike three.

CURTIS LESKANIC:
Struck out Cairo. That was the last pitch I threw in the major leagues.[406]

THEO EPSTEIN:
Leskanic was unbelievable. He had no right pitching in the big leagues with the way his shoulder was at that point. I mean, it was hanging on by a thread. And he comes out throwing slider after slider after slider and showed huge balls to record those key outs. A guy picked up off the scrap heap, we didn't expect to factor in at all and he's making huge pitches, getting huge outs for us.[407]

TROT NIXON:
Leskanic gave you every single ounce that he had. His arm was about to blow up. Literally. If you looked at it on an MRI machine, you'd say, "Oh, my gosh." Fantastic guy to have in the clubhouse and a great guy to have in that bullpen. I don't have a problem with baseball analysts saying, "Oh my goodness, there's *this* guy coming in?" But we thought, *This guy's gonna go get the job done.* That's the beauty about being on a team and believing in each other, having each other's back. That's what the normal fan doesn't really realize—the chemistry that we had.[408]

MIKE TIMLIN:
Going from when we tied it in the ninth through the 12th, it seemed like there was a whole other game. It was almost like starting the playoffs all over again for us.[409]

ALAN EMBREE:
It was a heavyweight title fight. You had two champs going at it, trading blows—and it was exhausting, emotionally and physically.[410]

Paul Quantrill was a 35-year-old right-handed pitcher who had come up through the Red Sox's farm system in the early 1990s. He signed with the Yankees as a free agent in December 2003 and pitched in a league-leading 86 games. In the 12th inning, Quantrill would face the toughest part of the Boston lineup.

Manny Ramirez started the inning by lining an inside fastball to left field for a single. Quantrill walked behind the mound, kicking softly at the dirt. Up next was David Ortiz, who Quantrill had struck out the night before.

DAVID ORTIZ:

I was pretty sure I knew how Quantrill would try to get me out. He didn't throw hard like Rivera. One of his best pitches was a sinker or what some guys call a two-seam fastball that usually gets the batter to hit a ground ball. Quantrill could start that pitch at my thigh and make it bend back toward the plate. With the pitch coming at you, your instinct is to back away a little, to move off the plate. But the ball would change direction and catch the inside corner, so you had to stay in the batter's box as long as possible and wait for the ball to break. At that stage of the season, my confidence was so high that I was sure I could hit anyone. I just had to be patient.

He has some kind of pattern, usually a ball, then a strike, and then he comes inside. He did exactly what I thought he would. He pitched me inside. I had to stay back and wait for the ball to break, and then I had to open my hips and try to pull. And when I finally got the pitch I wanted, when I got one I could handle, I did exactly what I wanted to do. I smoked it, bro.[411]

The crack of Ortiz's bat hitting the ball sent a charge through the crowd. Sheffield, in deep right field, tracked the ball to the wall and watched it sail over his head and into the Yankees bullpen for a game-winning home run. Red Sox 6, Yankees 4!

The Red Sox poured out of their dugout, leaping and dancing toward the plate. "Dirty Water," the Standells song played after every Boston win, blared from the PA, but it was barely audible over the din of the crowd.

Ortiz rounded third and saw the delirious welcoming committee forming a half-circle around home plate. With a goofy grin on his face, Ortiz tossed his batting helmet behind him, gave his waiting teammates a double point, leapt high in the air, and stomped down on the plate.

It was 1:23 AM, and the Red Sox were still alive.

David Ortiz was now the only player in baseball history to hit two walk-off home runs in the same postseason, and the Red Sox joined the 1910 Chicago Cubs as the only two teams down 0–3 to win Game 4 in extra innings.

JOHNNY DAMON:
Mark Bellhorn and I were back in the clubhouse grabbing a banana. It was a quarter after one in the morning, and we needed some energy to keep going. We started to walk back down the corridor to the dugout, and I could see on the TV that Manny was on first. We stopped to watch Ortiz bat. When he hit the ball out of the park, we sprinted down the concrete corridor and we ran out onto the field—about 10 seconds after everyone else, but in time to greet him at the plate.[412]

POKEY REESE:
It's a lot of ground to make up, but hey, Pedro's going tomorrow. We win that game and then we've got Schilling coming back. This is still wide open.[413]

KEVIN MILLAR:
Everything flipped with that game. One hundred percent. I said that before the game.[414]

CURT SCHILLING:
We felt like we had them when we won Game 4. Whether we did or not I don't think was relevant. We believed it. Which was all that really mattered.[415]

CURTIS LESKANIC:
I have a lot of New York buddies who are Yankees fans. And they told me after—it wasn't right after, it was years after—that after we won that first game, they were honestly thinking, *Uh-oh.* And that's funny for a Yankees fan to think, okay, they are up 3–0, and to lose one game, and they started questioning.[416]

TERRY FRANCONA:
We set out today to win. That was our only objective, and somehow we did it. Now our objective is to win tomorrow.[417]

After Game 4, the Red Sox officially announced that Curt Schilling would be the starter in a possible Game 6.

TERRY FRANCONA:

This is not a move of desperation. It's a move to try to win. Saying that, our fingers are crossed. But Schill's desire to pitch is so strong, and our medical people have gone through hoops to get him ready.[418]

CURT SCHILLING:

I never mentally shut it down after the first game.... The medical staff exhausted every scenario until we found something that could work. We've taken steps to ensure that we won't have the same problem we had the first time. That much I know.[419]

Asked to elaborate, Schilling politely declined.

Lost in the exhilaration of the extra-innings win was the fact that the best arms in the bullpen had thrown an extremely high number of pitches: Embree 30, Timlin 37, and Foulke 50.

Game 5 was scheduled to start in less than 16 hours.

Johnny Damon on the base path, ready to run. He scored five runs and drove in seven during the series against the Yankees. (Photo courtesy the Boston Red Sox / Cindy Loo)

Manny Ramirez, later named MVP of the World Series, was 2-for-5 with two RBIs in the deciding Game 3 of the ALDS. (Photo courtesy the Boston Red Sox / Brita Meng Outzen)

Red Sox captain catcher Jason Varitek readies to fire the ball to second base. (Photo courtesy the Boston Red Sox / Brita Meng Outzen)

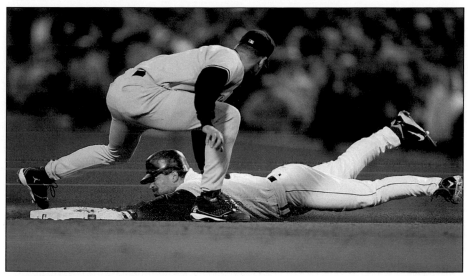

Dave Roberts slides into second base with "The Steal," beating Jorge Posada's throw to Derek Jeter by a fraction of a second. Roberts scored the tying run in Game 4 of the ALCS moments later. (Photo courtesy the Boston Red Sox)

Curt Schilling focused and firing the ball to the plate with his now-famous "bloody sock" on his right foot. (Photo courtesy the Boston Red Sox / Julie Cordeiro)

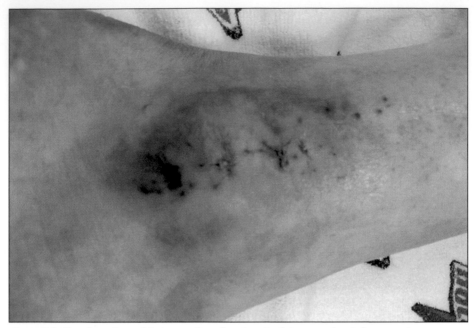

Curt Schilling's right ankle immediately after Red Sox medical director Dr. William Morgan performed his unprecedented surgical procedure. Schilling was operated on before ALCS Game 6 and World Series Game 2. Schilling won both games. (Photo courtesy Dr. William Morgan)

Doug Mientkiewicz celebrating the moment of victory after gloving Pokey Reese's throw to first base that won the ALCS and sent the Red Sox to the World Series. (Photo courtesy the Boston Red Sox / Julie Cordeiro)

Alex Rodriguez slaps the arm of Bronson Arroyo, as Doug Mientkiewicz backs off to get out of the way. Though initially ruled safe, A-Rod was called out for interference as the umpires consulted one another to get the call right. (Photo courtesy the Boston Red Sox / Julie Cordeiro)

Mark Bellhorn hit an eighth-inning two-run home run off Cardinals pitcher Julian Tavarez in Game 1 of the World Series. (AP Photo/Amy Sancetta)

Keith Foulke may well have been the MVP of the 2004 postseason. He pitched more than one inning in six of the team's 14 games and recorded an overall earned run average of 0.71. (Photo courtesy the Boston Red Sox / Cindy Loo)

Three-time Cy Young Award–winner Pedro Martinez won one game in each of the three series. He threw seven innings of three-hit shutout ball in Game 3 of the World Series, his last appearance in a Red Sox uniform. (Photo courtesy the Boston Red Sox / Julie Cordeiro)

The moment every baseball player longs for—winning the World Series. (Photo courtesy the Boston Red Sox / Julie Cordeiro)

David Ortiz atop a Duck boat with a big smile and a good grip on the 2004 World Series trophy. (Photo courtesy the Boston Red Sox / Cindy Loo)

More than 3 million people—about five times the population of Boston—turned out to celebrate the World Series win. This scene from the corner of Tremont and Winter shows how tightly packed the crowds were—an experience neither the fans nor the players will ever forget. (Photo courtesy the Boston Red Sox / Brita Meng Outzen)

15

American League Championship Series Game 5

Monday, October 18, 2004, at Fenway Park

GARY SHEFFIELD:

They're a walking disaster. They act like they're tough, like they care so much about winning, but it's all a front. They're just a bunch of characters.[420]

Monday morning's *Boston Herald* reprinted a quote from Gary Sheffield that had first been published in *USA Today Sports Weekly*'s ALCS preview.

ELLIS BURKS:

Kevin Millar and Billy Mueller clipped out the article from the paper and put a copy on everyone's chair so when we came into the locker room that night, we saw the quote. We took Sheffield's comments as a personal jab. It motivated us.[421]

DANA LeVANGIE:

That thing was posted on every door, every wall in our locker room, and in the bullpen. It didn't go unnoticed, that's for sure.[422]

The Yankees right fielder denied saying it.

GARY SHEFFIELD:

That's something somebody came up with on their own. I would never say anything to fire up a team. That's not me. It's something I didn't say. Who is accountable for writing what they want to write? I am surprised that somebody would stoop that low without even talking to me. That's the farthest thing from my mind.[423]

Bob Nightengale, the article's author, stood by his story's accuracy.

About three hours before the start of Game 5, in the treatment room behind the locker room, Dr. Morgan performed the radical procedure he had tried the day before on a cadaver's severed leg, but this time he performed it on the right ankle of Curt Schilling.

CURT SCHILLING:

I came to the park and I was pretty much resigned to not pitching. Then Dr. Morgan said, "Here's one last shot. I had an idea and I messed around with it and..." I was like, "Yeah, okay." He didn't even need to say it twice. I was like, "Whatever. Let's do it." It was a case of being out of options. Anything that let me pitch effectively was going to be tried.[424]

DR. WILLIAM MORGAN:

We did the procedure the day before Curt was pitching because I wanted to see how he would do with just the sutures, from the perspective of pain, how he felt after the anesthetic wore off. To see if he could walk! And to see if he was comfortable enough in daily activity before he really stressed it. It didn't take a lot. Just sterilized the area after numbing it up with lidocaine, which is a quick-acting anesthetic, and then mixed it with Marcaine. Dressed it. Had OR [operating room] sheets around there, for a sterile field. Then, on a sterile table, placed the sutures I was going to use. I had the needle holder and the surgical instruments I needed and went ahead and did it. It took probably 20 to 30 minutes. We tried to keep it quiet, but people who heard about it—like Pedro, I think, stuck his head in and quickly left. People don't like seeing those things. It was done with a small group, myself and the trainers.[425]

THEO EPSTEIN:

Although it seems extreme—we couldn't find a case of it ever having been done before—we thought it was almost a conservative approach in that it would be the best way for him to have his normal mechanics.[426]

CURT SCHILLING:

The logic made sense. The question was: would it hold? You're not asking it to hold for a long jump or a broad jump. You're asking it to work for 100-some pitches. It was uncomfortable, but it worked. I remember Bronson walking in, in the middle of it, and he was like gagging. I often wonder whose ankle he practiced on. I hope it was a Yankee fan.[427]

BRONSON ARROYO:

I was one of the first few guys to walk into the training room, right after they had done the surgery on his ankle, right there on the training table. It was amazing. At the time, I thought it was semi-barbaric.[428]

CURTIS LESKANIC:

It's something I've never seen in my years. And I've been around some training tables, believe me. They did some things to him to get him ready—they were using some utensils on him.[429]

KEVIN MILLAR:

It looked like a shark bite.[430]

About 90 minutes later, Schilling tested the ankle on the bullpen mound at Fenway Park. He felt fine.

It was Pedro Martinez and Mike Mussina in Game 5, with the first pitch at 5:10 PM. The Red Sox had won a thrilling game the night before—or, more precisely, that very morning. They were excited to get back on the field as soon as possible.

BILL MUELLER:

Coming right back for Game 5 was an advantage for us. There was no stoppage. The games were running real late, and then you turn right back around and do it again. I think that was a plus. You step out for two days and then come back in, some of that momentum could be squandered. Instead, it stayed at the ballpark and we kept carrying the weight of it. It kept going in our direction.[431]

then brought in another lefty, Alan Embree, to face three Yankee switch-hitters. With the Red Sox outfielders playing deeper than usual to guard against an extra-base hit in the gaps, Williams singled to right-center, and then Embree struck out Posada and Sierra.

In the bottom of the 11th, Quantrill stayed in with Esteban Loaiza warming up. Mueller blooped a single to right-center field. The Yankees expected a bunt, but Bellhorn swung away, lining a single to right. Now there were two on and no outs. Damon tried to bunt and popped up the first pitch to Posada in front of the plate.

JOHNNY DAMON:
That's why we don't bunt much on this team. I'm not a good bunter. We probably won't bunt much anymore.[446]

The Yankees' catcher considered letting the ball drop and trying to start a double play.

JORGE POSADA, *Yankees catcher*:
I did think about it. But in front of the plate in Fenway, especially, it's a little choppy. And we've got to get an out there.[447]

Quantrill slipped and turned his right ankle on the play. He was replaced by Loaiza, who got Cabrera to hit into a double play.

TERRY FRANCONA:
We took Alan Embree out of Game 5 when he wanted to keep pitching. We're constantly talking with our medical people, our pitchers, and our coaches.[448]

ALAN EMBREE:
I pitched with some bruised and sore ribs that whole series. We did what we could to get me ready for the game, and that's how it went. That saved me so I could be used the next night. If I remember right, I went in to catch my breath in the end of the tunnel and I think somebody saw that. I was upset that I was taken out. I was like, "No, this is my game."[449]

Tim Wakefield came in to pitch the 12th for Boston. With one out, Cairo singled to left and Ramirez misplayed the ball for an error, letting Cairo take second. Jeter lined a ball to right field. Kapler, who had been cheating toward the infield, raced in and caught the ball, likely saving a hit and a run.

GABE KAPLER:

I always shaded Jeter toward the line, and I played him two or three steps in because I knew that if he crushed a ball, it was going to beat me anyhow, and he loved to hit those line drives over the second baseman's head that fell in for base hits.[450]

Rodriguez flied to center on the first pitch, ending the inning.

In the 12th with one out, David Ortiz came to the plate. Would he do it again, as he had in the 12th inning of Game 4? The Yankees weren't taking any chances, and Loaiza pitched to him carefully, eventually walking him. Then, with Mientkiewicz at the plate, Ortiz took off for second base. Posada's throw was very high. Jeter leapt up, came down, and tagged Ortiz in the back. Ortiz was called out—although some replays appeared to show his hand on the bag before Jeter's sweeping tag.

DAVID ORTIZ:

I went because we had a hit-and-run, but there was no action from the hitter. You know I'm not a guy that's gonna steal bases. I saw the throw coming high. I tried to tag the back of the bag. I thought I got in.[451]

Wakefield, now in his second inning of work, struck out Gary Sheffield, but Sheffield reached first base on a passed ball by Varitek. Wakefield usually had Doug Mirabelli as his catcher; Varitek was not used to catching the knuckleball.

TIM WAKEFIELD:

I looked in, Varitek looked at me and said, "Let's go." I trust Jason's hands as much as anyone else besides Doug. But we just gave a look to each other and said, "It's okay." We've got to bear down and get out of it the best way we know how.[452]

Matsui forced Sheffield at second, and Williams flew out to right for the second out. Then the trouble began.

Wakefield's first knuckleball to Posada rolled away to Varitek's left, but Matsui didn't advance. After a called strike, another pitch hit off the heel of Varitek's glove for a passed ball; this time, Matsui did run down to second. Posada was then walked intentionally. With Sierra batting, Varitek was charged with his third passed ball of the inning—it rolled to the back-stop—and the Yankees' runners advanced to second and third. The tension was nearly unbearable. Wakefield had to keep throwing his signature pitch, rather than rely solely on medium-speed fastballs. Another pitch squirted out of Varitek's glove but did not get too far away. Wakefield's next pitch was in the dirt and smothered by Varitek. Finally, on a 3–2 pitch, Sierra swung and missed at an inside knuckleball for strike three.

JASON VARITEK:

Wakefield threw some hard ones—about 70 mph—that really had a lot of action. Usually his harder one doesn't have much. His knuckleball really had loops in their movements. That made it tough on me. But he really picked me up, striking out Sierra to end the inning.[453]

DOUG MIRABELLI:

When Wakefield was warming up in the bullpen, I was catching him. His ball was ridiculous; it was moving everywhere. It's hard enough catching Wake's knuckleball, but there are degrees of knuckleballs, and this was like a 10. I would have struggled catching him that night—and I catch him all the time. Even though Varitek wasn't accustomed to catching him, at the end of the day, he was going to make the plays. Somehow, some way, pretty or not pretty, it was going to get done. We were all watching him. He's catching a few, he's dropping a few. I'm sure his nerves were skyrocketing at that point, but guys like that find a way to make it happen. They never scored.[454]

The Red Sox went down in their half of the 13th, and Curtis Leskanic began getting loose. Wakefield had a much calmer 14th as Clark struck out looking, Cairo flied to center, and Jeter grounded to shortstop.

CURTIS LESKANIC:

I got up that night and thought, *There's no way*. If they put me in, they would have to move the third baseman and the shortstop back, or they might get killed if Gary Sheffield got a hold of one. I was warming up in the bullpen thinking, *I have absolutely nothing*. Not because I had pitched the night before, but my arm in general. It was gone at that point. I was biting a tissue just to get the ball to home plate.[455]

In the bottom of the 14th, Loaiza's fourth inning of work, Bellhorn struck out, Damon walked, and Cabrera struck out. With two down, Ramirez put on an outstanding at-bat, confidently taking pitches that were barely off the inside edge of the plate. He worked a seven-pitch walk, moving Damon to second and allowing Ortiz to bat. Despite how hot Ortiz had been, Joe Torre didn't pitch around him—even with two outs. That would have pushed the potential winning run to third.

DOUG MIENTKIEWICZ:

I tease Joe Torre about that. I played for Joe with the Yankees and in L.A. "What were you thinking? You did know I was on deck, right?" He says, "Yeah, I knew"—but my numbers against Loaiza were really good. At that point, Joe was up 3–1 still. He was playing with the house's money. I always said that was the toughest at-bat I never got.[456]

JOE TORRE:

There are too many things that can happen with a man at third base. I was comfortable with the way Esteban was pitching to David. Even the time before, he eventually walked him, but it looked like he had tremendous command. Looked like he put the ball where he wanted to and he was making some pitches.[457]

DAVID ORTIZ:

That's all I do—hit. I don't go in the field. Whenever I get the chance, I've got to get it done. I've got to do something every time I come to the plate. We were one loss away from going home for good. We couldn't let it end that way at home in front of our fans.[458]

Loaiza's first pitch was a fastball cutting down and away; Ortiz took a big swing and missed. Ortiz then looked at a ball outside and fouled off two pitches. On 1–2 he clubbed a fly ball to deep right, but it hooked foul. Ortiz stood at the plate, bat in hand, watching the ball arc its way into the crowd. Loaiza went outside again, and the count was 2–2. Ortiz fouled off the next three pitches, mostly sinkers, all to the third-base side, spoiling Loaiza's offerings and hoping the right-hander would make a mistake.

DAVID ORTIZ:

His best pitch was a cut fastball, the same pitch Rivera throws, but nobody's is as good as Rivera's. But Loaiza could throw that pitch to both sides of the plate—and he could throw it for strikes. Loaiza could start the pitch off the outside corner so that it would look like a ball, then bring it back over the plate for a strike. Other times he could start the pitch in the center of the plate and move it in on your hands—like Rivera did—making you think you had a chance to hit it. And then, after you had started your swing, the ball would move in on you, tie you up. He made some unbelievable pitches. I didn't know if they were balls or strikes, so I swung because I knew they were close.[459]

DOUG MIENTKIEWICZ:

Every time David took a good swing, I thought, *They're not...come on, David.... They can't pitch to him now.* This is my turn. I've got a guy I know. A guy I've faced a million times. One good swing and we're right back where we need to be. Three-two, going back to New York. It wasn't false. It wasn't fake. It felt like, *This game's over. Whether David does it or I do it, it's over. We're not going back out on defense.*[460]

The 10th pitch of the at-bat was a cutter up and in. Ortiz fought it off, flaring the ball over second base and into shallow center field. Damon was off on contact. Bernie Williams ran in to field the ball but didn't bother throwing home. Damon scored standing up—and Ortiz and the Red Sox had done it again! This time, the score was 5–4 in 14 innings.

DAVID ORTIZ:

Loaiza angled his pitches very well at the time. He was throwing the cutter back door and front door. It was a fight. It was a battle. But the good thing is, I was the winner.[461]

JOE TORRE:

The ball was in off the plate, but he's so strong that he was able to fight the ball off. And if you make a mistake out over the plate, he can kill you like he did in the eighth inning.[462]

TERRY FRANCONA:

What can you say about Papi? Has anyone ever done what he's done in this setting? In any setting?[463]

KEVIN MILLAR:

I'll bet there are a lot of great players who've never had a week and a half like this. What am I saying? There are some good players who haven't had whole seasons where they've done what he's done in—what?—six games.[464]

DOUG MIENTKIEWICZ:

To do it night after night, it's ridiculous. He's a freak of nature. He almost hit a home run around Pesky's Pole. This game is not that easy, but there are some nights he makes it look easy. To come up in situations over and over again and keep doing it, it's just unbelievable. You wonder, "Can he do it again?" And he does.[465]

JOHNNY DAMON:

The way he's going, there might be a nice monument for him around here some day.[466]

CURTIS LESKANIC:

Every time he was up, the magnifying glass was on him, and he came through. It was incredible. It was a one-man kick-ass contest, that's what it was.[467]

GABE KAPLER:

It was unbelievable. It was Jordan-esque. It was remarkable, unparalleled, unrivaled.[468]

THEO EPSTEIN:

That's one of the best at-bats I've ever seen. Loaiza was throwing nuclear stuff out there and locating. Ortiz is just fearless up there. To foul all those balls off the way he did and then to hit that ball to center was remarkable.... I might be in sort of a haze, but I think that was one of the greatest games ever played, if not the greatest. I'd like to hear some nominations. Everything was on the line, unlikely heroes, amazing game. I'd like to get the DVDs of this one when it's all over, kick back, and watch it on the beach somewhere.[469]

JOHNNY DAMON:

Playing a game like this is so stressful. I'll be interested to see how gray my hair looks after this season. I might need an instant dye job. But what a great feeling this is. We're still down, but we can see that it's within reach.[470]

KEITH FOULKE:

I truly believe the pressure's all on them. It's their job to finish us off. Because we aren't going to go away quietly. I will do whatever I need to do to help our guys win. We're not going to give up. We are going to fight until we have nothing left and they make us leave.[471]

PEDRO MARTINEZ:

The Yankees have to think about who is their Big Papi.[472]

Nearly a year after giving up Aaron Boone's walk-off home run in the 2003 ALCS, Tim Wakefield got his extra-innings win over the Yankees. In three innings, he allowed only one hit and no runs.

TERRY FRANCONA:

To get shutout innings out of your bullpen for that length of time [eight innings], it was an unbelievable performance. You can't imagine how happy I am that Wakefield got to end the game. We used everyone. The last few innings, Wakefield was on fumes. He pitched the last inning on heart. Everybody was trying to do something, even if it was just to cheer. They're beat, the whole group, and they keep wanting the ball.[473]

DAVE ROBERTS:

After we won Game 5, I think the series really changed momentum. We were in very good shape.[474]

DOUG MIRABELLI:

Now we're really feeling good. We've won two ballgames. We've gone five games now without seeing any offense. We lost three of them, and we won two by one run. And we think, *Okay, you know what? This is momentum. This is a momentum switch right here. Their bats got cold. Our bats haven't gotten hot yet. We've been cold for five days. It's our turn*. That's how we were looking at it. And going into Game 6 and Game 7, I think that's what we saw.[475]

MARK BELLHORN:

It gave us a huge mental boost, the way we won. Especially the first night, and then to do it again. Going into New York, the last two games, we felt like the pressure was on them.[476]

ELLIS BURKS:
Once we won Games 4 and 5, that was a wrap. We knew we were going to win it.[477]

BEN CHERINGTON:
Speaking for myself, it wasn't until we won Game 5 and forced it back to New York that I started to feel we had a chance.[478]

BOB TEWKSBURY:
Teams gain momentum, positive momentum. I don't think it happened at 0–3. They had to win that first game. They won that—Game 4—and then there was a little uptick in confidence. But then when they won the next game, it was 2–3, and that was it. We're going to win this. We're not only going to tie it. We're going to win it.[479]

DAVID McCARTY:
The days, the games, everything was just surreal. I was exhausted, going on very little sleep, plus I was sick. I had a cold. A lot of guys on that team had colds. I'd come home, and it would be just hard to wind down. I was taking NyQuil for the cold, so that pretty much put me to sleep.[480]

DOUG MIENTKIEWICZ:
Jokingly, after Game 3 we all brought one piece of luggage to pack up and send home. That was Johnny Damon's thing. "You know what? I'm going to bring my stuff to the park because we're probably going to lose anyway." Throw the bad luck right back at it. Reverse psychology. Everybody brought one thing to ship home per game. Game 4, we brought it. Game 5, we brought it. It was a reminder. "I'll send this home today." We had boxes everywhere. The media was freaking out. "These guys are already packing." I remember them saying, "These guys are frauds," and all that stuff. We didn't pay attention to it. Our thoughts of ourselves were probably higher than they should have been, but it worked.[481]

The Yankees left 14 men on base in Game 4 and stranded 18 in Game 5, one shy of the postseason record. Since the sixth inning of Game 4, New York had been 1-for-18 with runners in scoring position. They simply could not get past the Red Sox pitching staff. In the two games, Boston's bullpen allowed only one run in 14⅔ innings. It was the first time the Yankees had ever lost consecutive extra-inning postseason games.

JOE TORRE:
It's Groundhog Day.[482]

DEREK JETER:
We're still in an awfully good position. We're still the team with the three wins. Now we need to finish the job.[483]

GARY SHEFFIELD:
We're taking it back to New York, and we will win.[484]

MARIANO RIVERA, *Yankees pitcher:*
[Asked if the Yankees still had any momentum] We're going home, what do you think?[485]

ALEX RODRIGUEZ:
It's been three days, and it feels like we've been [in Boston] a month.[486]

After the game, Ortiz expressed some frustration.

DAVID ORTIZ:
Somebody else is going to have to step up. It's always me lately. That's fine, but if we're going to beat the Yankees, somebody else has to do it. Not me, not all the time. We can't win that way. If we keep playing that way, they're going to beat our asses.[487]

MANNY RAMIREZ:
Nobody's got to step up. Everybody's done a great job. Everybody's putting in little pieces and that's it.... I try to do what I can. I can't be thinking, *I've got to produce more*. When I'm in the playoffs, I'm not worried about my average or anything. You just have to go and do little things so you can win.[488]

CHRISTIAN ELIAS, *Fenway Park scoreboard operator:*
Kind of like the press box, we don't root back there [inside the scoreboard], but it was impossible not to get caught up in the energy and the feeling and the tension. We have it easy during the playoffs and the World Series because there are no other games to post scores for. There is not a lot of work, but even so, there wasn't a lot of talking going on during those games. There was a lot of watching. I recognized that something was going on that had never happened in the past, a different feel to the ballpark, to the crowd—a different energy. And those games were so long. It was an exhausting time. The other thing was the weather. It was freezing. We're working

surrounded by concrete and metal. There's no heat back there. I felt like the Michelin Man since I was so puffed up with all my shirts and sweatshirts. Since we weren't working putting up scores of other games, there's not a lot of walking around. By the third inning, you couldn't feel your feet unless you kept moving.[489]

DAVE JAUSS, *advance scout:*

We were in Houston for Game 5. The Red Sox game started before ours; the Houston–St. Louis game was a night game. The Yankees' guys—all 12 scouts led by Gene Michael—they are still really happy. They had a tough one the day before, but they're all set. They're up 3–1. They got a lead through the sixth inning. Seventh inning, everything's still all set. We're all hanging around together in the media room. All of a sudden, we come back and tie it up again and they bolt out of there. Get to their seats for the game. Because the Red Sox game went into extra innings, it didn't end until about the third inning of the Astros-Cardinals game. You've got the Sox game on one of the scoreboards, showing the men on base, the number of outs, everything. But it's a little bit delayed. Alan Regier, another scout, was with me and he had the ESPN broadcast on a transistor radio in his ear. He's telling me, "Okay, we got out of that inning," or "We got a runner on." Well, Ortiz's hit wins the game in the bottom of the 14th and Regier looks over and says, "We won. We won." There's no feed on the big scoreboard yet, and there's 12 Yankees scouts right in front of me. I told our staff, "Watch these guys when this thing goes up on the board." Sure enough, the score goes up and you should have seen everyone's necks just yank. They're ticked off! They weren't going to St. Louis for the last two games. Their report was done. They knew they were going to have to see Steinbrenner the next day, and he would be livid that his team hadn't finished off the series. It's still one of the funniest incidents I've ever witnessed.[490]

Dorr's Liquors in Brighton, Massachusetts, had supplied 10 cases of champagne that was on ice at Fenway Park for the celebration had the Yankees won Game 4 or Game 5. Now that the ALCS would be decided in New York, the champagne had to be returned.

LEO "SKIP" DERVISHIAN, *Dorr's Liquors***:**
I was happy to take it back. I always like to see the Red Sox move
forward in the playoffs. I put the bottles on display with a back card
saying, "These champagnes were in the Yankees clubhouse during the
playoffs." I didn't raise the price or anything like that, but everyone
went a little ga-ga over that.[491]

The three Fenway games had been long ones. Game 3 clocked in at 4:20,
the longest nine-inning game in postseason history, Game 4 ran 5:02, and
Game 5 was 5:49, the longest postseason game in history. Red Sox Nation
hadn't gotten much sleep; it was running on adrenaline. There was tension
and anticipation—and hope—in the air.

16

American League Championship Series Game 6

Tuesday, October 19, 2004, at Yankee Stadium

After winning an emotional Game 5—in the season that refused to end—the Red Sox boarded a train from Boston to New York, arriving in Manhattan in the wee hours of Tuesday morning.

JACK McCORMICK, *traveling secretary*:
We had a charter train, a three-car Amtrak train with a special engine. You go right in at South Station, right up at the train, and in 30 seconds you're gone. It lets you off in the city. You come into Penn Station. The buses are right there and take us to the Westin, 43rd and Eighth. A nice way to go. Builds camaraderie.[492]

URI BERENGUER, *Spanish language radio announcer*:
It was a very cheerful ride to New York. Very good spirits. I spent most of it fooling around with Ellis Burks. He was "interviewing" me, trying to interview me in Spanish. He was trying to play my role. I'm trying to play his role, giving the answers I would imagine he would have given. Johnny Damon was another one who chimed in. It was a very fun train ride. We actually even danced. We put some salsa on and

started dancing, and some of the guys who couldn't dance a lick—not salsa, anyways—tried it.[493]

CHRIS CUNDIFF:

They told me that Trot Nixon insisted that I go to New York with the team. So they flew me to New York with a bunch of the minority owners, and I did Games 6 and 7 in New York. I felt like I was going to throw up all through Game 6, it was so nerve-wracking.[494]

RON JACKSON:

After the fifth game I said, "I've got to get Johnny Damon and Bellhorn going. If I don't get these guys going so they can be out there on base, we're going to lose this thing. These guys gotta be out there." When we went back to Yankee Stadium, I got to the park early. I wanted to get down there before the Yankees got in, before they started their extra work in the cage. The guys were playing cards. I talked with Ellis Burks. I said, "Ellis, I need Johnny and Bellhorn down to the cage. Tell them to get their butts down there. I know what they're doing wrong." He said, "They'll be down there, Papa Jack. This is my last year. I need a ring."

Johnny Damon wasn't loading up like he normally does. His hands weren't getting up like he used to do, and he wasn't staying inside the baseball. The biggest thing in hitting is trusting your hands. And Bellhorn, the same way. Both of them weren't trusting their hands. Trust their hands means staying gap-to-gap. Staying up the middle, and not trying to do too much. You don't try to pull anything or cheat—I call that cheating, and when you cheat, that's when you get in trouble. We sat down and figured out what they were doing wrong with their mechanics. And the rest of it is history.[495]

MARK BELLHORN:

I never really stayed on top of the ball a whole lot. I always had a little bit of an uppercut, especially left-handed. When I struggled, it probably got a little worse. When you don't get hits, you get anxious, you lose confidence. I'd get a little aggressive. I didn't always stay back, keep my hands back. I'd go out to get it as opposed to waiting for it to get there. It was the first time I'd been involved in a series like this, and sometimes you try a little too hard. I did some extra work and tried to not put so much pressure on myself. Everybody encouraged me. They knew I could get it done, that it was bound to happen sooner or later. They knew you could not do anything one night and be a star the next night.[496]

The Red Sox were concerned about how Curt Schilling's surgically positioned right-ankle tendon would hold up under the strain of throwing as many as 100 pitches in cold, damp weather. They had kept the procedure a secret. Word had not gotten out. The media was still talking about braces in Schilling's shoe.

THEO EPSTEIN:
It's always nice to have some secrets in October.[497]

DR. WILLIAM MORGAN:
Curt tolerated it that first night very well. He slept okay. He said it was a little sore. But the sutures were still in. I again injected it with Marcaine. He did a bullpen. He went out and did some pitching, and he felt good.[498]

Red Sox fans, and all the new fans who had taken notice of this scrappy Red Sox team in the last few days, had no idea what Schilling had gone through to make this start. They simply hoped his ankle was more stable that it had been for Game 1.

CURT SCHILLING:
There was no precedent for what I was about to do. I was excited, but I was also terrified. I was getting ready to pitch in Yankee Stadium against the Yankees in front of Yankee fans. As I am wont to do in my career, before Game 1 I made a comment about shutting up 50,000 people from New York. I always enjoyed saying and doing those things because I felt it put extra pressure on myself, which I liked. But before Game 6, I didn't do any of that.

It was a significant moment in my life and my faith, that whole day. I tried to muscle up and be a tough guy in Game 1, and in Game 6 I was very emotional about it. I prayed and went and talked to some of my fellow Christians on the team. People mocked me after it was over about how God doesn't want anybody to win, blah blah. I never prayed to win. I never prayed for Him to score runs. I prayed for the ability to compete. It was always centered around giving me the strength to compete. I wanted to be able to pitch the game that they had assigned me to pitch.[499]

Terry Francona indicated Derek Lowe and Bronson Arroyo, who had thrown only 17 pitches in his one inning of work in Game 5, were his first options out of the bullpen behind Schilling. Tim Wakefield would likely get the ball in a possible Game 7, although Francona did not say whether Jason Varitek or Doug Mirabelli would catch him.

> **TERRY FRANCONA:**
> Some of it will depend on who doesn't get used tonight, but Wakefield has already been told to prepare for that. If we get into 16 innings, you don't know what's going to happen. But that's our outlook—to have him prepare as if he's not going to pitch tonight so he can get ready for tomorrow.[500]

The Red Sox took batting practice under the stands instead of on the field before Game 6, but not because of the raw weather. They wanted to avoid being exposed to "Yankeeography"—video biographies of famous Yankee players, which the home team played during opposing batting practice, perhaps hoping the grandeur of the franchise's storied past would intimidate in the present.

> **KEVIN MILLAR:**
> That was the first night of the Jack Daniel's. And it started with one simple thing: "Yankeeography." That caused the Jack Daniel's. When the Yankees take batting practice at home, they got music, everybody's hip-hopping and having fun. When the visiting team comes out—here's the Boston Red Sox—they put on this Yankeeography crap. It lulls you to sleep. My whole theory was, we're not falling for Yankeeography. I yelled about this a lot during the year as a joke, "We're not falling for it, boys. Don't fall for it." I was always pretty loud on the field, so I'm yelling during BP. Well, today, we're not going on the field and falling for Yankeeography. I told Francona we're going to hit in the cages. And he looked at me like I was crazy. Well, if you guys want to hit in the cage, go ahead. It's like the Super Bowl now, it's a little bit misty, rain, 47 degrees, you got your Red Sox–Yankees Game 6 and there's a bazillion media, and the Red Sox are hitting in the cages. Francona says, if you guys want to do it, figure out if everybody else wants to do it. So I walked into the locker room, told everybody, "Let's hit in the cages, we're not falling for Yankeeography." Next thing you know, as I'm walking to the cage,

there's this huge bottle of Jack Daniel's that the clubbies have. So I put my eyes on it, and grabbed it, and we had a symbolic toast. We hit in the cages, and I got the bottle of Jack and was pouring—you know, in these Gatorade cups, for fun.[501]

ORLANDO CABRERA:
We were in the back, doing shots. Millar was giving it to some people and he called me and I took it—I didn't even know what I was drinking—nothing much. But it was getting cold, too, cold and windy. He was just trying to make people part of the team.[502]

POKEY REESE:
I went along with what my teammates were doing. It was cold and liquor kind of heats up the system. Everyone just took a shot. I don't see anything wrong with that. Nobody went back and had five or six shots.[503]

THEO EPSTEIN:
I saw the Jack in New York. Millar came up to me and offered me a cup, and I said, "I don't see that shit," and turned and walked away.[504]

TERRY FRANCONA:
I never knew about it until the World Series.[505]

Millar first told the Jack Daniel's story a few days after the Red Sox had defeated the Cardinals in the World Series. "I went around and got a thing of Jack Daniel's and we all did shots of Jack Daniel's about 10 minutes before the game," said Millar, a guest on *The Best Damn Sports Show Period* on Friday, October 29. "And we won Game 6. So Game 7, of course, we had to do shots of Jack Daniel's. And we won Game 7, so guess what? I'm glad we won [the World Series] in Game 4 because these Crown Royal shots and Jack Daniel's shots started to kill me.... It's out there now, baby—we were drunk."[506]

When Millar repeated the story later in the show, he added, "We got Francona involved in Game 4 because he's not really good under pressure."[507] After the story got out, Millar backtracked, saying the players didn't do shots but merely took "sips" of whiskey from one small cup. Millar also said, "I wish I'd never opened my mouth."[508]

A few days later, on November 2, Millar said, "It was one of those group team things, like shaving our heads last year. What we had was one small Gatorade cup with a little Jack Daniel's in it. We passed it around, and everyone symbolically drank out of the same cup because we are a team. It wasn't as if guys were drunk. Can you imagine Trot Nixon or Jason Varitek or Mike Timlin actually sipping alcohol before a game? No way.... It's not a story about 25 shot glasses, it's one small Gatorade cup that we shared as a symbol. And once we won Game 6, we had to do it before Game 7, just like the lucky coin I had in my pocket every game."[509]

In 2013, Pedro Martinez said that some of the team drank a Dominican drink called Mama Juana, not Jack Daniel's. Ellis Burks remembered Pedro bringing it out, but when Millar was asked about it, he was mystified. "Mama Wanna?" When told what Martinez had said, David Ortiz burst out laughing.

Curt Schilling took the mound at Yankee Stadium in the cold rain. There was a blood stain visible near his right ankle.

DR. WILLIAM MORGAN:
Sutures will pull with movement, and we expected a certain amount of blood to ooze from the wound. Socks are like sponges. Even a small amount of blood can soak a sock.[510]

THEO EPSTEIN:
Dr. Morgan told me there would be some oozing. Never a word you want to hear on a baseball field.[511]

CURT SCHILLING:
No one was more nervous than I was before Game 6. I was nervous as hell. That's part of the motivation, the fear of failure. I always felt good players use the fear of failure in a positive way.... Everybody in the bullpen and dugout was questioning whether it was going to work or not.[512]

Schilling and catcher Jason Varitek anticipated that the Yankees, having lost two games and desperate to avoid playing a winner-take-all Game 7, might be anxious at the plate, especially in the early innings.

CURT SCHILLING:
I keyed in on their aggression. That was definitely part of the game plan. They were aggressive. Everybody on the Yankees was feeling it

at that point. Now you're down 3–1—"Wow, that would be unbelievable"—to down 3–2, and if we win this game, we're tied. The pressure
was gone from our end. It was exciting for us at this point. They had
to be dreading what could happen.[513]

THEO EPSTEIN:
Early on, there was a lot of tension with Schilling. Was he going to go
out and throw one warm-up pitch and fall down and have to be taken
off on a board? Was he going to throw 82 mph? Was he going to be
able to throw strikes? Were they going to bunt on him? Was he going
to be able to field his position? Would it matter anyway because in
Game 1 they beat his ass all around the ball park? We were holding
our breath with every pitch.[514]

Derek Jeter swung at Schilling's first pitch and flied out to right field.
Trot Nixon battled the wind but made the catch. While Schilling needed
eight pitches before Alex Rodriguez lined out to shortstop, Gary Sheffield
popped out to first on the second pitch. Schilling was showing far more
consistent velocity than he had in Game 1—plus the ability to drive hard off
the rubber. His right ankle was handling the pressure. The questions were:
Would it last, and would he be able to locate, to get on top of his splitter?

THEO EPSTEIN:
After the first pitch, I was pretty happy with his delivery. When he
showed that he had good mechanics, it took a huge lump out of my
throat.[515]

In the top of the second, Boston strung together three singles off Yankees
starter Jon Lieber and had the bases loaded with one out. Mark Bellhorn,
dropped to the ninth spot in the lineup, fouled off four inside pitches before
hitting a double-play grounder to second.

MARK BELLHORN:
I didn't have a whole lot of confidence. I didn't feel real comfortable
at the plate for probably the three games before that. But that was
probably the best I felt that whole postseason. It was a pretty big
situation, bases loaded. I grounded into a double play, but I felt really
good during that at-bat. I hit a two-hopper to the second baseman,
but I hit it right on the sweet spot. I felt like I had a great at-bat; I
just hit it right to him.[516]

Schilling retired the Yankees in order in the bottom of the second. With two outs, Jorge Posada smashed a 2–1 pitch to deep right field. On another night, it likely would have been a home run, but the wind and rain knocked it down. Trot Nixon caught the ball at the base of the wall. Back on the mound, Schilling took one look at the ball in the air and turned around—no fist pump, no display of emotion at all—and began walking to the third-base dugout, secure in knowing the ball would stay in the park.

Through three innings, Schilling retired nine of 10 Yankees batters.

CURT SCHILLING:
As each inning went by, I felt like something special was happening—you can just feel it. It was like an out-of-body experience. I always feed off the crowd's energy, even on the road, but on this night I was so locked in, concentrating so hard, that I didn't even notice the fans. Nothing like that had ever happened to me before.... During all this, one of the stitches busted, and the blood started really coming through my sock. I knew the tendon was still okay, and that's all I cared about. I just prayed that it would hold out for a while.[517]

LYNN JONES:
We were all wondering how long he was going to hold up. That was the key, how long was he going to be able to hold up. And he put mind over matter. Just taking the excruciating pain, the process, and taking it and putting it aside. And delivering what needed to be done.[518]

Lieber got the first two outs in the top of the fourth, then Millar smoked a first-pitch fastball down the left-field line. It hit off the wall for a double. Varitek battled Lieber for 10 pitches—one of them a wild pitch that moved Millar to third—before lining a single into center field. Millar scored, and the Red Sox led 1–0.

Orlando Cabrera pulled the first pitch he saw into left for another hit. That brought Bellhorn to the plate. The Yankees were continuing to pitch Bellhorn inside, but when Lieber finally threw a pitch away, the quiet second baseman was ready for it. He drove a high fly to left-center. It was hit well enough to just get over the fence. Hideki Matsui gave up on it and watched the ball strike a fan's bulky black winter coat. The ball bounced back onto the field, and Matsui tossed it into the infield. Left-field umpire Jim Joyce ruled that the ball had struck the wall. Bellhorn pulled up at second base.

MARK BELLHORN:

I was always better hitting the ball away than in, so the Yankees were throwing everything inside the whole time. I fouled a couple off and then it got to 1–2. And then he went away. I kept telling myself I wasn't going to let this guy get me out. I need to come through here. Probably just more positive talking to myself. I hit it and definitely didn't think it was going to be a home run. I knew I hit it pretty good. I thought it was probably going to be a double down the line and it ended up hitting off a fan's chest—home run. I never saw it hit the person. I rounded first and got to second, then saw Matsui throwing it in. I stopped at second instinctively. Then I saw [third-base coach] Dale Sveum run out there, saying that it was a home run, arguing with the ump.[519]

TERRY FRANCONA:

In our dugout, we have a horrible view. But I saw Dale right away yelling it was a home run, and when I got out there Dale explained to me what happened. All I cared about was just getting together and getting the call right. It was very obvious after being out there for a minute or two. Our whole dugout was on the field.[520]

The six umpires gathered on the infield grass to discuss the play. About 30 seconds passed. Then crew chief Randy Marsh broke from the umpires' huddle and twirled his index finger in the air, the sign for a home run. Bellhorn resumed his trot around the bases. Boston led 4–0.

RANDY MARSH, *umpire (crew chief)*:

When we got together, everyone else felt that the ball was a home run. Sometimes when a ball goes and ricochets that fast, if you're moving at all, it makes it hard to see. I don't know if Jimmy [left field umpire Jim Joyce] was still moving on that, but obviously he was taking some heat on it. We all started walking toward him. "Let's get together." He came in. All five of the other umpires agreed that the ball was a home run.[521]

As Schilling began the bottom of the fourth, his velocity began to wane. Rodriguez singled up the middle. Sheffield hit a grounder that rolled down the third-base line. Bill Mueller watched it, hoping it would go foul, but it stayed fair and bumped the bag for a single. Schilling bore down and retired the next three hitters, keeping the ball in the infield: Matsui fouled out to first, Bernie Williams grounded out Millar-to-Schilling—the ball hit off Millar's glove, and he led a hobbling Schilling to the bag—and Posada grounded out to Millar, who made the play himself.

THEO EPSTEIN:
I was pretty nervous through the whole thing, especially when he had to cover first because you never know what kind of force might impact the sutures and the tendon.[522]

CURT SCHILLING:
I felt like I was pushing it at that point. I was struggling. It was kind of hard to get around on.[523]

Schilling's velocity reappeared in the fifth inning. He struck out Ruben Sierra and Tony Clark and retired Miguel Cairo on a grounder to shortstop. Schilling also retired the Yankees in order in the sixth.

TERRY FRANCONA:
His velocity was a little inconsistent, but it seemed like every time we started to get a little worried, he would pump it back up to 94 and hit his spots.[524]

In the seventh inning, Bernie Williams hit a one-out, solo home run, cutting Boston's lead to 4–1. But Schilling gave the Yankees nothing after that, finishing strong as Posada popped to second and Sierra struck out swinging.

TERRY FRANCONA:
Some people said they were surprised he came out of the game after the seventh, but we were actually keeping an eye on him from the fourth in case he was starting not to feel great. After the fourth, he got a little—I don't know if cranky is the right word, but he looked good in the fifth and sixth. We kept a close eye on him, though. When you see Schill go to the umpires after the seventh and say, "Good job," you know he's done. I don't think any of us have any idea what he went through to pitch tonight.[525]

CURT SCHILLING:
I had enough. I'd been struggling since the fourth.[526]

Schilling's performance would have been superb under any circumstances, but considering what he had gone through to take the mound, it was nearly miraculous: seven innings, four hits, no walks, one run, and five strikeouts. He threw 99 pitches.

BERNIE WILLIAMS, *Yankees center fielder:*
We definitely had our chances. He left the door open. He left some pitches there for us, and we didn't take advantage. He wasn't as sharp as he normally is. That was especially true with the fastball. He didn't have the velocity he usually has. He knew he had to hit his spots. He pitched like Pedro. He was saving his bullets. He wasn't adding on his fastball until late in counts, and when the game got tight. He would wait until he got two strikes on you, and then add a few miles to the fastball.[527]

CURT SCHILLING:
My ability to stay out there for seven innings was because the ankle was better. I made a lot of mistakes and they missed them, as opposed to Game 1 when they didn't. There were a couple different situations—the sixth inning, the front-door slider I threw Sheffield—a couple of situations where I needed to make pitches and we made the pitch and got away with it. I don't attribute it to any one thing. We were in a situation going into that game where I knew they would be pressing. Outside of Jeter and his aggressiveness, I was not sure how aggressive the rest of the team was going to be, and they were aggressive, which was huge, because my pitch count was down. I fully expected them to bunt and to test me, which I never really thought was going to be much of an issue, as far as getting off the mound and fielding my position. The only major adjustment for me was what Dr. Morgan did for me in between games. That was the one thing that allowed me to stay out there and pitch.

I don't remember the weather. I don't remember it being cold, other than being on the bench and I had a towel on my head because it was chilly and my ears were cold, but I don't remember thinking about it. I saw my breath as the game went on, and I used that as a trigger for breathing and taking my time. When I'm on the road and I'm in front of hostile crowds, I have always been able to kind of use that. They are yelling, you make a pitch, and they shut up. I don't remember hearing anything that night. I know after the seventh inning when they sang "God Bless America" that the fans were getting into the game, but I don't really remember hearing it.[528]

TERRY FRANCONA:
I expected him to pitch well, and that wasn't fair. He was a mess. He had wanted this moment so bad. He wanted to be on that stage and be the guy. He wanted to stick it up their ass. We all talked, and I said, "Schill, this will probably hurt your career." He had no business pitching in that game, let alone winning.[529]

Bronson Arroyo came out of the bullpen for the eighth inning, pitching on back-to-back days for only the second time in his career. Gabe Kapler had pinch-hit for Trot Nixon in the top of the inning and was now playing right field. Francona had also put Doug Mientkiewicz at first base in place of Millar.

BRONSON ARROYO:
I felt fine coming in. We had a three-run lead. I thought if I got the first lefty out in Clark, then I'd have no problem getting a hold on my nerves.[530]

Arroyo had no problem with Clark, striking him out on a 2–2 slow curve. Miguel Cairo fouled off several pitches before lining a double into the right-field corner. Mike Myers was throwing in the Red Sox bullpen as Derek Jeter jumped on Arroyo's first pitch and singled to left. Cairo scored easily, cutting Boston's lead to 4–2. It was the first run allowed by a Boston reliever in the last 13⅔ innings.

With one out, the Yankees had the potential tying run at the plate in Alex Rodriguez. Arroyo was working Rodriguez away and threw ball one. Pitching coach Dave Wallace came out for a quick chat. Arroyo got two breaking balls over the outside edge of the plate and was ahead 1–2. An outside fastball just missed, then Rodriguez fouled off a pitch. Both bullpens were busy with Timlin and Rivera now warming up.

BRONSON ARROYO:
I took a little bit off on a curveball, and Alex just squibbed it right off the end of the bat.[531]

The ball was chopped down the first-base line. Arroyo's follow-through took him in that direction, and he was quickly off the mound to field the ball. Mientkiewicz had come in a few steps, which meant that Arroyo would have to tag Rodriguez himself instead of tossing the ball to his first baseman. Arroyo went to make the play on Rodriguez, and the Yankee third baseman slapped Arroyo's forearm with his left hand.

The ball rolled away, down the right-field line, into foul territory. First-base umpire Randy Marsh's view of Rodriguez and Arroyo was blocked by Mientkiewicz, so when he saw the ball roll loose, he signaled that the ball was still in play.

Jeter raced around the bases and scored, and Rodriguez went to second. Boston now led 4–3, with the potential tying run in scoring position and only one out.

BRONSON ARROYO:

He karate-chopped me in the arm. It was so obvious to me. Then I looked at some of the umpires and they were reacting like it's not that big of a deal. I'm thinking, *There's six umpires here, somebody had to see what just happened.*[532]

DOUG MIENTKIEWICZ:

On a little dribbler, you're always taught to go get the ball until the pitcher calls you off. But with 58,000 screaming maniacs, you're not going to hear. The last thing you want to do is have Bronson run to first and I'm already there and the ball just rolls to me. As I got closer, I saw Bronson was going to get it, and I started back-pedaling. Now I was too close to him. If A-Rod got by him, he gets to first base. A-Rod slapped the ball out of Bronson's hand and my first reaction—I started giggling. I was like, "Are you kidding me?" I was laughing. I said to the umpire, "Randy, please tell me you saw that." And he says, "No, you blocked me out." And then my laughter turned to, "Are you shitting me?" I remember walking toward Joe West, saying, "Joe, please tell me you saw that. That can't be fucking legal." He threw his hand up at me like, "Hang on. Hang on. Just stay there. We'll take care of it." Joe's look was stoic, and I'm thinking, *I don't think he saw it.* I was going to go to every umpire until they agreed with me.[533]

TROT NIXON:

The last time I saw something like that was probably in a Wiffle Ball game in the backyard. I never saw that in high school. You'd see guys that would maybe try to throw an arm or a shoulder into the guy and see if they could dislodge the ball because the glove was away from the body. But not to actually swing their hand down. Everybody on the bench, we were saying, "Did he really just slap the ball out of his hand?"[534]

THEO EPSTEIN:

In Yankee Stadium, I had sat in the scouts' section behind the plate for the 2003 ALCS and the first two games in 2004, so by the time we went back for Game 6, just because of superstition, I was going to mix it up. I ended up watching with Josh Byrnes in the manager's office. We watched the game on a small color TV. Shoes off, you know, leaning back in Tito's chair, sometimes in the fetal position. And when A-Rod slapped the ball, and Jeter crossed home plate and pumped his fist and A-Rod was at second base with a big grin on his face, and the umpires didn't call anything, I ran out to the main clubhouse. Dave Roberts was there, watching the big TV with some of the bench play-ers, and we were both apoplectic. We watched the replay, and it was clear that A-Rod had slapped the ball. I told Dave, "Go down to the dugout. Go right now! Tell Tito what you saw on TV! Tell him to go out there and argue that!" I remember the look on his face—he couldn't get out of there fast enough. I don't even think he had his shoes on! He sprinted down the tunnel, but by then Tito was, of course, out on the field arguing.[535]

TERRY FRANCONA:

You could see Alex take a swipe at the ball. I couldn't get on the field to say anything till the play was over because the guys were circling the bases.[536]

ORLANDO CABRERA:

It didn't feel right how the whole thing happened. I said to myself, *I'm pretty sure that's not legal. He can't do that.* A-Rod got to second base—and he's doing this [shrug]. I was like, "Are you fucking crazy?" He said, "I didn't do anything!" I said, "Dude, they got you on video. They're watching that in Japan right now! They're going crazy." And he's sort of like, "What did I do?" I'm almost in his face. I was like, "Are you trying to get away with murder here? I mean, come on!"[537]

RANDY MARSH:

Mientkiewicz came right between me and Arroyo. I saw Arroyo come over, and the next thing I know the ball is flying past me. Arroyo said, "He hit my arm! He hit my arm!" and then Francona came out, and I thought, *Maybe something happened here that I didn't see.* So I got the crew together. Plate umpire Joe West was coming down the line, and he could see it clearly. He really helped us out. When we got together, he was the guy who had the best view. He said, "Randy, it looked like he hit his arm. Like he swiped at it." I said, "All right." When we work a six-man system in the playoffs, we ask the right-field umpire to drift into foul territory and up toward the base itself on a play at first base. Jeff Kellogg drifted in and observed the same thing Joe said. Jeff said, "Yes, that's exactly what I saw." I said, "Good enough. Listen, we're going to switch it."[538]

BILL MUELLER:

It was a desperation play, obviously. And if the umpires didn't see this guy slap the ball out of Bronson's glove, that's devastating. It would make you pissed off because it was so blatant. I was waiting for things to unfold, for the umpires to talk, let them dictate what should happen. And they did, and it was great that everybody saw the right stuff. That was a good feeling.[539]

According to Section 6.1 of the MLB Umpire Manual, "a runner is not allowed to use his hands or arms to commit an obviously malicious or unsportsmanlike act." Rule 2.00 (Interference) of the Official Baseball Rules states, "Offensive interference is an act by the team at-bat which interferes with, obstructs, impedes, hinders, or confuses any fielder attempting to make a play.... In the event the batter runner has not reached first base, all runners shall return to the base last occupied at the time of the pitch."

The umpires ruled that Rodriguez had interfered with Arroyo and was called out. Jeter had to return to first base.

JOHNNY DAMON:

The umpires got it right. That's the beauty of it. If they got it wrong, who knows what situation we'd be in.[540]

TROT NIXON:
In all the years I played at Yankee Stadium, you don't see too many calls get reversed and go to the opposing team—especially the Red Sox.[541]

ORLANDO CABRERA:
They called the play, and I'm like, "Yes!" He wasn't thinking that if he hit that ball out of his glove it was going to go that far. He probably thought it would just drop. Oh my God, it was crazy.[542]

BRONSON ARROYO:
Without question the call gave me a boost. Jeter had to go back to first, which made the inning so much easier. I could pitch to Sheffield and not worry about him getting a hit to tie up the game.[543]

ALEX RODRIGUEZ:
I don't know what I tried to do. Maybe I should have just run him over, like a catcher. But I came out of my way to knock the ball out of his hand. My reply [to the umpires] was, "Well, if he's coming to touch my stomach, why am I going to sit there dumbfounded and let him touch me?" I was perplexed by the whole situation.[544]

JOE TORRE:
I was upset that it turned out the way it did for a couple of reasons. First off, they said that Arroyo was in motion, too; it's not like he was just standing there. And Mientkiewicz was in the line and didn't have the ball, which can be an obstruction play.[545]

BRIAN CASHMAN:
He was trying to find a way to get a win. It wasn't malicious. He was trying to knock the ball free.... It took me two innings to confirm that the right call was made.

ALEX RODRIGUEZ:
I don't want those umpires to meet anymore because every time they meet, it goes against the Yankees.[546]

When the call was announced, the Yankee Stadium fans went berserk. It was the second time in the game that the umpires had changed a call, and both results had gone against the Yankees. Now instead of trailing 4–3 with one out and a man on second, the Yankees trailed 4–2 with two outs and a man on first. In the stands, euphoria over New York's apparent rally quickly turned to rage. Bottles and other garbage rained down on the field.

DOUG MIENTKIEWICZ:
After they talked about it and called Alex out, Joe West walked over to me and said, "We had it under control. We just had to get you guys in the middle of the field because we knew in the aftermath, you were going to get it." The fans throwing stuff and everything. He said, "We wanted to make damn sure we were in the middle of the field and not going to get hit by bottles." Okay, but next time give me a little hint so I'm not standing over there with a 300-beats-per-minute heartbeat.[547]

Terry Francona motioned for his players to leave the field. Bob Sheppard, the longtime public-address announcer, asked fans to "Please refrain from throwing anything on the field. Yankees sportsmanship is still the best. Please continue that tradition."[548]

CHRIS CUNDIFF:
They were throwing full bottles of soda from the upper decks. It was like bombs. You could hear them hit the roof of the dugout. I was thinking, "I'm not going out there."[549]

BRONSON ARROYO:
I wasn't really worried about the trash. Trash was the furthest thing from my mind. I was just worried about getting a new ball and pitching to Sheffield.[550]

While the Red Sox waited for order to be restored, Cabrera glanced back toward the Red Sox dugout and flashed two signs. First he made a crying gesture, miming wiping tears from his right eye. Then he held up seven fingers.

ORLANDO CABRERA:
There were two wise guys there, out past the Red Sox dugout toward left field. Front row. Suits. Italian guys. I was pretending I was crying. "Waaaa." Then I held up seven fingers. "That's right! Game 7. Tomorrow." I was sending it to those two guys. They were going nuts. When I'd be coming in, they'd be screaming some shit at me. They were going like [pantomimes pointing a pistol at his head].

I'm thinking, *That's all right.... I'm from Colombia. That doesn't bother me.*[551]

The game was delayed about 10 minutes while the debris was cleaned off the field.

When play resumed, Arroyo wasted little time with Sheffield. One foul, a ball, a second foul, and then Sheffield popped out to Jason Varitek in foul territory. The Yankees, trailing 4–2, were down to their last three outs.

Boston tried adding to its two-run lead in the top of the ninth. Varitek grounded a hard single back through the box, past pitcher Paul Quantrill, and into center field. Varitek was forced at second by Cabrera, who narrowly beat the relay to first. Fans in the stands, annoyed at the safe call on a close play, threw more trash on the field. Tanyon Sturtze came in to face Bellhorn. During the pitching change, dozens of police in riot gear came out of the dugouts and took positions in foul territory on both sides of the field.

RANDY MARSH:
They were throwing things, bottles, especially around third base. These things could hurt somebody. Kevin Hallinan was senior vice president of security for the Commissioner's office, and he was at the end of the Yankees dugout. I went down and said, "Kevin, I want a sign of security down the lines." Meaning not the field side of the fence. The fan's side of the fence. In other words, have the police in the stands right by the fence so they could see if anybody was throwing anything on the field. Unbeknownst to me, they had security ready to line the field after the game. I think they were guys who were going through the police academy. They were all down in the tunnel. When I told Kevin, "I want a police presence down the fence," all he said was, "Got it." I didn't know that he had all those guys down there.

Next thing we know, those guys are coming out in riot gear. They were there for just a half-inning or so. Then we got them off the field and got the police down in the stands by the fence so they could keep an eye on what was happening.

I didn't expect it to go that way. I don't think Mr. Steinbrenner was happy that it turned out like that. I had the plate in Game 7 and I was thinking, *This'll be interesting when we walk on the field.* You know what? We didn't hear a thing. I think the New York people knew that we did what was right. We didn't hear a peep.[552]

ORLANDO CABRERA:
We had some incidents like that in Colombia, but I was surprised to see it in New York. With riot gear. I'd never seen that many police on a field in the United States before. In Colombia, they do it at soccer games. They really thought things were getting out of hand. Fans in the park saw the replay on televisions in the park's concourses and came back and they said okay. That was the moment they started hating A-Rod.[553]

CHRIS CUNDIFF:
Penny Marshall, of *Laverne and Shirley*, was sitting behind me. She came over and congratulated the team in the seventh or eighth inning, and I was thinking to myself, "Shut up! We've already been here before. I don't want you to jinx this one." Then they brought out the SWAT teams. I didn't know they were lined up in the hallway. I sat on the field right in front of the wall. I went down to put some stuff away, and I turned around and they just started coming. It was like the Army came out.[554]

Cabrera stole second and Bellhorn walked, but Sturtze was able to work out of the jam, getting both Damon and Mueller to pop up to shortstop.

For the bottom of the ninth, Terry Francona had no hesitation about using Keith Foulke for a third straight night, even after his closer's heavy workload in Games 4 and 5.

KEITH FOULKE:
I don't think that I've ever worked four innings in two days and still been available.[555]

Hideki Matsui led off with a seven-pitch walk, which immediately brought the potential tying run to the plate. Umpire Joe West seemed to be calling a very tight strike zone. Foulke would have to earn every strike. Bernie Williams took three pitches, two of them strikes, before swinging and missing for the first out. Foulke got ahead of Jorge Posada 1–2 and got him to pop out to Bill Mueller at third. One out to go. Foulke walked Ruben Sierra, and Matsui advanced to second. New York now had the potential tying run at first base and the potential pennant-winning run at the plate in Tony Clark.

Foulke had been working all of the Yankee hitters away, every so often coming inside just enough to get a called strike or a foul ball. It was both working—he had recorded two outs—and not—he had walked two batters.

Foulke's first two pitches to Clark were up and away for balls. Foulke then split the plate with a fastball for a called strike, prompting the Fox television announcers to wonder what in the world Clark was waiting for.

KEITH FOULKE:

I had pressure on myself every single pitch. Every time, I had a purpose in my mind before I made the pitch. This is where I want to go. If it didn't go there—even if I got an out—I'd get a little disappointed. I wanted to be perfect every time. At that point, I was battling. The tank was empty, and I was struggling to get the ball down in the zone. My control wasn't there, and I was just gutting it out.[556]

THEO EPSTEIN:

The single most anxious moment of the whole series for me was the end of Game 6. The Yankees got a couple of guys on and Tony Clark came to bat against Keith Foulke, representing the winning run. Foulke had been superhuman through the whole series and had thrown so many pitches, his arm should have been falling off—and in fact, it probably did negatively impact the rest of his career, which went downhill after that postseason—but Clark comes up against Foulke, and I was thinking that one swing of the bat could end this thing when we're so close to getting to Game 7. I could barely watch. I think I watched that whole at-bat through the cracks of my fingers, covering my eyes. The strike zone got real small for that at-bat, and he just started pumping fastball after fastball—small strike zone, tired closer, Tony Clark who had been having some pretty good swings, short porch in right field. I couldn't watch. I felt like a year after the Aaron Boone experience, we were potentially going to see it again, and that might have been more than I could have handled.[557]

JOHN HENRY:

I have never felt such intense stress—*ever*.[558]

Clark fouled off the next pitch to the third-base side of the field. Foulke's 2–2 offering was in the dirt. Full count. Foulke's 28th pitch of the inning was a fastball, 88 mph, up and possibly out of the strike zone. Clark took a big cut at it and missed. Strike three. The game was over!

With the 4–2 victory, the Red Sox had done what no major league baseball team had ever done before: battled back to force a Game 7 after being down 0–3.

TONY CLARK, *Yankees first baseman*:
I got a pitch I could handle—one I should have done something with—and I swung right through it.[559]

JOHN HENRY:
With the final out, I was so overcome with relief, I couldn't muster even a silent cheer.[560]

Henry was not at Yankee Stadium for Game 6. He watched the game, along with fellow Red Sox owners Tom Werner and Larry Lucchino, at Lucchino's house in Brookline, Massachusetts.

TOM WERNER:
We didn't want to go to New York and watch the Yankees clinch. The nightmares of 2003 were such that we felt we'd rather be in Brookline if we lost. If we won Game 6, then we'd go down to New York for the seventh game. None of us wanted to be in Yankee Stadium and watch the Yankees jump up and down and celebrate on the pitcher's mound. We all take this extremely seriously. It's very exhausting and tense. By the time Game 6 ended, we were so exhausted we could hardly raise our arms over our heads.[561]

The Red Sox bounded out of their dugout and congratulated one another in the infield. Foulke, beaming, hugged Bronson Arroyo. Foulke started to walk away, then turned back to Arroyo and said, in a voice barely above a rasp, "Gotta make it interesting!"

With his 28 pitches in Game 6, Foulke had thrown an even 100 pitches in five innings in three must-win games over a period of roughly 48 hours. It was a mind-boggling amount of work for a closer.

THEO EPSTEIN:
We had expectations that he could do more than what a traditional closer is used to doing. But what he's done the last three or four days is almost superhuman. I couldn't imagine a relief pitcher assuming

this workload and pitching this well. It's shocking to me, but I'm loving every minute of it. He's seemingly as strong now as he was three or four days ago. He's not making mistakes. He's not getting lucky. He's locating really well. He's been representative of the bullpen as a whole. Those guys are pitching on guts.[562]

KEITH FOULKE:

We've kept the ball out of the middle of the plate. It sounds like a simple philosophy, but it works. Sometimes when you are tired, you take a look at what you are doing. I made a few adjustments to my mechanics and I stopped trying to overpower the ball, and I felt fantastic. I don't rely on trying to blow the ball by people. I don't tax my arm like other guys do. I don't have as much wear and tear. I've trained all my life to be in a position like this. I look forward to the challenge. They put us down 0–3, and now the pressure's on them to put us away. In 20 years, no one's going to remember if Boston lost the series 4–0, 4–1, or 4–2, but everyone will remember how we did it if we go to the World Series.[563]

After the game, there was nothing but praise for Curt Schilling's performance in what was immediately dubbed the "Bloody Sock Game."

DOUG MIENTKIEWICZ:

The fact that the man is even walking around is amazing. To pitch like that completely healthy would have been one hell of a performance, let alone do it with arguably one foot. To do it in that atmosphere, that's the guttiest pitching performance I've ever seen. Hands down.[564]

GABE KAPLER:

Just the fact that he got himself prepared to pitch this game energized the club, energized everybody around the team. You know, "Is Schill gonna pitch? What's he gonna be like?" And when we saw him get through those first couple of innings, we breathed a huge sigh of relief, not because we knew we were going to win the game, but we knew we were going to compete.... I don't know how many of us noticed, but his stuff wasn't there early on. It just *got there*.[565]

DAVID ORTIZ:

I never thought in baseball you might find somebody with that kind of heart. This guy, he's got like 100 stitches in his ankle. It's swollen, painful, and everything's going on. Before the game, I asked him how he felt and he told me, "I got no pain, and I don't think nobody can beat me today, so you better follow."[566]

MIKE TIMLIN:

I've seen some pretty gutty performances, but he stood on a hurt ankle and threw 92, 93, 94 and kept one of the best lineups in baseball off balance for a long while. That shows a lot. It shows what he's made of, where his faith lies, and where his heart is.[567]

In his *New York Post* column, former Yankees catcher Joe Girardi said it was "really disappointing" that no one attempted a bunt on Schilling. "On the couple of times that Schilling had to go to first," Girardi wrote, "he didn't look to me like he had the same velocity immediately afterward. I just don't understand why the Yankees didn't bunt."[568]

CURT SCHILLING:

I don't know why the Yankees never bunted on me. I think they felt that if I was out there, I was okay. Maybe they felt that people were over-playing the injury and were trying to deke them into doing it. Maybe they thought we were trying to trick them. I don't think that would have mattered at all. I had to cover first a couple of times. I think it would have been uncomfortable. I think they would have seen that as "gimmicky." I think they thought, *We're going to beat them.* They expected to beat me, doing the things they'd done.[569]

KEVIN MILLAR:

I couldn't believe they didn't get him moving. They swung at a lot of first pitches, popped up, he had to cover first one time on a play to me. But they didn't get him moving. I mean, if you're looking at a wounded duck, the media attention is all over the place, the Yankees know, so why not? But I guess that lineup, besides Jeter, is Bernie Williams going to bunt? Is Jorge Posada going to bunt? Matsui? No, no, no. A-Rod? It wasn't like you were playing the St. Louis Cardinals in the '80s. Still, I was surprised that somebody didn't move him.[570]

BILL MUELLER:

I was a little bit surprised. But they were probably doing things they were comfortable with. Maybe they felt like if he was out on that mound that he had enough mobility. They probably didn't know the extent of what was going on, so they might have thought it was fabricated. Who knows? If they don't know anything, they are going to go about their business the way they do it. Schilling is kind of a tough guy to bunt against anyway because he likes to ride that fastball up in the zone, yet it's still a borderline strike. Those pitches are tough to bunt because you have to make sure that your barrel stays at an angle where you can get that downward projection. It's never easy to bunt against him.[571]

JOE TORRE:
Bunting is an individual choice. And we were not necessarily of a mind to believe that there was a lot wrong with him. It's not that we're saying that he wasn't telling the truth [about being hurt], but we have to deal with him, the pitcher we know, instead of seeing that there's something drastically wrong with him physically. We don't want to take away from ourselves. I hate to think, *A-Rod, here, drop one down so you don't hit one out of the ballpark*. I'd rather take my chances with him swinging the bat.[572]

After the game, Bronson Arroyo was asked if he thought Rodriguez had intentionally slapped the ball out of his glove.

BRONSON ARROYO:
Without question. That's like asking me if I'm breathing.[573]

CURT SCHILLING:
That was freakin' junior high baseball at its best. Let me ask you something—does Jeter do that? You know for a fact he doesn't because Derek Jeter is a class act and a professional, that's why.[574]

KEVIN MILLAR:
It was a classless play. That was unprofessional. If you want to play football, strap on some pads and go play for the Green Bay Packers.[575]

DOUG MIENTKIEWICZ:
After I saw him do that, I thought, *Hell, I might as well tackle him*. If he's going to play that way, so can I.[576]

With the series tied at three games apiece, Francona reconsidered his options for Game 7 and tapped Derek Lowe for the start instead of Tim Wakefield. Once it had been clear that Schilling would go deep into Game 6, Lowe was sent back to the team's hotel to get some extra rest.[577]

TERRY FRANCONA:
We think Derek can give us more innings, more pitches than Wake could if they are throwing well. Whoever is pitching for both teams isn't going to have a big rope, but if Derek can get outs, we think he can stay out there longer. Derek is a little younger, he's a sinkerball pitcher, and I think that works to his advantage a little bit.[578]

BRONSON ARROYO:
We're all available. Even Pedro will be out there.[579]

KEVIN MILLAR:
I wish we could play right now. I wish we didn't have to shower and we could get right back out there.[580]

JOE TORRE:
It was supposed to come to Game 7. Sometimes it happens in a weird way.[581]

ALEX RODRIGUEZ:
If we win, it won't be embarrassing. Everyone wanted to see a one-game showdown. Now there is one.[582]

DEREK JETER:
Forget about the first six games. We've got to play better for one day. They've responded well in three do-or-die games. Now we're going to find out how we respond.[583]

While rushing to his car after Game 6, Yankees principal owner George Steinbrenner was asked if he was worried. "Sure, I'm worried. The whole team should be worried. We've got to win it." Steinbrenner refused to answer any questions about the umpiring. When asked if he was upset that the Red Sox had extended the series to a seventh game, Steinbrenner said only, "Good night."[584]

17

American League Championship Series Game 7

Wednesday, October 20, 2004, at Yankee Stadium

KEVIN MILLAR:

We have a chance to shock the United States of America.[585]

Peter Gammons called it "the most anticipated game in baseball history," and the pronouncement didn't even sound like hyperbole. Dan Shaughnessy wrote that New Englanders—and Red Sox fans everywhere—are "at once sleepless, breathless, and full of hope." Mike Lupica wrote that the game "feels as big as any ever played, in a World Series or anyplace else."

KEVIN MILLAR:

We wanted to play Game 7 the second Game 6 ended last night. This morning, I was up at 8:00 with my eyes wide open, just ready to get here.[586]

Wherever they were, Red Sox fans felt awe and disbelief at the roller-coaster ride of the last three games, elation at Boston's resurrection, and anxiousness over Game 7. Fans no doubt struggled to keep their minds on their work, school, or families that day, anticipating the action that would begin at 8:20 PM.

The front page of the *Boston Herald* featured a picture of Mark Bellhorn's home-run swing with the headline: "Believe It! Brilliant Schilling Leads Sox To Game 7 Showdown Tonight." The back page proclaimed the Red Sox were "Back From The Dead."

KEVIN MILLAR:
This is it. There's no pressure. We have a chance to do something nobody's ever done in baseball, and that's come back from being down 0–3 and win a seven-game series.... Right now we're all running on straight adrenaline.[587]

Everyone sipped a little more Jack Daniel's (or Mama Juana, or whatever...) before the game. In the manager's office, Terry Francona and Theo Epstein drank their glasses of Metamucil.

ELLIS BURKS:
Baseball players are very superstitious. If you do something a certain way and you win or have a great game, nine times out of 10 you're going to do it again the next day. Especially when you're talking about a team like the Red Sox that had a history of letting down at the end. All of a sudden we get an opportunity and we keep winning, we're going to continue doing the things we were doing.[588]

In the Yankee Stadium outfield before Game 7, Mike Mussina, bullpen catcher Mike Borzello, and a few other players were talking. Mussina revealed in a later interview that the general sentiment was, "We're finished. That was the feeling after Game 6. As soon as Game 6 ended."[589]

MIKE BORZELLO, *Yankees bullpen catcher*:
There's just no chance of winning this game. People didn't trust [Kevin] Brown. He was never part of the team, and now our hopes were on him. We let it get to that point. And there's no way we're going to be able to survive. We had our shots. We had three games to do it, and now it's come to this. We deserve to lose.[590]

With the Yankees' pride and reputation on the line, the *New York Post* beseeched ghosts to assist the 2004 pinstripers. The tabloid's front page featured a huge picture of Babe Ruth with the headline: "Put Me In! Yanks

Need Babe's Curse In Game 7." The *Daily News* also alluded to the spirit world: "Seven Help Us!"

The Yankees themselves pulled out all the stops. They invited Hall of Fame catcher Yogi Berra to deliver a locker room speech. Bucky Dent—the former Yankees shortstop who had struck an unlikely three-run home run at Fenway Park in the one-game playoff for the American League East title in 1978—threw out the first pitch. The *Daily News* said those gestures "smacked of desperation by a team desperate not to be on the wrong side of postseason lore."[591]

John Henry, Tom Werner, and Larry Lucchino made the trip down from Brookline and were in attendance for Game 7.

JOHN HENRY:

You know where they put us? In the Babe Ruth Suite.[592]

Derek Lowe was getting the ball in one of the most important games in Red Sox history.

DEREK LOWE:

I came in fully confident. You can look at the two days rest, but you can also look at the fact that I only pitched once in 16 days, so it wasn't like I was pitching every five days. It was a personal challenge for me to see if I could come back in the Stadium after the disaster I had in September, giving up seven runs in one inning. We had no idea how long I was going to go, and they didn't, either.... Game 4, we really didn't have anything to lose. Tonight is a different story. Games like this can make or break your career.[593]

JOHNNY DAMON:

I was confident Lowe was the perfect pitcher for the job. I knew he'd be tired, and I knew he'd be sharp, because when he's tired, his sinker sinks even better.[594]

DEREK LOWE:

They should do that on *MythBusters* because it's not true. I would much rather pitch at full strength. You still need your legs under you, and you still need your arm in the right arm slot. If you get too tired, your ball doesn't move any more. I promise you.[595]

CHRIS CORRENTI, *trainer:*

We periodized the pitching program. When we hit August 15, the last 45 days of the season, it was no holds barred. We didn't worry about rest. Everybody's workouts were cut back. It was about pitching and getting outs at that point. As far as "rest" or "tired"—those words were not in our vocabulary. The goal was to peak out at the end of the season. Theo was getting impatient, and I said, "Relax. Once we get to the end of the season, that is when we're going to peak out" and sure enough, we sure did.[596]

When Lowe arrived in the visiting clubhouse at Yankee Stadium, something was missing.

DEREK LOWE:

My game shoes. The old Yankee Stadium was notorious for having stuff miraculously disappear. There was this constant gamesmanship—how can you out-screw the other team. You'd come in, all the coffee was decaf, the air conditioning never worked when it was hot, the heat never worked when it was cold, how do you screw the other team with tickets. They always messed with Nomar because Nomar had so many things that he had to have, and they would constantly take stuff. We had left Boston two nights before and there are certain things you always make sure you pack: your shoes and your glove. We looked through the whole place—no shoes. They figured the Game 7 pitcher didn't need his shoes. I tried on some other players' shoes to see if they fit. We ended up going to Sports Authority, getting these off-the-shelf size 12 Reeboks. If you look at video from the game, you'll see we had to black them out with a marker because by contract I was supposed to wear only Nike.[597]

LYNN JONES:

We had a bunch of players, coaching staff, at the ballpark early, 12:30, 1:00. So what do you do? You put on *Miracle on Ice* [a movie about the 1980 U.S. Olympic men's hockey team]. And Theo Epstein walks through and he says, "Look at this phone call." And it's a text message from Jim Craig, the goalie of that U.S. hockey team! He ends up talking with Derek Lowe on the phone. That gave me chills, that we were watching *Miracle on Ice* and Jim Craig calls. I felt good after the movie, the phone call, and Derek talking with him.

DEREK LOWE:

Theo called me over and put me on the phone, and Craig explained how they did it against the Russians. It sounds kind of corny, but it's true. He said to try and break the game down, break the game into small increments. Don't try to throw seven shutout innings. Just try to make it simple.[598]

CHRIS CUNDIFF:

I'd always go over on the early bus. I remember they watched *Miracle on Ice* before Game 7. I think Schilling brought it in. Everybody was watching that, which was pretty funny because it's not a big clubhouse. They had everybody crammed in there.[599]

THEO EPSTEIN:

The clubhouse was kind of quiet. Everyone was coming to grips with what we were hopefully about to go do.[600]

The Red Sox were hoping to complete their own Miracle on Grass.

Kevin Brown, who had lasted only two innings in Game 3, had an equally rough start in Game 7. Damon began the evening by grounding a single to third, under Alex Rodriguez's glove, and into left field.

JOHNNY DAMON:

I needed to make something happen. I have the green light so whenever I want to steal, it's okay with Terry. I didn't think we'd score too many runs off Kevin Brown, so I figured we should play a little small ball. He doesn't have a particularly good move to first.[601]

Mark Bellhorn was back to his usual second spot in the Boston order. On Brown's 1–2 pitch to Bellhorn, Damon got a big jump and easily stole second base. Bellhorn struck out, but Manny Ramirez hit a hard ground ball to the left of shortstop. Damon waited to see if Derek Jeter would make the play, so he got a late start toward third. The ball got through into left-center, and Damon rounded the third-base bag. Hideki Matsui threw the ball in to Jeter, who turned and fired a perfect throw to the plate. Jorge Posada blocked the dish and tagged Damon out.

The Yankees fans had barely stopped cheering when David Ortiz crushed Brown's first pitch to deep right field for a home run. The Red Sox fans in attendance erupted. Boston led 2–0.

DAVID ORTIZ:
It was like having flashbacks from what happened to me in 2003. We went to Game 7. In New York. In 2003 we had a day game—a 4:00 game—for Game 6. We won that game. Then I went straight to my room. My family and friends were in New York, and they wanted to go out for dinner. It was like 9:00 when I got back to the hotel. I was so focused on the next day that I stressed out too much. I went and locked myself in my room. I wanted to be disconnected from everything so the next day I'm good to go. But it was the opposite. I was worn out the next day. So in 2004, same situation. We won Game 6 in New York. But I changed a few things. This time, I went with my family to this one friend of mine's restaurant. Have dinner. Good time, you know. Have a couple of glasses of wine. And then I'm like, "Okay, now I'm ready to go to sleep."

When I was walking out of the restaurant, there was a table with some Yankees fans. And when they saw me walking out, they were like, "Huh. I don't think this guy's going to make it tomorrow." I turned my head and told them, "Hey, I'm going deep on my first at-bat tomorrow." They were like, "Yeah, whatever." That was my boy's restaurant right there. His name is El Rubio, from the Dominican. He's got a restaurant in Queens. My boy's watching the whole thing. These fans were customers of his. Everybody was laughing. The next day, he went to watch the game at the restaurant, and he caught my first at-bat. Against Kevin Brown—pow! I went deep my first at-bat. They started going crazy. They couldn't believe it—I said I was going deep on my first at-bat, and I did. I think the Yankees were done, just because of that.[602]

DEREK LOWE:
When he hit that, we all relaxed.[603]

Lowe retired the Yankees in order in the first inning. Jeter flied to center, Alex Rodriguez grounded to third, and Gary Sheffield struck out looking. Strike three was a filthy curveball that started high in the zone and broke down to Sheffield's waist.

DEREK LOWE:
Striking out Sheffield on a 3–2 breaking ball. We were trying to throw him curveballs inside. We were trying to start the ball directly at him, knowing full well that the ball would end up right down the middle

of the plate. We were fine with that. We figured that he would take it, and he did.[604]

In the second inning, after Trot Nixon grounded out to shortstop, Kevin Millar lined a single to center and Bill Mueller walked. New York pitching coach Mel Stottlemyre came out, hoping to settle Brown while Javier Vazquez warmed up in the bullpen. Orlando Cabrera battled Brown through eight pitches and worked another walk, loading the bases.

In this must-win game, Yankees manager Joe Torre couldn't afford to let Boston establish an early advantage; Torre yanked Brown after only 1⅓ innings and 44 pitches. Brown had been a complete bust against the Red Sox, pitching only 3⅓ innings in two starts and allowing (in the end) nine runs. When Torre came out to get the ball from Brown, he didn't even clap his pitcher on the back, a clear sign of displeasure.[605]

Now Vazquez faced Damon with the bases loaded. Vazquez had given up two home runs to Damon in consecutive at-bats back on June 29, one on the second pitch and one on the first pitch.

JOHNNY DAMON:

I had a feeling Vazquez would try to get ahead of me because then he could go to work on me, throwing his change-up and changing speeds. I knew he was going to throw me a fastball, and I guessed that he figured I'd be leaning over the plate, looking for a fastball away. I was actually looking for a fastball in, and I was thinking if he threw it there, I'd hit it out of the park. *Come on, big fellow, pitch it in. Let me see it.* Vazquez's first pitch was a fastball in. He didn't throw me a bad pitch. He actually jammed me. But from the hard work I had been doing in the cages, I was able to adjust, get my balance back, and when I swung, I was hoping I'd gotten enough of it for it to go out. Thank goodness right field in Yankee Stadium is short![606]

Grand slam! Boston led 6–0.

MIKE MYERS:

Once Damon hit the grand slam, we started counting down outs in the bullpen. How many outs do we have left? Me and Dana LeVangie looked over at each other, and Leskanic, and we started counting down how many outs we had left before we could run out on that field.[607]

Vazquez walked Bellhorn but retired Ramirez and Ortiz to end the inning.

DEREK LOWE:
We tried to keep throwing first-pitch strikes. That was the key. And I never took the score for granted. Getting six runs was huge, there's no denying that. But I kept trying to think of it as a one-run game.[608]

In the second, Lowe gave up only a two-out walk. In the third, with one out, he hit Miguel Cairo with a pitch. As Jeter batted, Cairo stole second base then scored when Jeter grounded a single through the shortstop hole.

Mike Myers began warming up for the Red Sox. By the time Lowe had thrown three pitches to Alex Rodriguez, Curtis Leskanic had joined Myers in the bullpen. Terry Francona was taking no chances. If Lowe didn't have it tonight, he would not last long. Rodriguez grounded back to Lowe, who threw him out at first, and Jeter took second. In the Boston bullpen, Pedro Martinez took off his jacket. With two outs, Lowe faced Gary Sheffield.

DEREK LOWE:
Sheffield hit a bullet to third. It was a hanging breaking ball, and Bill Mueller made a great play at third base. Even though we still had a big enough lead [6–1], you could sense that they wanted to strike. The Bill Mueller play was—you don't want to say it was game-changing, because it was the third inning—but to me, personally, it could have been the end to my night. I looked down to the bullpen, and if there were three mounds out there to throw off of, we'd have had a guy on all of them.[609]

GABE KAPLER:
We were sitting in the clubhouse. It was about the third inning. I'm stretching, trying to get ready. I was telling Ortiz how impressed I was that Curt Schilling still gets nervous before a big game. I told him I thought it was amazing a guy of his caliber still has the jitters. David looks at me and says, "I never get nervous." Now my first inclination was not to believe him. But he says, "When I start feeling that way, I think about what I've gone through in my life, and then I put

things in the proper place." By prioritizing baseball, it allowed him to be at ease, and to relax. It shows on the field. There is always this calmness about him. And when pitchers see that calmness, I think it worries them.[610]

Vazquez was still on the mound for New York in the fourth inning. Orlando Cabrera had a seven-pitch at-bat and walked.

JOHNNY DAMON:

After hitting a grand slam the at-bat before, I was feeling totally relaxed and comfortable. I figured he'd start me out with a fastball on the other side of the plate—outside—and that's what he did, and I drilled it into the upper deck in right field.[611]

Damon's second home run of the game gave Boston a commanding 8–1 lead. Through the first six games, Damon had batted a paltry .103. He had one stolen base and had scored only three runs. Now, with two swings of the bat, he had knocked in six runs.

Vazquez walked Bellhorn. After he retired Ramirez on a pop-up to third, he walked Ortiz. And that was the end of his night.

Jason Varitek, facing Esteban Loaiza, hit a hot shot off Cairo's glove at second base. The ball rolled into right field, and the Red Sox had the bases loaded, with only one out. Loaiza prevented any further damage by striking out Nixon and getting Millar on a grounder to second.

DEREK LOWE:

I had just pitched against them 72 hours earlier, so I had a fresh thought of what I wanted to do. Our game plan was to throw a lot of breaking balls. We threw a lot of them, and I was fortunate enough to have good command of my off-speed stuff. We figured they'd be ultra-aggressive because of how the series had gone.[612]

After his rough patch in the third, Derek Lowe retired the next nine Yankees hitters, setting them down in order in the fourth, fifth, and sixth innings. Only one of those nine outs left the infield.

DEREK LOWE:

I settled in and got a lot of ground balls. Once they had that chance to strike, and didn't—I don't recall having any stressful pitches. I got ahead of a lot of guys, and the crowd was at a standstill. There wasn't a lot of noise.[613]

TERRY FRANCONA:
We were trying to get innings out of D, and he had just pitched two days ago. If we got three, four, whatever we got, we could have gone to Wakefield. We had lined up a lot of different scenarios, but he was so special tonight. I mean, the runs helped.[614]

At the end of the fifth inning, Francona and Lowe talked in the dugout. Francona asked Lowe how much he had left in the tank, and the right-hander replied, "This will pretty much be it."[615]

TERRY FRANCONA:
Derek Lowe had no more in him. The last thing he said to me when he went out for the sixth was, "Don't leave me out there to die." I said, "Okay." He had three hitters in that inning. If he got to Matsui, who was due up fourth, Myers was coming in.[616]

Lowe needed only 10 pitches for the sixth, getting Jeter and Rodriguez to ground to shortstop and striking out Sheffield.

DEREK LOWE:
I struck out Sheffield and just let out a deep breath. It was over. It was what you dream about the night before. It was how you see the game going, and I was able to do it. To be honest, it was also a big relief.[617]

Lowe had allowed only one hit in six innings—Jeter's RBI single in the third. He walked one batter, hit another, and struck out three. He threw 69 pitches, and he was exhausted.

DEREK LOWE:
I was fortunate to have a good change-up. More than half my outs probably came on change-ups. I figured I'd keep throwing it until they made an adjustment.[618]

CHRIS CUNDIFF:
When the Yankees batted, I'd run back to the clubhouse...I think I watched every inning of Game 7 from the video room. They set it up in the front of the clubhouse, just to the right when you come in the front door. Dave Roberts was next to me. You'd be amazed how many

people were in there. You couldn't move in there. Then we'd all run down to the dugout when the inning ended. We'd do that inning, and then we'd all run back and get in the exact same spot. I was a nervous wreck.[619]

Pedro Martinez began tossing in the bullpen while his teammates were batting in the top of the sixth. Now, in the bottom of the seventh, Martinez came out of the bullpen and walked across the outfield to the Yankee Stadium mound.

TERRY FRANCONA:
We got him loose in the inning before. If we got Pedro up and we sit him down and then there's a rally, you're risking a lot because we've got so many outs left. So if we got him up, we were going to get him in. We were trying to minimize fatigue on guys' arms and win the game. We didn't exactly have an abundance of fresh arms down there. I was excited about bringing him in. I know he gave up some hits and some runs, but he actually threw the ball very well. We wanted him to be standing on that mound with some success and having the lead. It also bridged the gap to where we got to Timlin.[620]

DAVE WALLACE, *pitching coach*:
You pull out all the stops. There's no conventional way to do it. Our bullpen's taxed. Foulke had thrown 100 pitches in three days. It was Pedro's side day. He wanted to be a part of it. And really, that was a huge inning. We had to bridge. We had to get to the eighth to get to Timlin and Embree and Foulke. We had to do it.[621]

Despite trailing by seven runs, just the sight of Martinez was enough to spark the crowd.

CHRIS CUNDIFF:
We were up 8–1, and I ran out to get Pedro's coat when he came in. I was out in the middle of the outfield where you take the coat from the new pitcher coming in the game. The place started to chant, "Who's your daddy?" Despite the fact they were down by so many runs. The place was rocking. You could feel it. Each side was just off a bit from the other; they weren't doing it in unison. They were doing it two different ways. It was like stereo speakers. And you could feel

it! It was unbelievable. Indescribable. I stopped and looked around for a moment thinking, *This is the coolest thing ever.*[622]

Martinez threw two pitches out of the strike zone, then Matsui ripped a double into the right-field corner. Bernie Williams fouled off two pitches and then he also doubled—to the gap in right-center—and Matsui scored. Williams had hit a fastball that registered a weak 87 mph. Martinez's velocity was way down.

Timlin started warming up as Posada grounded out to first base. Now the crowd was taunting Martinez with a sing-song chant of "*Paaay*-dro! *Paaay*-dro!" Kenny Lofton singled to center and Williams scored, cutting Boston's lead to 8–3.

CURT SCHILLING:
The game was never as close as I think everybody in our dugout felt.[623]

Red Sox fans may have wondered why Francona didn't call in Timlin. But Martinez remained in the game. With John Olerud pinch-hitting for Tony Clark, Martinez suddenly regained his velocity. After a 1–1 start, Olerud fouled off three pitches, then took ball two—which came in at 97 mph. Martinez's 2–2 pitch was up and away at 95, and Olerud chased it for a strikeout. Facing Cairo, Martinez threw nothing but gas: foul, ball, swinging, then a fly out to Nixon near the right-field corner. It had been a bit scary, but Martinez finished strong, and the Red Sox still had a five-run lead with two innings left to play.

THEO EPSTEIN:
It brought such life back to Yankee Stadium. Even being up by as many runs as we had, all those probably unjustified fears that we had came up in one split second, you know, when they started to rally off Pedro. The crowd started to go crazy. It was almost a huge surprise when we got out of that inning and still had the lead. That was harrowing.[624]

DEREK LOWE:
We always questioned why Pedro went in. That was something that was always kind of weird. Because the place was so silent. We had all the momentum, and then Francona woke them up by bringing Pedro into the game. It re-energized not only the crowd but the

Yankees, and they ended up scoring a few runs. I think if you bring in anybody besides Pedro, they may not have scored. So it was one of those things—why are we giving these people any reason to get rejuvenated again?[625]

In the top of the eighth, Mark Bellhorn drove a Tom Gordon fastball off the right-field foul pole for a home run, and Boston's cushion increased by one 9–3.

MARK BELLHORN:

That might have been the first hit I ever got off Gordon. He threw that cutter—I don't know if Mariano taught it to him. It's crazy what one big hit can do for you. I hit the home run the night before and—I don't know, I just kind of reacted. Every once in a while, you'll take a swing and you'll be surprised that you hit the barrel of the bat. That was one of those swings where I swung and I was like, "Oh!" I was surprised how good I hit it. And it stayed fair and hit the pole.[626]

Timlin faced the top of New York's lineup in the bottom of the eighth inning. Pokey Reese was now playing second base; Doug Mientkiewicz had gone in to first in the seventh. Timlin set the Yankees down in order—Jeter grounded to third, Rodriguez struck out, and Sheffield grounded to shortstop. Thousands of Yankee fans began streaming for the exits.

In the ninth, facing Tom Gordon, who pitched in six of the seven games, Nixon and Mientkiewicz began the inning with singles. Nixon took third on Mueller's fly to center, and when Cabrera flied to center, Nixon jogged home. The score was now 10–3, and it sounded like most of the remaining crowd was made up of Red Sox fans. A loud chant of "Let's go, Red Sox! Let's go, Red Sox!" could easily be heard.

KEVIN MILLAR:

It was like we were at home. We took the stadium over.[627]

BILL MUELLER:

To see it that way was almost a complete turnaround. I never imagined seeing Yankee Stadium in that fashion. From the first moment I walked in there and heard people chant "19–18"—and then two years later, being in that same stadium and hearing all the

Red Sox fans, knowing that we're going to go to the World Series and we beat them coming back from that deficit—it was surreal.[628]

After Cabrera's sacrifice fly gave Boston a seven-run lead with two outs, Joe Torre summoned Mariano Rivera to face Johnny Damon. As always when Rivera came in to pitch at home, Metallica's "Enter Sandman" blared from the stadium PA, but it seemed grossly out of place. Rivera got Damon on a routine comebacker to the mound for the inning's third out.

LARRY LUCCHINO:
John Henry turned to Tom Werner and me and he said, "With a seven-run lead, everyone in America except us thinks we're going to win this game tonight." We weren't doing any premature celebrating.[629]

TOM WERNER:
We've all seen crazy things in baseball, and I didn't really relax until the game was over.[630]

Timlin was on the mound for the bottom of the ninth. Hideki Matsui singled to right, then was forced at second by Bernie Williams. Jorge Posada popped out to Cabrera. There were two outs. Williams took second base on defensive indifference as Kenny Lofton walked on four pitches.

With Ruben Sierra batting for John Olerud, Francona called for lefty Alan Embree.

It was one minute past midnight when Sierra hit a 1–0 pitch on the ground toward Reese at second base. Reese easily scooped up the ball and in one fluid motion threw it to Mientkiewicz. First-base umpire Jeff Nelson signaled "Out!"

The Boston Red Sox were the 2004 American League champions!

POKEY REESE:
Sierra kind of corkscrewed it my way. It was in slow motion to me. Make sure you stay down, and this ball does not get by you. It was hit pretty slowly and I gathered and did my normal routine and I tossed it over to Mientkiewicz and that was that. We went crazy! It was one of the best feelings I've ever had in baseball.[631]

ALAN EMBREE:
I thought, *If I throw a fastball away, he's going to roll over on it.* He was going to hit a ground ball. And it worked. It was the longest,

slowest play of my life. It took *forever* for the ground ball to get to him—in my mind. I could almost read the ball as it was going by me. Knowing it was the last out, knowing there were runners on—the whole deal. But watching the ball, it was like slow motion.... The adrenaline rush that went through my body when the umpire signaled the final out, I just can't describe it. Not many guys get that opportunity, and I thank God I was there.... Sweet revenge. We felt like we had unfinished business all year long with these guys. We played them tough. They thought they had us. We were the only ones that believed we could do it.[632]

TIM WAKEFIELD:

When we got that final out, I wanted to stand on that mound as long as I could and relish the fact that I got to walk off the field a winner this time. For us to win four in a row from these guys really shows our determination.[633]

The entire Red Sox team rushed to the middle of the infield to celebrate. They had accomplished what no team in the history of Major League Baseball had been able to do—win four straight games after losing the first three of a best-of-seven series. After decades of playing second fiddle to the Yankees in the American League—and one year after a soul-crushing defeat at Yankee Stadium—the Red Sox had won two marathon games in Boston, then returned to the Bronx to vanquish their longtime rivals. In tandem with Boston's improbable comeback, the New York Yankees had suffered the greatest postseason collapse of all time.

In the visitors' locker room, the celebration was only beginning.

JOHN HENRY:

You can't do this. You just can't do this. To come back and be in this very spot where we were last year, and succeed this time from where we were just a few days ago? The performances we got...from Curt and Derek, Ortiz, Johnny Damon, Bellhorn. I could name everybody I'm looking at right now. Can you believe it? It has to be the best comeback in the history of sports, right? How could it be anything else?[634]

TOM WERNER:

It was the greatest evening that I've ever enjoyed as a fan. You don't get many chances to repeat. After the seventh game in 2003, I felt that it would take us a long time before we got back to a time like that. And there we were the next year.[635]

TERRY FRANCONA:
There was no room for error. We concentrated on every single pitch, every single play to win it.[636]

THEO EPSTEIN:
We did it. We did it in their fucking house.[637]

LARRY LUCCHINO:
All empires must fall, sooner or later.[638]

PEDRO MARTINEZ:
Wakefield told me, "We were in the clubhouse last year crying, and now we came back to have the last laugh."[639]

MIKE TIMLIN:
How many times have we walked out of this place with our heads down? Finally we walk off this field with our heads high.[640]

TROT NIXON:
I know how much these fans want the opportunity to win a world championship. I hear it when I go to the doctor's office. I hear it when I walk out in the streets. Let those fans know that I remember what they say. I don't forget those kinds of things.[641]

After the Yankees won Game 7 of the 2003 ALCS, George Steinbrenner was spotted waving to the Red Sox team bus, yelling, "Go back to Boston, boys!"[642]

KEVIN MILLAR:
Where's George at? Where's Steinbrenner at?[643]

JOHN HENRY:
What were they saying? "Go back to Boston, boys?" Tell them don't forget to turn off the lights today.[644]

TIM WAKEFIELD:
This is as big as the World Series. It's tremendous, not only for this organization, but for the city and the fans that stuck around through thick and thin for us.... I still scratch my head and try to figure out how the heck we did what we did, but we did it.[645]

TERRY FRANCONA:

Four or five days ago, no one gave us a chance, but here we are, going to the World Series. We didn't want to be down 0–3, but we fought back. We didn't give up, just like we didn't give up in July when we were treading water there. And we're still not going to give up.[646]

KEVIN MILLAR:

We beat the Yankees, and we're going to the World Series. They get a chance to finally watch us on the tube.[647]

THEO EPSTEIN:

There's been so many great Red Sox teams and players who would have tasted World Series champagne if it weren't for the Yankees. Guys in '49, '78, us last year. Now that we've won, this is for them. We can put that behind us, move on to the World Series, and take care of that.[648]

DEREK LOWE:

I gave myself the nickname "Cockroach" in the Anaheim series. They kept trying to kill me. I'd find a way to wiggle back to life.[649]

KEVIN MILLAR:

How many times can you honestly say you have a chance to shock the world? It might happen once in your life, or it may never happen. But we had that chance, and we did it. It's an amazing storybook.[650]

David Ortiz, responsible for so much throughout the series, tried to take credit for Damon's resurgence at the plate.

DAVID ORTIZ:

I tried to keep him away from his fiancée. I told them, "Hey, Michelle, listen, you are sleeping in somebody else's room. You've got to stay away from my boy for the next couple of days." And I think it helped. Look at my man today.[651]

Damon had swung the biggest bat in Game 7, but it was no surprise that Ortiz was named Most Valuable Player of the ALCS. He went 12-for-31 (.387), with three home runs, six runs scored, four walks, and an LCS-record 11 runs batted in. In addition to his extra-inning, game-winning hits in Games 4 and 5, Ortiz also hit Boston's only triple in the ALCS.

Orlando Cabrera also had a big series with 11 hits, five runs scored, and five RBIs. Manny Ramirez was on base a lot, with nine hits and five walks, many of which prolonged innings, and gave David Ortiz a chance to do some damage with runners on base. But Ramirez did not drive in a single run in the seven games.

MANNY RAMIREZ:

It doesn't matter. I hope I go 0-for-40 and we win the World Series.[652]

Ortiz's 11 RBIs shattered the Red Sox's previous record, which had been six, set by Rich Gedman and Jim Rice in 1986 and tied by Ortiz in 2003. Ortiz came one RBI shy of the Boston record for any postseason series; John Valentin drove in 12 runs in the 1999 ALDS against Cleveland.

THEO EPSTEIN:

David Ortiz picked us up on his back, delivered a couple wins, and then every single player followed suit. These players looked at the 24 guys around them and said, "I'm not letting you down." The next thing you know, we're drinking champagne in the Yankee Stadium clubhouse.[653]

LARRY LUCCHINO:

He's got big, broad shoulders, and he used them this entire series to carry this team. He does it on the field, and he does it off the field.... Theo Epstein deserves a big kiss for getting David Ortiz.[654]

Toward the end of Boston's celebration, Wakefield got a phone call.

TIM WAKEFIELD:

We were wrapping up our celebration and I was walking into the training room and one of the clubhouse attendants said, "Hey, the phone's for you." I thought, *That's kind of weird*. It was Joe. He said, "Wake, this is Joe Torre. I just wanted to congratulate you. You're one of the guys over there that I respect. Just remember to have fun. You guys deserve it." Afterward, I wrote him a note and told him how much that meant to me. That's one of the highest compliments you ever get from an opposing manager at that point. I said it meant the world to me. It really touched me deeply for him to call me.[655]

In the Yankees' clubhouse, the mood was subdued.

ALEX RODRIGUEZ:
We have no excuses. They beat our asses.... I'm embarrassed right now. Watching them celebrate—being up 3–0 and not being able to deliver the knockout punch. It's crushing. I don't have the words to describe my disappointment.[656]

BRIAN CASHMAN:
All year long, Boston was kind of like Jason from *Halloween*.[657]

JOE TORRE:
They can put winning streaks together before you blink your eye, and we knew that. That why we wanted to close the deal. That's why I brought in Mariano in Game 4 with two innings to go, even though we were up 3–0.[658]

DEREK JETER:
Sure it hurts a little more because of who we lost to.... I never thought this would happen. We had so much confidence going in.... I can't explain it. They played better than us. That's all I can say. We couldn't stop them.... When you look back, it's shocking.... It's upsetting to lose. But in terms of being the first team to lose after being up 3–0, I couldn't care less.[659]

Curt Schilling and Doug Mientkiewicz came back onto the field to shower the remaining fans crowded behind the Red Sox dugout with champagne.

CHRIS CUNDIFF:
The Yankees let all the Red Sox fans stay after Game 7. We dug the hell out of the field, with people taking chunks of earth and bottles of dirt and this and that.[660]

DAVID ORTIZ:
I don't know who made up the phrase, "Keep the faith," but they were the best words ever created.[661]

18

Advance Scouting

THE 2004 RED SOX WERE ADVANCED in their use of baseball statistics. The front office had hired statistics iconoclast Bill James as senior baseball operations advisor, and many others in the Baseball Operations group were also comfortable using data known as sabermetrics. General manager Theo Epstein also relied on veteran baseball men like Bill Lajoie, special assistant to the general manager/scouting. The Red Sox organization as a whole thirsted for information and used it to great effect.

THEO EPSTEIN:

Advance scouting is huge. It's fundamental. [Advance scout] Dave Jauss and [advance scouting coordinator] Galen Carr don't get enough credit. Advance scouting was the key to beating Oakland in 2003, and it was the key in the Anaheim series this year. It also helped against the Yankees, although the impact was lessened somewhat because the teams are so familiar with each other. We started scouting the Cardinals in September. We focused on them throughout the postseason. And we spent two days taking our reports to the coaching staff and then to the players.[662]

CURT SCHILLING:

I couldn't sleep at night if I thought I lost a game because I wasn't prepared. My goal is to never be caught off-guard on the mound. I want to be prepared for any hitter, any count, any situation. I keep notes on umpires, which guys call on what corners. In the eighth inning with a runner on third, if I know I've got an umpire who calls a wider outer half to the strike zone, I'm going to throw the ball off the plate.[663]

BRIAN O'HALLORAN, *coordinator of major league administration*:

I would work with an intern, watching the last four or five games of an umpire who would be working our games. We were looking for their tendencies—ball/strike calls, does this one have a high zone, that sort of thing. With Pitch f/x, we can get that information much more easily now.[664]

CURT SCHILLING:

I've had some great advance scouts in the past. The Red Sox guys are probably the most detailed, the most thorough. It's a thankless job. People have no idea. That's a tough life. They travel every bit as much as we do. They never see their own team. Billy Broadbent [video/advance scouting coordinator] does a lot of work for all of us. He puts so much time and effort into helping me.

If I can see 10 at-bats against a guy from four years ago, that's 10 at-bats better than seeing nothing. The day I pitch—from the minute I wake up until I throw my first pitch—every minute I'm like a batter waiting in the on-deck circle. Every moment that I can, I'm thinking about a hitter or a situation or a count or a pitch. In between innings I'm looking at the game charts.

I'm very big on defensive placement. I do my own spray charts and I position my infielders when I'm on the mound. In my preview meeting, I go over with the defensive coach where my outfielders will be with each guy, where my infielders are going to be for a variety of circumstances.[665]

JASON VARITEK:

It takes me close to three hours to go through what I need to know before the start of a series. When you add in my own notes to the advance scouting, Billy Broadbent with the video, and the pitching coach's work and the bullpen coach's work, you have a huge pool of information. It always comes down to execution—utilizing that information properly and making on-field and game-time adjustments.[666]

TERRY ADAMS:
Varitek was extremely prepared. It was almost like he was going to school every day with his books.[667]

MIKE TIMLIN:
The relievers work as a group. We sit down before a series and put a game plan together. It's not really chaired by anybody. The catchers are in there, too. You bring your strengths and weaknesses into the meeting, match them up against the hitters, and form a game plan. They're very comprehensive—hot and cold zones, if this guy's a pull hitter or he likes to go the other way—things like that.[668]

DOUG MIENTKIEWICZ:
We had so much data on every team we played. We knew what they ate before the game. It was crazy. We were as well prepared as any team I've ever been on before October. Advance scouts—they're the bloodline. All that info that they gave us was invaluable.[669]

GALEN CARR, *advance scouting coordinator:*
When a relief pitcher comes in, you'll see guys in the dugout go over to the bench coach or the hitting coach and take a look in their advance report binder to get information about the new pitcher. I feel like that started back around 2004 when we provided these binders—close to 100 pages—for guys to use in the dugout.

Each coach requires his own information. We had player reports—a full-page report on every single player, no margins, single-spaced—a ton of information. A lot of subjective analysis, but a lot of numbers, too. First-pitch swing percentages, that sort of thing. The reports take three or four days to prepare. And as you progress in the playoffs, you don't know who you're going to play next, so we'd have to work up each team.

Before each series, we had PowerPoint presentations with a slide on each player with objective and subjective data. All the major league staff would be present, the scouts who had followed that club, and Jason Varitek and Doug Mirabelli would be there. They'd both receive a folder on all the hitters. Jason would pore through the report himself.

He'd make his own notes based on his experience, based on what he'd seen on video. The meetings would last a good three hours.

We provided reports to Schilling. Johnny Damon liked to get the pitcher reports to get an idea of how long it took the guy to get rid of the ball when there were runners on base. He wanted a good idea of who he could run against.

Varitek was impressive in his preparation, but his recall was unreal. In addition to the PowerPoint presentation, we'd have another screen with video pulled from our BATS [Baseball Analysis and Tracking System], a huge reservoir of sortable video clips. We'd be sorting through video on certain players and there would be a random at-bat in the seventh inning of a 6–1 game in the middle of July, and Jason would say, "Oh, look at this next pitch. He hits a splitter down and away." You begin to realize how different that experience is for the catcher as opposed to watching from the stands or on TV.

The pitching coach would get hitter reports and the hitting coach would get pitcher reports. But then we added BATS, which has the ability to produce pretty much any chart or grid with any objective information that you could think of. Pitch types and percentages on certain counts. All kinds of spray charts. We would print out opposing player spray charts versus right- and left-handed pitching. Sometimes we'd break it down further, versus right-handed off-speed, right-handed fastballs. We also had specific spray charts based on past history against Tim Wakefield, since he was such an outlier. We would base a lot of defensive positioning on those spray charts.

There were also eight to 10 pages of general team approach: how the opposing manager used his bullpen, what lineups we might expect against lefties or righties, how they utilized guys coming off the bench, who might be the hit-and-run guys, the straight-steal guys, and pickoff tendencies. We'd have sheets of every time an opposing player showed bunt or actually executed a bunt. We'd have a running list of catcher's throws, as well.[670]

DAVE JAUSS, *advance scout:*
We began watching teams in mid-September. We'd put two scouts on every team that we thought was going to make the postseason. In 2004, there were five teams, 10 scouts. During the ALDS, we had two guys on the Yankees and two guys on the Twins. Same thing for the Cardinals and Astros in the NLCS. I had one guy do the hitters and one guy do the pitching. That's just my personal preference. The

Yankees would have 12 guys on one club. We never had more than four plus myself.

The only time a coach or advance scout has done his job or a report has done its job is when the player executes on the field. The due diligence of coaches and advance scouts is always done, so it comes down to execution. Everybody's got the information. The same report that put us down 0–3 against the Yankees also won us four in a row. It was the same report.

I stayed with the team during the World Series, and Papa Jack and I ran the hitters' meetings, and Dave Wallace ran the pitchers' meetings. We knew the Yankees really well, but St. Louis, being in the other league, was a bit different. That was more day-to-day information during those four games. Those were the only four Red Sox games I got to see all season.[671]

19

World Series Preview

THEO EPSTEIN:
Time to play Finland.[672]

But wait...there's more! Red Sox fans, exhilarated and exhausted after the Greatest Comeback in Sports History, had only two days to rest before their team met the St. Louis Cardinals in the 100th World Series. While the comeback against the New York Yankees may have given Red Sox fans eternal bragging rights over their pinstriped rivals, they could not be content with anything less than the ultimate prize—a World Series championship.

DEREK LOWE:
People have quickly shifted to, "All right, let's win the World Series. I don't want to wait 18 more years for these clowns to get back in." Today they can talk about the Yankees all they want, but I know, come Saturday night, the Yankees are going to be the furthest thing from people's minds.[673]

The Red Sox arrived in Boston at 4:20 in the morning following their pennant-winning victory and celebration at Yankee Stadium.

CHRIS CUNDIFF:

The most unbelievable thing was when we came back from New York. People surrounded the plane when it landed. The whole airport staff was clapping. When we drove back to the ballpark, there were people everywhere. All the cars stopped. People were getting out and clapping. They were lined up on buildings on the route home. And it wasn't a marked route. Even going through the tunnel, people were stopping.[674]

Boston had World Series fever. It had been nearly a generation since the Red Sox had played in a World Series (1986 against the New York Mets). It had been 86 long years since they had emerged victorious—way back in 1918, when World War I was raging in Europe and women weren't allowed to vote. The day after the Red Sox clinched victory in New York, hundreds of long-suffering fans—having enjoyed what Red Sox general manager Theo Epstein called "a collective, cathartic exhale"—were buying World Series caps and American League Champions shirts from souvenir shops near Fenway Park. Tickets for the first two World Series games in Boston were going for as much as $5,000 each on eBay.

KEVIN MILLAR:

We finally had a chance to relax and have time to think about what we did. Everybody had 50 voicemails of congratulations and folks asking for World Series tickets. We all went out to Jillian's [a restaurant and bowling alley near Fenway Park] and watched the Cardinals-Astros game to see who we were going to play. We had a great night, but now it's back to work.[675]

TERRY FRANCONA:

I was watching ESPN and saw a chronology of the series. I saw all of these chances we had to lose if something did not go our way. It astounded me.[676]

Millar and the Red Sox would face the St. Louis Cardinals, who led all major league teams with 105 regular season wins and had defeated the Houston Astros in seven games to win the National League pennant.

TROT NIXON:

I heard Tony La Russa talking about going to the World Series to win a championship ring. I told my wife, Kathy, "It's finally dawning on me right now. We've got to try to win four games to win a ring."[677]

Terry Francona watched most of NLCS Game 7, but he was also studying the reports the team's scouts had prepared.

TERRY FRANCONA:

I actually fell asleep for an inning. I had the scouting reports, but we didn't know which team we were going to be facing. I had some Chinese food and chocolate. There was chocolate on the Houston report. I couldn't make out some of their hitters. Fortunately, St. Louis won.[678]

GABE KAPLER:

We felt invincible after the Yankees series. We had so much momentum, we were going to steamroll that club. It had nothing to do with them, either. It had everything to do with where we were at the time.[679]

DAVE ROBERTS:

It didn't matter who we faced at that point. We were going to go right through them. We had something special going. We weren't going to be denied a championship.[680]

KEVIN YOUKILIS:

After beating the Yankees, we didn't think we could be beat. That was our attitude. We thought the Cardinals were pretty good, but from what I saw—being a young guy in my first year in the big leagues and not knowing any better—we thought we could beat anyone.[681]

DOUG MIRABELLI:

Our confidence was sky-rocketing. It wouldn't have mattered at that point who we were playing because when you get a team that's hot, you don't want to play that team.[682]

KEVIN MILLAR:

The Cardinals had an offense like an American League team. That was their strength. The one thing the Cardinals didn't have, on paper—and this is not discounting any of those guys—but their starting pitching wasn't a great matchup against our offense. But at that time, we were on such a roll, I don't think it mattered.[683]

GABE KAPLER:

Everybody in this clubhouse and the fans here and around the country thought the Yankees series was "World Series I." This is going to be "World Series II." For the city of Boston, New England, and Red Sox Nation, we understand the Yankees series was hugely important for historical reasons. But this series is more important. This is the pinnacle. This is what we play for.[684]

CURTIS LESKANIC:

Sweeping the Yankees, that felt like my World Series. And nothing against the Cardinals, but this was going to be quick. They had no idea what they were getting. They had no idea what was about to be bestowed upon them. There is no chance in hell that they are going to win any of these games.[685]

The 2004 Cardinals had a powerful offense that ranked nearly as high as the Red Sox. They were second in the majors behind Boston in team slugging, thanks to a powerful mid-lineup trio of Albert Pujols, Jim Edmonds, and Scott Rolen. The Cardinals scored 855 runs and allowed 659—a run differential of 196 runs, even better than Boston's 181.

Pujols had yet another spectacular year at the plate, batting .331 with 46 home runs, 123 RBIs, and 133 runs scored. Edmonds (42 homers and a team-high .418 OBP) and Rolen (34 home runs, 124 RBIs) each also had an OPS better than 1.000. Larry Walker had played in only 44 games, but he also swung a big bat. Most of the Cardinals' punch came from those four hitters.

Like the Red Sox, the Cardinals' starting rotation had enjoyed good health all season. The quintet of Chris Carpenter, Jason Marquis, Jeff Suppan, Woody Williams, and Matt Morris started all but eight of St. Louis' 162 games. Four of the five starters had at least 15 wins. But Carpenter, who led the staff with a 3.46 ERA and 1.14 WHIP, had suffered nerve damage in his right forearm in September and was unable to pitch in the postseason.

St. Louis was also missing one of its key bullpen arms. Steve Kline had torn a tendon in the index finger of his pitching hand during the NLCS. That left Julian Tavarez and closer Jason Isringhausen as the Cardinals' strongest relievers. Overall, the St. Louis pitching staff had a 3.75 ERA, just a hair behind the league-leading Atlanta Braves (3.74).

JOHN HENRY:

When the World Series began, Theo was a completely different person. He was so confident. I have never seen a man in the game of baseball who was as confident as Theo was. He said we knew how to stop three of the four big guys [Pujols, Rolen, and Edmonds], and we knew how to hit their pitchers. He said that all of them are essentially the same pitcher in different forms. He was telling me from Game 1, "Don't worry, we're gonna beat these guys." It was amazing how confident both Theo and Tito were.[686]

THEO EPSTEIN:

It was a combination of things. We all felt like no matter who we played or what came next, we would handle it. And we had spent a lot of time building up our advance scouting operation, and that was going to be a key for us in the postseason. We had to scramble after Game 7 to find time for our advance meeting. We held it in the conference room in our basement baseball operations offices at Fenway Park.

We had the catchers in there, the coaches, the advance scouts, and we went through the Cardinals' lineup, talking about how we're going to get each guy out. We went through their pitching staff and what to expect from each pitcher, and what our game plan would be. One thing we did really well as a team is we would punish right-handers who had average-to-solid stuff who could pitch but didn't have a plus-plus fastball, didn't have a swing-and-miss secondary pitch, didn't have a devastating change-up, but would try to sink the ball down in the zone, get groundballs—we would punish those guys. We were so lethal left-handed, we had so much power, we would force pitchers into the zone and then do a lot of damage.

And so as we went over each of the Cardinals' starters, it seemed like each guy that we went through, in my mind, unless something unexpected happens, we should really have good swings against this guy. And the next guy, we should have really good swings against him. And this guy's a perfect matchup for us. And I don't see how this guy is going to get us out. You never want to get too optimistic in baseball, but it seemed that after the meeting, not only did we have momentum and emotion and brotherhood and everything else on our side, but we also had a really good technical matchup against their pitching. When we were coming out of that advance meeting, I remember John Henry being a little anxious. He asked, "What do you think?" And I said something like, "Oh, we've got this. It's a great matchup for us. They can't play with us."[687]

Before Game 7 of the ALCS began, Tim Wakefield got the word that he would be the likely starter for Game 1 of the World Series at Fenway Park.

TIM WAKEFIELD:
If Derek [Lowe] was pitching well enough in Game 7 even to get to the fifth or sixth inning, then they were going to try to save me to be the Game 1 starter.[688]

Curt Schilling would get the ball for Game 2 at Fenway because the designated hitter would be used in the American League park, so Schilling wouldn't have to bat or run the bases on his bad ankle. Pedro Martinez and Derek Lowe would pitch Games 3 and 4 in St. Louis.

BRONSON ARROYO:
Derek came up to me on the plane back from New York and he said, "What game are you pitching?" I said, "What game am I pitching? Are you a retard? You have to pitch Game 4. I'll be in the bullpen."[689]

Despite having arrived in Boston at dawn, several players came out to Fenway Park for an optional workout. Among them was Keith Foulke. The Boston closer had thrown 100 pressure-packed pitches in three of the four must-win games against the Yankees. He had pitched in seven of Boston's 10 postseason games, throwing a total of nine shutout innings, striking out 11, and allowing only three hits. He had also walked seven batters.

KEITH FOULKE:
I know this sounds funny, but I feel like I'm getting stronger. I feel better now than I did in April. With my style, I don't put a lot of stress on my body. And I think failing a lot in the playoffs the past couple of years helped me become mentally stronger.[690]

The entire Boston bullpen had logged a huge number of innings in the ALCS. Of the 69 innings played against the Yankees, the starters had pitched barely more than half (35⅓). The bullpen's work had been fraught with immediate danger—facing elimination inning after inning in Games

4 and 5 and then holding the lead in Game 6. Fortunately, in the final two games, Curt Schilling had gone seven innings and Derek Lowe six, giving most of the relievers some rest.

In 2003, most observers felt that the Yankees were emotionally and physically drained from the ALCS against Boston, and that had been a big factor in their World Series loss to the Florida Marlins. Would the Red Sox suffer a similar letdown?

TROT NIXON:
We have been reminded all day today about how tough it could be to bounce back, but I don't think so. We're at zeroes now, and we have to play every game like it's our last one. There are going to be some nerves out there Saturday night. A lot of us haven't been in this type of atmosphere before.[691]

TIM WAKEFIELD:
I think having Thursday off really helps and gets us to focus on our main goal, and that's to try to win the World Series. I don't think it will be too big of a letdown for us.[692]

BRONSON ARROYO:
The best way to avoid any letdown is by realizing the Cardinals have won more games than anyone in baseball. This is the World Series. You don't get this opportunity often, so you can't take it for granted. You don't want to be down 0–2 or 0–3 again. You don't want to go to that well too many times.[693]

JOHNNY DAMON:
That was a stressful week we went through. We were able to get through it, but we're not finished. We're just a step closer to erasing all the chants, all the myths and, of course, the curse.[694]

BILL MUELLER:
St. Louis is my home town. The last World Series game I was at was in 1982. I was 11 years old, sitting in the nose bleeds with my dad, watching the Cardinals beat the Milwaukee Brewers in Game 7. Now I'm playing in a World Series on the same field. This is as big as you can get for me.[695]

THEO EPSTEIN:

It's a nice historical parallel. First we went through the Yankees, the team that kept us from our goal many, many different times. Now we've got to go through St. Louis, which cost us that chance in '46 and '67. If we're able to get this done, it will be like clearing the whole slate at one time.[696]

DEREK LOWE:

Is this team going to be happy just getting here? No way. This is a chance of a lifetime. A lot of guys play their whole careers and don't make it past the first round of the playoffs, let alone get to the World Series. We realize we are four wins away from one of the best parades in the history of sports.[697]

A sign on the Red Sox clubhouse door read, "We can change history!" Lowe suggested they put up a new sign saying that they were already losing three games to none. Whatever it takes.

20

World Series Game 1

Saturday, October 23, 2004, at Fenway Park

During the afternoon before Game 1, Dr. Morgan again performed the suturing procedure on Curt Schilling's right ankle in preparation for Schilling's start the following night. This time, Morgan sewed four sutures into the ankle, one more than Schilling had received before ALCS Game 6. Morgan also moved the internal "wall" of stitched-up tissue keeping Schilling's dislocated peroneal tendon in place.

DR. WILLIAM MORGAN:

[The tendon will be] a little more secure, a little higher. He felt some motion in there the last time. This time, there shouldn't be so much.[698]

CURT SCHILLING:

I've been in a lot of situations with team doctors who wouldn't have spent the time away from the field trying to come up with something. It says a lot about him. He's earned all the accolades he's gotten over the last 10 days. Because without him, I would not be out here.[699]

Immediately after the procedure, Schilling went out to the Fenway outfield and did some light throwing.

CURT SCHILLING:
As far as pain goes, I'm not feeling anything right now. We were not as rushed as the first time we did it, so Dr. Morgan allowed the painkiller to actually work this time.[700]

ALAN EMBREE:
I was in the training room getting my ribs taken care of. We would do ultrasound heat packs, an anti-inflammatory injection, massage work. Lube, oil, and filter. That was for every game. I was getting treatment as they were laying him on the table. It was quite an invasive little procedure to get him to be able to pitch. He's in there and he's laid open and they're suturing stuff with whatever. I don't know exactly the procedure they did, but it looked like an operation. Dr. Morgan got him out there. He could have very easily said, "I can't go."[701]

DR. WILLIAM MORGAN:
I may go into the seamstress industry next.[702]

For Tim Wakefield, this would be an emotional night. He had been penciled in to start Game 1 of the 2003 World Series, but those plans had gone awry. Wakefield had been pressed into action in extra innings of Game 7 of the ALCS and had given up Aaron Boone's pennant-winning home run. Wakefield would be the first knuckleballer to start a World Series game since 1948 when Cleveland's Gene Bearden faced the Boston Braves. Game 1 of the 2004 World Series would be Wakefield's first start in 22 days.

TIM WAKEFIELD:
Considering what had happened the year before, it was pretty special. To be the starting pitcher opening the World Series, it was amazing.[703]

JASON VARITEK:
Tim's been through the wars in this city for a long time, and I couldn't be happier for him.[704]

Doug Mirabelli, the backup catcher who caught all of Wakefield's starts during the regular season, would be behind the plate in Game 1. Jason Varitek had no qualms about being a spectator at his first World Series game.

JASON VARITEK:

It'll be hard, but I'm also happy because we did this as a team. Doug and I have built a tremendous bond over the years. We help each other offensively, defensively, with the pitchers. We both want to accomplish the same thing. We want to win a championship. There's no question we go with Doug tonight.[705]

DOUG MIRABELLI:

There's a bunch of emotions in my body right now. Excitement, nervousness, anticipation. I'll be ready.... I might be more tired watching the games than the guys playing.[706]

In addition to Mirabelli, Terry Francona's lineup included Mark Bellhorn at the bottom of the order and Orlando Cabrera in the No. 2 spot behind Johnny Damon. Playing with the designated hitter in the American League park, Cardinals manager Tony La Russa put So Taguchi in left field and used Reggie Sanders as his DH.

From Wakefield's point of view, weather conditions in Boston were terrible. The wind was blowing in from center field at a brisk 15–20 mph, and the game-time temperature was only 49 degrees with the wind chill dipping into the 30s.

TIM WAKEFIELD:

It was probably the worst conditions that a knuckleballer could pitch in. It was not only the wind. It was cold, which makes it hard to feel, and then the rain on top of that, it makes the ball a little slippery.[707]

Carl Yastrzemski threw out the first pitch, and Aerosmith lead singer Steven Tyler sang the National Anthem. There was also a moment of silence for Victoria Snelgrove, a 21-year-old college student who was killed by a projectile fired by police into the celebrating crowd in Kenmore Square after the Red Sox won the pennant on Wednesday night.

Despite the wind and the cold, Wakefield began the game well. He struck out Cardinals leadoff hitter Edgar Renteria. After Larry Walker doubled into the right-field corner, Wakefield got both Albert Pujols and Scott Rolen on infield pop-ups.

Boston wasted little time going on the attack against Woody Williams. Johnny Damon looked at 10 pitches before doubling to the opposite field toward the left-field corner.

JOHNNY DAMON:
You want to make an impact out there. You don't want to let your team down in something like this. I never want to go back to what happened in the ALCS where I didn't get the job done until the end.[708]

Orlando Cabrera made two bunt attempts and then was hit with a pitch on his left shoulder, the ball glancing off his jaw. Unhurt, Cabrera jogged down to first base. Manny Ramirez flied out. Then David Ortiz made his World Series debut by launching a 1–0 pitch high and deep to right field. The ball sailed over the "Pesky Pole"—just fair—for a home run. Big Papi's spectacular October continued; it was his fifth home run of the 2004 post-season. Only four batters into the game, Boston had a 3–0 lead.[709]

DAVID ORTIZ:
Cutter or a slider, and I hit it pretty good. It wasn't fair by that much...I thought it would go foul. That's why I stayed at the plate watching it. I hit it really good, and before it started hooking, it was past the pole.[710]

GABE KAPLER:
It's definitely amazing. I seem to be saying that over and over. I mean, he's not going to win every game for us. There has to be another hero, or heroes, in here. But I wouldn't put it past him, either.[711]

Kevin Millar banged Williams' next pitch off the left-field wall in left, about 10 feet from the top, for a double. Millar took third on Trot Nixon's fly ball to right, then scored the fourth run of the inning on Bill Mueller's single.

The Cardinals got one run back in the top of the second. With the Red Sox shifted over to the right side of the infield, Jim Edmonds dropped a routine bunt into no-man's-land near third base for a single. Reggie Sanders walked, and Tony Womack bunted the runners to second and third. Mike Matheny's fly to center was deep enough to score Edmonds.

Mark Bellhorn, the only Boston hitter to not bat in the first inning, opened the second with a single. After Williams got two outs, he allowed a single to Manny Ramirez and walked David Ortiz. With the bases loaded, the Cardinals bullpen was already stirring. Williams wiggled out of trouble as Millar grounded into a force play. In the third inning, Larry Walker homered, cutting Boston's lead to 4–2.

In Boston's third, Mueller walked with one out and Doug Mirabelli lined a single high off the Green Monster.

DOUG MIRABELLI:
I hadn't played in about 20 days at that point. I had one at-bat in Game 3 of the ALCS, popped up to second base. That's the only at-bat I had in a long time, so I had some nerves going, for sure. Woody struck me out in my first at-bat, and then in the second at-bat, he had me 0–2 and he tried to sneak a fastball inside. I was prepared for that and got to it. I hit that ball really well. It was one of those hits that you can't even get to second base on because it bounces right back to the left fielder.[712]

Bellhorn drew a full-count walk to load the bases. Damon singled to right, Mueller scored, and Boston led 5–2. Cardinals manager Tony La Russa made the call to his bullpen—12 of the 19 batters Williams faced had reached base.

WOODY WILLIAMS, Cardinals pitcher:
I let everybody down. I'm not taking anything away from the Red Sox, but I wasn't sharp at all. When I made a good pitch, they fouled it off. When I didn't, they hammered them.[713]

The change in pitchers did not slow Boston's momentum. Orlando Cabrera greeted Dan Haren by knocking his first pitch off the left-field wall. Mirabelli came around and Boston led 6–2.

ORLANDO CABRERA:
That should have been a homer. When I hit it, first I said, "Yes! I got it!" and then, "Too high! The wind's going to take it." And the ball hit the wall. When they showed the replay, you see the people in the back,

their hair was going wild because of the wind. That wind was coming in. That's why I only got to first. I was batting second, so sometimes you can't try to do anything with those guys hitting behind you. You have to stay on first, not risk going to second.[714]

Manny Ramirez brought home Boston's seventh run when his ground ball allowed Bellhorn to score; it was Ramirez's first RBI since the Division Series against the Angels. Amid a deafening chant of "Who's your Papi?" David Ortiz walked again, re-loading the bases. Millar—batting with the sacks full for the second straight inning—grounded out. Boston sent 23 batters to the plate in the first three innings.

Wakefield, with the gift of a 7–2 lead, suddenly lost his feel for the knuckleball. He walked three consecutive hitters—Edmonds, Sanders, and Womack—to start the fourth inning (which tied a World Series record). Twelve of Wakefield's 14 pitches to the Cardinals trio were out of the strike zone.

DOUG MIRABELLI:
The nature of the knuckleball is a wild pitch. It's coming at the hitter at 70 mph, and hitters miss it. There's a reason. Just like there's a reason it's very difficult to catch. Its very nature is its unpredictability. Sometimes it's a strike down the middle, and you can't catch it. Other times the ball is all over the place. We tried to get Wake back into a count where he throws a four-seam fastball. He usually has pinpoint control with that thing. But at that point, he couldn't even throw the fastball for a strike.[715]

TIM WAKEFIELD:
It was so cold that I had a tough time gripping the ball. It was very slick, and the field was slippery. I wasn't getting any resistance to my knuckleball because the wind was at my back. And there started to be a little bit of sleet and snow in the second inning.[716]

Matheny hit another sacrifice fly—this time to right field—and Edmonds tagged and scored. Millar, as the cut-off man, took Nixon's throw from the outfield. He turned and saw a chance to cut down Sanders, who was headed to third. Rushing, Millar made a low throw and the ball skipped past Mueller and into the Cardinals' dugout. Sanders walked home with another run.

KEVIN MILLAR:
I didn't have a grip on the ball. I never should have thrown it, but I tried to make the play anyway.... They don't pay me to think. If they paid me to think, I'd make about $4 an hour.[717]

Womack took third on Millar's throwing error, and he scored when Taguchi grounded out. St. Louis had scored three times in the inning without the benefit of a hit, and Boston now led 7–5. Wakefield walked Renteria, bringing Larry Walker to the plate as the potential tying run. Francona called on Bronson Arroyo to relieve Wakefield. Walker lined a single to right, and Renteria went to third. Arroyo got Pujols to ground to shortstop to end the inning.

For the next three innings, Dan Haren held the Red Sox at bay while the Cardinals tied the game against Arroyo in the sixth. After two quick outs, Taguchi singled back to the mound and advanced to second on Arroyo's throwing error. Renteria doubled in Taguchi, and Walker doubled in Renteria. It was Walker's fourth hit of the night and the game was tied at 7–7.

In the bottom of the seventh, St. Louis' third pitcher of the night, Kiko Calero, issued a walk to the ever-patient Mark Bellhorn, then another to Cabrera. Manny Ramirez singled to score Bellhorn and give Boston an 8–7 lead. Lefty Ray King came in to face Ortiz with runners at first and third. Big Papi smashed a hard ground ball that took an unexpected hop and struck second baseman Tony Womack in the chest. Cabrera scored on the hit, and it was 9–7. Womack left the game and was taken for X-rays.

TONY WOMACK, *Cardinals second baseman:*
It really hurt when I got hit. I lost feeling in my fingers and arm. It got one of the nerves, the one near your collarbone that pushes up against the bone. I lost feeling for five or 10 minutes.[718]

The Cardinals rallied in the eighth. Matheny singled with one out, and Alan Embree was summoned from the Red Sox's bullpen. Embree surrendered a bloop single to pinch-hitter Roger Cedeño, and Francona made the call for Keith Foulke, hoping for a five-out save.

DAVE WALLACE:
When you get that deep into the game, you want your best guy.[719]

Foulke was facing the top of the Cardinals' lineup. Renteria skidded a single into left field. The ball skipped by Manny Ramirez for an error, but Ramirez recovered and threw the ball in. The play at the plate was close, but pitcher Jason Marquis—who had pinch-run for Matheny—got in safely. The next batter, Larry Walker, hit a fly ball to left that should have been the second out. But as Ramirez ran in, his foot caught in the grass, and he stumbled forward. The ball banged off the back of his glove and rolled toward the foul line. Cedeño scored easily on Boston's fourth error of the night, and the game was tied at 9–9. It was a blown save for Foulke.

MANNY RAMIREZ:

I caught my foot in a drain out there. I shouldn't have made a dive for that ball. If I keep running, I catch that ball very easy. I'm just lucky I didn't hurt my ankle or knee.[720]

JOHNNY DAMON:

From my angle, Manny's foot got stuck in the ground. It looked to me like he'd hyperextended his knee. I thought there was a chance he could go down for the rest of the series.[721]

KEITH FOULKE:

As a pitcher, you can't worry about plays behind you. It's the same thing as if I give up a hit. I still have to make the next pitch, and that's what I focus on. I'm worrying about the next hitter.[722]

That was Albert Pujols, and Foulke walked him intentionally, loading the bases with only one out. Scott Rolen swung at Foulke's first pitch and popped up to Mueller for the second out. It was a critical out for Foulke in a tie game. Facing Jim Edmonds with a 1–1 count, Foulke hit the inside corner for a called strike and then did the same for strike three, ending the threat. Edmonds voiced his displeasure over the call to home plate umpire Ed Montague.[723]

JIM EDMONDS, *Cardinals center fielder*:

I took a ball I thought was a ball. It was a ball on TV. It was a ball on the overhead.[724]

KEITH FOULKE:
You got to come inside to get tough outs in those situations. The pitch to Rolen was a fastball in, and the one to Edmonds was just another fastball that tailed in and caught the corner.[725]

RON JACKSON:
Right there—when we struck out Edmonds with the game tied 9–9— right there, I knew we were on our way.[726]

TERRY FRANCONA:
It's easy when things go wrong to put your head down for a minute, or take a deep breath, or even feel sorry for yourself. But then Foulke gets rolling on Edmonds. If they take the lead there, that's a whole different game.[727]

When Ramirez got back to the bench, he made light of his adventures in the outfield.

MANNY RAMIREZ:
Snipers got me.[728]

DAVE ROBERTS:
We were laughing at him. He was demoted from silver to bronze to green glove. That's why this team is so special. There's no reason to get down on a guy for trying.[729]

DOUG MIENTKIEWICZ:
Manny was making jokes after that inning in which he dove kind of goofily and took out a big chunk of sod. Manny comes in and sits next to me and says, "The grounds crew hates my guts." I'm like, "Manny, we've got to win the World Series." That's the way we were.... I had to break Manny's gloves in because he felt that because I won a Gold Glove, that would make him better defensively. That's Manny being Manny.[730]

THEO EPSTEIN:
The atmosphere was almost relaxed, maybe because for the first time in a week we were playing a game that wouldn't end our season. We had a safety net.[731]

Julian Tavarez pitched the bottom of the eighth for St. Louis. With one out, Doug Mirabelli reached on an error by shortstop Renteria. Tavarez got a called strike on Mark Bellhorn, and then Bellhorn hit a long drive to right that hooked foul in the wind.

On the Boston bench, Curt Schilling turned to pitching coach Dave Wallace.

CURT SCHILLING:
You know what we need? How about the wind blowing that ball *into* the foul pole?[732]

Bellhorn took a ball, making the count 1–2. Then he drove a pitch harder and straighter down the right-field line. It hit high off the right-field foul pole. Home run! Boston was up 11–9.

DOUG MIENTKIEWICZ:
When Curt said that, and the ball went out, you knew something special was going on.[733]

MARK BELLHORN:
The first pitch he threw me, he threw the sinker inside. It started at me…and then strike one. I figured he was going to throw it again, and he did. The wind was blowing straight from center field to right field, so it was blowing everything foul. I honestly thought that the first foul ball should have been a fair home run, but the wind must have blown it 30 yards. He threw another pitch. Then he threw a slider, and it was the same as Game 7. I just reacted to it. I hit it, and then I was thinking it was going to be foul just like the other one. But the ball stayed straight. The pole got in the way.[734]

TERRY FRANCONA:
Bellhorn's ball, the first ball he hit, I thought was a home run off the bat, and it went so far foul, I was afraid to even get up and get excited on the second one.[735]

LARRY WALKER, *Cardinals right fielder*:
If the pole wasn't there and the stands went back another 15 feet, I would have caught it. Unfortunately, it didn't work that way for us. I was talking to Bellhorn before the game, and I know he's had some rough times here, getting booed. He hit a big three-run home run at Yankee Stadium and the game-winner tonight. I think he redeemed himself pretty good.[736]

BRAD MILLS:

Bellhorn always had good at-bats. The strikeouts? That went into seeing a lot of pitches. He came through with some big hits for us. He fit in pretty well, and it was kind of a surprise to some people how he was able to add to that ballclub. Offensively, even though you had all the strikeouts, he was able to do a lot of good things for us.[737]

KEVIN MILLAR:

I'm telling you something right now. That guy has been the unsung MVP for this team. The guy has been so awesome. And he doesn't change his demeanor, no matter what's going on. We have never lost confidence in him. When all the TV people and the papers and the radio shows were on him, he was getting nothing but positive feedback from us.[738]

Bellhorn had now homered in three consecutive postseason games. Unlike his foul-pole home run in Game 7 at Yankee Stadium, which sounded on the broadcast audio like a metal tray clattering on a cement floor, this one off the Fenway pole resonated with a deep clunk.

With the Red Sox now up by two runs, Foulke had some breathing room. He struck out Reggie Sanders on three pitches. After Marlon Anderson, who had replaced Womack at second base, sliced a ground-rule double to left, Foulke stayed cool. He got Yadier Molina to pop-up to first, and he struck out Roger Cedeño.

The first notes of The Standells' "Dirty Water" marked Boston's fifth consecutive postseason win. The 20 total runs scored in the 11–9 win set a new record for a World Series Game 1. The Yankees (12) and Chicago Cubs (6) had scored 18 runs on September 28, 1932. Boston was also the first team to commit four errors in a World Series game since the Milwaukee Brewers did it against the Cardinals in Game 6 in 1982.

JOHNNY DAMON:

We made four errors and left 12 guys on base. We have to shore up our defense. We have to tighten things up out there.... That puts a lot of pressure on our pitching staff and our hitters. We can't do this again and expect to win.[739]

TERRY FRANCONA:

That was not a video to send to the instructional league. That was rough. We did some things wrong, we didn't catch the ball cleanly, but we persevered and we won. I don't think the players were nervous. They made *me* nervous.[740]

KEVIN MILLAR:

This is the Red Sox. Nothing comes easy for us.[741]

DOUG MIENTKIEWICZ:

We haven't played a normal game since I got here on August 1. And I don't think we'll be playing one this week, either.[742]

DAVE ROBERTS:

It doesn't matter how it gets done as long as it gets done. And now, to have Schilling and Pedro coming up? Let's just say we're going to keep having fun.[743]

21

World Series Game 2

Sunday, October 24, 2004, at Fenway Park

KEVIN MILLAR:

I don't know who they should get to play him in the movie. Maybe Mel Gibson. What was that movie? *Braveheart*? He could be Brave Ankle.[744]

CURT SCHILLING:

That was one of the scarier mornings of my career. I woke up at about 7:00 AM in one of those mindsets where you know something's wrong. I looked around and wondered, *Why am I up? It's 7:00 AM.* I would normally sleep until 10:00 or 11:00, given game time. And as soon as I turned to my left, I felt like my leg was in a fireplace. I rolled the cover back, and my right ankle was swollen as thick as my right calf. And it was red, very red. It was so sensitive. Just the covers touching it hurt. Shonda woke up, and she was in shock: "Oh, my God. What is that?"

I got on the phone and I called Chris Correnti, and I said, "You've got to get ahold of Derek Lowe immediately, because there's absolutely no possible way I can pitch. I don't even know if I can drive to the park." I couldn't step on it. I couldn't walk. Nothing. I waited a while, and nothing changed. They called Derek. I drove to the park an hour earlier than normal, around noon or 1:00. I was trying to drive with my left foot because I couldn't use my right foot. As soon as I hit the end of my driveway, there were like 200 signs on the way in from Medfield.[745]

Knowing Schilling's route from his home to Fenway Park, fans had hung up signs along the way.

CURT SCHILLING:

There were signs on fire stations, on telephone poles, wishing me luck. I was listening to WEEI, and everybody was talking about the game. "What do you expect from Schilling tonight?" I thought, *These people have no idea that I'm not going to pitch tonight.*

When I left the house, I told Shonda not to rush to the game because there was no way I was going to pitch. I got to Fenway and Doug Mirabelli was in the parking lot, filming with his handheld video camera. He was talking pictures of guys showing up at the park for Game 2. I opened the car door and he's got the camera on and he started making a joke, and I said, "Turn it off." He said, "Dude..." and I said, "Turn it off." I stepped out of the car and he said, "Oh, my God. What happened?" I said, "I have no idea." Doug helped me get into the clubhouse. They called Dr. Morgan and he said, "Ah, I know what it is. I'll be there in a minute."

This is like 2:00, 2:30-ish, and I've got it in my head that I'm not pitching. Dr. Morgan comes in, looks at it, and goes into the training room. He'd put an extra stitch in this time to hold the tissue down, and the extra stitch had punctured a nerve. Once he popped out that stitch, you could literally see my foot—in real time—shrinking. Immediately. And I'm walking around going, "What the hell?" He said, "Yeah, that was my fault, blah, blah." And I was like, "Oh, my God, I'm fine! I can pitch!"

Now I panicked! I'm a routine guy. I'm doing email and getting my notes together. I've got to hurry up. That Cardinal lineup wasn't something to laugh at. Pujols, Renteria, Rolen, Larry Walker. So now I'm going to pitch. I completely disregard calling my wife. I'm not even thinking of any of that. I'm just trying to hurry up and get ready.

I had missed chapel that day because I was off in the training room, and so Walt Day, our chapel leader, I asked him to hang around so I could have a private moment. You could imagine the emotional roller coaster I'm on since I woke up at 7:00 AM. I sat down and—this is like 3:00 in the afternoon—and I just broke down. I was sobbing uncontrollably for a good 20 minutes. Walt asked, "What's wrong?" I said, "Listen, the amount of guilt I have, I can't ask Him to help me again. I can't." And Walt said, "It's not up to you. Just put your trust in God. Put your faith in God, and you go out and pitch." We prayed for the strength to compete again.[746]

Matt Morris was the surprise starter for the Cardinals, working on three days rest. Manager Tony La Russa decided to save pitcher Jason Marquis for Game 4 in St. Louis, where there would be no designated hitter and the team could take advantage of Marquis' .292 batting average.

MATT MORRIS, *Cardinals pitcher:*
I think the last time I pitched on short rest was a Wiffle Ball game when I was 10. But there's nothing to rest for. This is the whole point. It's all or nothing right now. I'm not saving myself for anything.[747]

Morris and Schilling had faced off in the postseason once before, in Game 1 of the 2001 NLDS. That game had been a pitchers' duel and a 1–0 win for Schilling's Diamondbacks. Morris had made two starts against the Astros in the 2004 NLCS and allowed three earned runs in five innings during each game. Morris had seen Fenway Park only once before.

MATT MORRIS:
I played in the Cape Cod League as a freshman when I went to Seton Hall University. We came up here for a day off. Actually, Varitek was my catcher in the Cape Cod League in Hyannis in 1993.[748]

Tony Womack was still sore from where David Ortiz's grounder had struck his collarbone, but he was back in the lineup for Game 2. Fenway's head groundskeeper, Dave Mellor, had spoken to Tony La Russa about the bad hop on Ortiz's ground ball. "I wouldn't want to see a bad hop if I was taking care of a high school field, let alone in a World Series game on a field that I care for. I want to say I'm sorry for that happening." La Russa said, "I can't believe you came to see me. It certainly wasn't your fault. It's just how the ball bounces." Womack added, "Anything hit hard in the middle of the game, it could have been my fault just as much, how I played it. Don't worry about it."[749]

Before the game, the Standells performed "Dirty Water," the Red Sox victory song.[750] James Taylor sang the National Anthem. The ceremonial first pitches were thrown out by Dom DiMaggio, Bobby Doerr, and Johnny Pesky. All three former Red Sox players had played against the Cardinals in the 1946 World Series.

> **DAVE MELLOR, *Fenway Park director of grounds*:**
> Curt very respectfully asked me if it was possible to make the top part of the mound next to the rubber soft so he could put his foot in, so it wasn't hard to kick out, but firm underneath, so that there wasn't a big hole there. You know when a starting pitcher comes in you see him kick against the rubber? He didn't want the ground to be packed in so hard that it would hurt his foot to kick. So the top three-eighths of an inch, I made soft. I measured exactly how big his foot was and found out where he put his foot, and I made that just a little bit softer and then down below made it firm so that the hole wouldn't get dug too deep and twist his ankle.[751]

> **CURT SCHILLING:**
> I expect them to bunt, absolutely. I expect them to try to get me to move off the mound, push the envelope a little, and make things happen. I would love to see Pujols come up and try to lay down a bunt. Or Edmonds. Or Rolen.[752]

> **TERRY FRANCONA:**
> If Larry Walker, Pujols, Edmonds want to bunt, please go over and tell them I said, "Go ahead." You know what I'm saying? There are some guys that do bunt and we know will bunt. And Schill is actually very good at that stuff. It might hurt him a little bit, but I don't think they are going to get by by doing things they normally wouldn't do.[753]

Curt Schilling, knowing the television cameras would show his ankle multiple times during the game, had written "K-ALS" on the side of his cleat: strike out Amyotrophic Lateral Sclerosis, the neurodegenerative disease once known as Lou Gehrig's Disease.

Schilling had a battle right away, needing 12 pitches to retire the first batter of the night, Edgar Renteria. Renteria fouled off seven of eight pitches before grounding out to shortstop. With two outs, Albert Pujols hit a gap double to left-center but was stranded on second as Scott Rolen slashed a line drive directly at Bill Mueller at third.

In the bottom of the first inning, Morris retired the first two Boston batters and had an 0–2 count on Manny Ramirez. Morris was one strike away from a clean inning, but he began nibbling around the plate. Ramirez refused to swing at anything outside the zone. He watched four balls go by and trotted down to first.

MATT MORRIS:

I got too cute with Manny. I didn't finish him off. I gave him a curve, and he didn't offer. I gave him a cutter, and he didn't fish for it.[754]

David Ortiz battled Morris for eight pitches before he also walked. Jason Varitek, a switch-hitter, was batting fifth, giving Terry Francona a little extra protection for Ortiz. Batting left-handed, Varitek tripled into the triangle in deep center field. Boston led 2–0, and the Fenway crowd began chanting, "*Mor-ris, Mor-ris!*"

KEVIN MILLAR:

The whole team is clicking. You look at Varitek's big hit in the first inning. Manny and Ortiz drew big walks. You make those two-out walks hurt.... Our lineup isn't built around a single guy. We have balance and a lot of good, patient hitters who can hurt you.[755]

TERRY FRANCONA:

Two-out hits, two-out runs are huge. When teams get them against you, they're damaging. When you do it, it's awesome. The way they're approaching Ortiz, I don't blame them. Varitek swinging the bat like that gives us an added dimension, another weapon in the middle of that order.[756]

On the first pitch of the second inning, Jim Edmonds lifted a foul ball to the left side of the field. Bill Mueller called for it, but Varitek was also attempting to catch it. Neither man made the play.

BILL MUELLER:

One thing I learned is don't bump the captain when he's trying to make a catch. We were both going for that ball, and it went off his glove and they gave me the error. They don't give errors to the captain.[757]

The dropped ball was not costly; Edmonds grounded out to first. Schilling walked Reggie Sanders then allowed a single to right-center by Tony Womack. Sanders advanced only one base.

REGGIE SANDERS, *Cardinals left fielder:*

I missed second base. It was a hit-and-run. I was running, and I looked to see where the ball was and where the outfielders were. The umpire said he thought I hit the base, but I knew there was no way I had touched it. So I said to myself, *I'd better go back and really be safe rather than sorry.* If I'd gone to third and been called out at second, I would have looked like an idiot.[758]

There was a microphone in the second-base bag, and on the televised replay, it sounded as though Sanders' foot had hit the base. The replay also showed what appeared to be a new footprint on the side of the bag. But Sanders played it safe and went back to second.

Mike Matheny lined a pitch directly to Mueller at third. A split second later, Sanders ran into Mueller, his shoulder colliding with the third baseman's jaw, knocking him to the ground. Mueller held onto the ball for an unassisted, inning-ending double play.

CURT SCHILLING:

When I wound up to throw the 2–0 pitch and I looked back, Reggie was getting a break. He was stealing third. He didn't see me look at him. Matheny fouled the ball off. My first thought was, *He had that bag stolen easily.* So I thought, *Okay, next pitch I'm going to spin and throw to second.* I've done it a million times in my career. I get the sign, and I come set. Then I go to my windup and I can't spin. I can't explain it. I couldn't turn and throw. I couldn't. I don't know why. It wasn't physical. So I throw the pitch. Matheny hits a line drive to Bill Mueller at third and he tags Sanders, who was stealing third on the pitch again. Inning over. That was one of those times I'm like, *Okay, this is way beyond me.*[759]

TONY LA RUSSA, *Cardinals manager:*
I thought early on that [Schilling] wasn't at his best, like the first two or three innings, he wasn't quite as sharp. That's when I thought we deserved better than we got. After that, though, whenever we got a smell, he made quality pitches.[760]

Schilling needed only nine pitches to set down the Cardinals in the third, collecting his first strikeout on the final pitch.

In the fourth, Pujols collected his second double of the game then advanced to third on a fly ball to right by Scott Rolen. Jim Edmonds struck out swinging. Reggie Sanders grounded to third, and it looked like Schilling had escaped any damage—but the ball short-hopped Mueller and struck him in the chest. Mueller kept the ball in front of him but couldn't make a throw. Pujols scored on the error, and Boston led 2–1.

In the home half of the fourth with one out, Morris hit Millar with a pitch. After Nixon fanned for the second out, Mueller atoned for his error by hooking a double down the right-field line. Bellhorn took ball one then hit a long drive to straightaway center over Edmonds' head and off the base of the center-field wall. Both runners scored. Boston led 4–1.

MARK BELLHORN:
That might have been the hardest ball that I hit in the whole Series. I'd seen Morris a lot before. He always liked to throw me a lot of curveballs. I always liked hitting the fastball. He threw me a bunch of curveballs, and then he threw me a fastball. It was up, and I hit it really good to center. The wind was blowing in so Edmonds might have been playing in a little, but I still hit it hard enough to get it over his head. It was more of a line drive than a fly ball.... I liked being up in those situations, no matter if I was 1-for-16 or not. I had the confidence that I could come through as opposed to a normal at-bat.[761]

After throwing 40 pitches in the first two innings, Schilling had a nine-pitch third and an eight-pitch fifth. In the sixth, he stranded runners at first and second—and headed to the bench with a pitch count of 94.

Matt Morris lasted only two batters into the fifth inning before getting the hook. Cal Eldred came in and stranded two Boston base runners.

MATT MORRIS:

I beat around the bush with my pitches and gave them good counts to hit. I should have changed my approach. I got ahead of guys, but I didn't finish them off. I should have been more aggressive. I was trying to throw curves and cutters and make them fish, but they wouldn't.[762]

The Red Sox's defense sprang more leaks in the top of the sixth. With two outs, Rolen chopped a routine grounder to third, but the ball hit the heel of Mueller's glove and he was charged with his third error of the game. Mueller was the tenth player (and third third baseman) to commit three errors in a World Series game.

CURT SCHILLING:

I told Billy I was going to get the next out. I mean, you can't understand unless you're in that clubhouse. I care more about these 24 guys than anybody I've ever played with. I'd do anything for these guys, and I think they feel the same way about me. Very few times on the mound do you get a chance to pick up the fielding for the guys playing behind you, and there was a chance for me to do that. I wanted that to happen so bad. I wanted to get out of that inning and make it all right for him.[763]

It took Schilling two batters to get the final out. First, Jim Edmonds bunted toward second base and the ball hit off Bellhorn's glove for another error, Boston's fourth error of the night. The inning ended when Sanders hit a ball to Mueller, who gloved it and stepped on the bag for a force out. (In 15 World Series innings, the Red Sox had now committed eight errors.)

Trot Nixon opened the bottom of the sixth with a ground single to center off Eldred. With two outs, Johnny Damon singled through the infield. Orlando Cabrera lined a single off the left-field wall, which scored both runners. Boston led 6–1.

ORLANDO CABRERA:

It was a good at-bat. Eldred made tough pitches, but I was looking for that pitch. That was how Morris was pitching me the whole game. I was able to pull my hands in and put a good swing on it.[764]

After Manny Ramirez singled for Boston's third consecutive hit, Ray King came in and struck out David Ortiz.

BRAD MILLS:

Being on a team with better players in a winning atmosphere has given Cabrera a chance to have his talents really come out. Up in Montreal, not many people saw him. People saw his numbers, so they said he was a good player, but now he's come to a winning team and it brings out his skills.[765]

RON JACKSON:

That is a big momentum swing. They are maybe one pitch from getting out of an inning, and then all of a sudden runs are scoring. Our main goal is to work the pitcher into throwing a lot of pitches, and when we do that, we get guys on base and open up some holes.[766]

ALAN EMBREE:

Take a look at who we've got coming up next, and there's no relief. One guy after another is a tough hitter. I'm glad I don't pitch to us. There's never a chance to say, "Whew!" when we're at bat.[767]

With the Red Sox ahead by five runs, Francona and Wallace decided the bullpen would finish the game. In six innings, Schilling had allowed four hits and one walk. The one run he allowed was unearned. He struck out four.

DAVE WALLACE:

It looked like he was in some pain. A couple of times, I went out or Tek went out, just to give him a breather. But he's mentally strong He's dealing with a lot, physically. His pain tolerance is pretty extreme.[768]

Alan Embree was the first man out of the bullpen in the seventh, with Pokey Reese subbing for Bellhorn at second base. It took Embree 18 pitches, but he struck out the side: Womack (swinging), Matheny (swinging), and Taguchi (looking).

ALAN EMBREE:

I felt awful. It was cold. It was rainy. You're stiff. The one thing you try to do is break a sweat. You can do that on the way in. Then after the first pitch or two, you're in the game. Just knowing you're going into the game, that gives you a little extra energy. At that point, you're working on adrenaline.[769]

Mike Timlin pitched the eighth in a slight drizzle. Renteria led off with a walk and came around to score on Rolen's sacrifice fly. Keith Foulke came in to get the final out of the eighth and also took care of the ninth. Sanders struck out, Womack lined to right, and Matheny grounded to shortstop.

Boston took a 2–0 lead in the series with the 6–2 win. It was Terry Francona's ninth postseason win, putting the rookie skipper first all-time among Red Sox managers.

Schilling became the first pitcher in history to win a World Series start with three different teams—the 1993 Phillies, the 2001 Diamondbacks, and the 2004 Red Sox.

CURT SCHILLING:
Every memory I'm going to take away from this season revolves around the fans' energy at this ballpark. On the way to the park today I was thinking about stepping on to the field and beginning that walk to the bullpen. Regardless of what happens in my career, I'll never get a feeling like that ever again in my life, like I had tonight. These fans believe in me to the nth degree, and a lot of times I tell the other guys, "Don't be the only guy not believing in yourself. Everybody here believes in you." That's what I tried to walk out there with tonight.[770]

ALAN EMBREE:
When Curt first hurt his ankle, he wasn't even supposed to pick up a ball. It was our worst nightmare. And now look at it. You cannot describe what is happening out there with Curt. You just cannot describe it.[771]

DAVE WALLACE:
It's unbelievable. Not only the circumstances but who he's doing it against. The Yankees and the Cardinals? Two of the best batting lineups in a long, long time. Amazing.[772]

CURT SCHILLING:
I've been on some great teams and had some close teams, but this environment creates an entirely different scenario for us in the clubhouse. I don't question for a second any of these guys doing it for the team. Pain was not a very relevant issue. I was numbed up. Once we got past the initial thing this afternoon and I got numbed up, I'm not really dealing with a lot of pain out there. I just have to go

in and understand that mechanically things are different and I have to be different. I have some different thoughts that I have to pitch with right now. I was more concerned with that lineup. I mean, one to nine, that's as good of a lineup as I've ever faced.[773]

After the game, Dr. Morgan removed the sutures from Schilling's right ankle to guard against infection. If it were necessary, could Schilling go through the procedure *again*?

DR. WILLIAM MORGAN:
Honestly, we may not be able to do it a third time. It depends on what his tissues look like. He's more uncomfortable because it's the second time around. The line may be drawn there, depending on how he looks over the next five days.[774]

Morgan's remarks were construed as if he had offered a definite negative answer. Replying to that report, a high-ranking Red Sox official said, "That's news to me."[775] Theo Epstein said simply, "He's our Game 6 starter."[776]

CURT SCHILLING:
I don't know.... I'm a little beat up now. It's the first time in my life I think I've felt my age. We'll see what happens.[777]

DR. WILLIAM MORGAN:
When you put sutures in through the skin and then tie the skin down with everything else, that particular small area doesn't see a blood supply real well. The tissues actually become a little ischemic. That's the reason I had said it's not clear how frequently we could do that. The tissues become like...bad meat. And they could pull through, pull right out.[778]

Mark Bellhorn's two-run double in the fourth had been the difference in the game.

JOHNNY DAMON:
Manny and David and myself, we weren't too big a factor tonight. But that's what's great about our team. It can be someone different every night. Take your pick of who the offensive hero was tonight: Bellhorn or Cabrera or Varitek.[779]

TERRY FRANCONA:
It's not like Bellhorn walks in and lights up the room with his personality. He's a great kid. But when you first meet him, he's just kind of the way he is. You say, "Hey Bell, how are you?" He says, "Okay." I called Jamie Quirk, a coach with Colorado, who I had coached with in Texas, who had Bell. I said, "Give me the lowdown on Bellhorn. I think I [upset] him somewhere along the way." He said, "No, he doesn't talk. His nickname was 'Mute.'" So I felt a little better about it.[780]

All of Boston's runs in Game 2 scored with two outs. In the two games, the Cardinals had walked 14 Red Sox batters, hit three others, and saw eight of those 17 base runners score. The Red Sox left 21 men on base in the first two games and still scored 17 runs.

THEO EPSTEIN:
I would love to lead the league in men left on every year. That's a sign of a great offense.[781]

MIKE MATHENY, *Cardinals catcher:*
The walks and the hit batsmen came back and got us almost every time. You give guys a free pass and it usually comes back to haunt you.

DAVE DUNCAN, *Cardinals pitching coach:*
Our pitchers are trying to do too much. They're trying to make the perfect pitch, and it's not always necessary to make the perfect pitch. So we'll be a little bit more aggressive in the next few games, and we'll see how that works.[782]

The eight errors by the Red Sox were the most by a team in the first two games of a World Series. The old record was six, set by the Detroit Tigers in 1909.

JOHNNY DAMON:
You know what? If it takes making four errors to win Game 3, we'll do it.[783]

After Game 2, Schilling showed his appreciation for his teammates' support by taking the entire group out to dinner.

LYNN JONES:

During the evening, I asked Johnny Damon, "How many games is this going to take us, to finish this up?" And he raised his hand up to his face and put two fingers down the side of his face. In other words, two more.[784]

22

Travel Day

Monday, October 25, 2004

ST. LOUIS CAB DRIVER TO DAVID ORTIZ:
Are you going to give us a chance to win one game or what?[785]

The Cardinals must have been looking forward to getting back to Busch Stadium in St. Louis, where they had a 53–28 record during the season and a 6–0 mark during the postseason. They might have been looking forward to coming home for other reasons, as well.

Because the World Series games, the Head of the Charles Regatta, and Parents Weekend for several local universities had all coincided, no rooms were available for the Cardinals in any downtown Boston hotel for Games 1 and 2. The Red Sox found a block of rooms for the Cardinals at the Marriott in Quincy, about seven miles from downtown Boston—or, according to the *St. Louis Post-Dispatch*, 15 miles away.[786]

TONY LA RUSSA:
I understand the home team has the responsibility for making the hotel accommodations. It was a real bummer to the point where a lot of us were upset and embarrassed. For most of these guys, this is their first World Series experience, right? When the game is over, there are all kind of restaurants by the park. In Quincy, there wasn't

anything except for the hotel that stayed open for us. We shouldn't have had this problem.[787]

After Game 2, the Cardinals' bus got separated from its police escort and didn't get back to the hotel until 2:00 AM. Room service had closed at 11:30. La Russa suggested that the Cardinals cancel the Red Sox's reservations at a hotel two blocks from Busch Stadium and relocate them to Jefferson City, Missouri.

With the series shifting to St. Louis, the games would be played under National League rules without a designated hitter. That meant in order to keep David Ortiz's bat in the lineup, Terry Francona would put the big slugger at first base.

TERRY FRANCONA:

Losing our DH is a disadvantage. We're not playing the team we put together. You saw our best team in Boston. But that's the rule, and we'll make do. I'm more worried that our pitchers will take a swing and maybe twist a back muscle. I told them if there's a guy on second, naturally they'll want to try to drive him in. But mostly, I'd be happy if they could just drive up the pitch count a little. If a pitcher is leading off, we don't want him making an out on the first pitch.[788]

DAVID ORTIZ:

I don't think I'm that bad of a first baseman. It's about getting the opportunity. When you go out there only every once in a while and you make an error, everybody looks at you like you're bad. But if you're not out there all the time, you're going to make mistakes. I always went out and caught a couple of grounders even though I knew I was going to be DH that day. I'm not going to be diving around like Mientkiewicz or Superman. God didn't give that kind of ability to everyone. But whatever's around me, I'm going to catch.[789]

MANNY RAMIREZ:

David is such a sweet first baseman. People judge him wrong. David's got a lot of skills at first base for a big guy. He's also got sweet hands. We believe in him.

DOUG MIENTKIEWICZ:
I've always felt that he's got fantastic hands. He's played a ton of games. Every winter he plays first base. Obviously him not playing every day is going to be different. But he's only got three possible games at first. He's going to be fine.[790]

KEVIN MILLAR:
This is a time when you've got to check the egos. It's all about winning baseball games. I can move to the bench and make the bench a little deeper. I'm going to be moving around, keeping the muscles loose. I'll go in the locker room and ride the bike, watch videos. I just want to be ready. It's tough because you want to be a part of this club and help this team win. But there's going to be a point in the fifth, the sixth, or the seventh when I could have a chance to help this team win. That's part of the double switches. And maybe a lefty comes for Trot, and I go to right. The flexibility that I'm able to bring will help us get deeper on the bench.[791]

On the off-day, the Red Sox players voted on playoff shares. The team decided to give a full share to former teammate Nomar Garciaparra, who had been traded in July.

TROT NIXON:
Mike Timlin brought it up. I'm not interested in the money. The championship is what I'm interested in. The prize is what every professional athlete strives for. Anybody who spills their blood on the field out there even one time helping a club win a ballgame deserves as much as anyone else, in my opinion.[792]

JASON VARITEK:
Nomar was such a big part of getting us to this point and helping this organization. I'm not taking anything away from the job Orlando has done. I love everything about him. I just wish we could have both of them here.[793]

Despite their 2–0 lead in the Series, the Red Sox weren't taking anything lightly.

DEREK LOWE:
If you were on that plane to St. Louis, you'd have no idea of what the score of the Series was so far. And that's the way it should be. The

beauty of our team is that we play the same way down three-nothing or up two-nothing.[794]

ALAN EMBREE:

It's a long way to go. These are the four toughest wins in baseball to get.[795]

CURTIS LESKANIC:

I want to get this over with. Without a doubt that Yankee experience helped us; we learned a lot from that series. If we're up two-nothing, three-nothing, that doesn't mean it's over. We still have to win four games. We're a relentless bunch of guys. If you get us this inning, we're going to get you next inning. If you get us this game, we're going to get you next game. We're going to keep coming after you.[796]

23

World Series Game 3

Tuesday, October 26, 2004, at Busch Stadium

JOHNNY PESKY, *former Red Sox shortstop*:
[Asked what he would do if the Red Sox won the World Series] I'm
gonna take off all my clothes and run around the ballpark. Then I
can die happy.[797]

BILLY BROADBENT:
I saw Orlando Cabrera coming into the stadium, and one of the St.
Louis security guards must have thought he was a fan and stopped
him. I went over to say something, but Orlando seemed amused and
motioned for me to hold off. A few moments later [director of public
relations] Glenn Geffner came along with the rest of the team and
explained he was our shortstop.[798]

Pedro Martinez celebrated his 33rd birthday on the off-day and got
the gift of a World Series start the following day. Despite a poor end to
the regular season, Martinez had rebounded in the playoffs, dismissing
the Angels in the ALDS and going toe-to-toe with the Yankees in Games
2 and 5.

THEO EPSTEIN:
I expect him to rise to the occasion. Pedro's one of the all-time greats, and it would've been a shame if his career ended without him ever having pitched in a World Series.[799]

Everyone was aware that the game could well be Pedro's last appearance in a Red Sox uniform, as Martinez was a free agent at the end of the 2004 season.

Facing Martinez would be Jeff Suppan, who won the clinching game for the Cardinals in both the Division Series and Championship Series, much as Derek Lowe had done for Boston. Suppan had originally been drafted by the Red Sox and pitched for them from 1995–97. Theo Epstein had brought Suppan back in a mid-2003 trade, but the pitcher then signed with the Cardinals as a free agent during the winter. Suppan may have been the Cardinals' best pitcher in the postseason, having made three starts and given up six earned runs in 19 innings. About his former teammates, Suppan smiled and said, "They're definitely idiots."[800]

TONY LA RUSSA:
I believe that the club that is playing well goes in with some momentum, as long as they don't take things for granted. But I definitely believe the most important thing is the pitcher for each side because you can go in feeling great and the guy just stops you. So if you had to pick one, I'd pick the starting pitcher as the more important one.[801]

As the Red Sox had done at Fenway, the Cardinals brought out some royalty of their own. Stan Musial threw the ceremonial first pitch to Bob Gibson. Both stars had defeated the Red Sox in past World Series.

The game was only six minutes old when Manny Ramirez launched a two-out solo home run into the left-field seats. The hit extended Ramirez's consecutive postseason hitting streak to 16 games.

BILLY BROADBENT:
Manny had a real video work ethic. I wasn't exactly sure what he was looking at, but I would see him pull out little note cards and he would write down things in Spanish. Maybe he was writing the pitch sequence the guys approached him with.... If he didn't have an at-bat against the guy, then he would look at some other big guy like

Miguel Tejada for Baltimore or somebody like A-Rod. Another righty. Manny would look at his stuff. That's something he came up with all on his own. It's nothing we suggested. He was one of the hardest workers that you'd ever want to see. I think he wanted to work and to be left to his work.[802]

RON JACKSON:
Manny comes out to the park and he works hard. He studies his video, the tendencies of the opposing pitcher that night. He makes little notes. He's checking this guy out. First pitch. Second pitch. His out pitch. How big a breaking ball he has, all that stuff.[803]

Despite the 1–0 lead, Pedro Martinez had a tough time getting established in the bottom of the first. He retired Edgar Renteria but walked Larry Walker and saw Albert Pujols reach safely on an infield hit. Martinez walked Scott Rolen, and the bases were loaded. Jim Edmonds flied to shallow left field. Ramirez caught the ball with ease and threw a perfect one-hop strike to Jason Varitek at the plate, who tagged Walker for an inning-ending double play.

Walker had seen Pujols ranging far off second base after the ball was hit—he'd gotten three-quarters of the way to third.

LARRY WALKER:
I didn't know what else to do. Albert was hanging out there, he was a sure out, I figured I'd take a chance and try to steal a run. There was no way I was going otherwise.[804]

MANNY RAMIREZ:
When I was in the outfield, I set my mind to go home, so that's what I did.[805]

Ramirez collected 11 outfield assists in 2003. Although he had only four during the 2004 regular season, he led the majors with 17 the following year.

ORLANDO CABRERA:
Manny is not a great outfielder, but he can throw. I didn't think it was deep enough for them to try to score. But they did, and Manny was able to make that good throw and cut that guy down.[806]

TERRY FRANCONA:

That was a big play. I thought Varitek on the receiving end did a great job, stood there nonchalantly and then put the tag on. There were 50-some thousand people screaming, going crazy. Bases loaded and we come out of that inning not giving up anything. It was a big boost for us.[807]

JASON VARITEK:

He threw the ball right on the money and allowed me to make the play.[808]

Martinez backed up the play behind the plate—then on his way to the dugout, he passed Walker and playfully swatted him on the ass with his glove. The two had been teammates together on the 1994 Montreal Expos.

Martinez was the leadoff batter for the Red Sox in the top of the third. Three of the four pitches were right down the center of the plate—and Martinez just stood there. Francona may have tipped his hand the day before by admitting he didn't want his pitchers risking injury by swinging too hard. After he was rung up, Martinez cracked a little smile and walked back to the dugout. Derek Lowe reached over and whacked Martinez's bat a couple of times.

DEREK LOWE:

I shook his bat to see if I could wake it up. I've never seen a guy take four fastballs right down the middle without moving his bat.[809]

RON JACKSON:

Pedro can hit. But he hadn't been swinging, and they didn't want him to pull a muscle. He was probably thinking, *Let's get this thing over with*.[810]

In the bottom of the third, it was Cardinals pitcher Jeff Suppan's turn to lead off. Suppan had two hits in the Division Series and an RBI on a suicide squeeze in Game 7 of the NLCS. Suppan collected his third hit of the postseason on a dribbler toward third base, beating Mueller's strong throw to first. Renteria followed with a double to deep right. Trot Nixon slipped in a puddle on the warning track—a rainstorm had passed through St. Louis about 90 minutes before the first pitch—and fell flat on his wallet.

TROT NIXON:
It's like getting tackled in football. You get hit hard, you get right
back up. The ball bounced off the wall right into a big puddle. I just
picked it up and threw it back in.[811]

Now there were runners on second and third with nobody out and the
Red Sox holding a 1–0 lead. The Cardinals had sent 10 batters to the plate
against Martinez, and five of them had reached base. Larry Walker came
up, and the Red Sox played their infield back, conceding the tying run.

PEDRO MARTINEZ:
I just wanted the out. It was early in the game, and we all knew Suppan
was going to be around the plate. I knew we had a pretty good chance
of scoring a couple more runs.[812]

JOSE OQUENDO, *Cardinals third-base coach:*
The first thing I saw was that everybody was playing deep. So I said,
"On a ground ball, you're going as soon as it's hit."[813]

Walker swung at Martinez's first pitch and grounded it directly to
Bellhorn, who was back on the outfield grass between first and second. He
scooped up the ball and threw it to Ortiz at first.

JOSE OQUENDO:
I started yelling at Suppan, "Go! Go! Go!"

Ortiz looked towards third, and saw Suppan moving back and forth
indecisively. Suppan started toward the plate, then turned back, then went
toward home again, only to turn back a second time. Ortiz took a few steps
toward the mound and fired a laser across the diamond to Mueller as Suppan
darted back to the bag. The throw was on the home plate side of the base,
in the perfect spot for Mueller to snag it and tag Suppan.

JEFF SUPPAN, *Cardinals pitcher:*
I made a bad baserunning mistake. I didn't do what I was supposed
to do.[814]

ORLANDO CABRERA:
Of course, that's the run that we have to give up. And Larry Walker,
as a veteran, all he wanted to do was hit a grounder to second so he

could move both runners. Fortunately for us, there was a pitcher on third, and he got confused.[815]

Suppan said after the game that when Oquendo said "Go, go, go," he heard "No, no, no." Longtime Boston fans might have been reminded of another World Series baserunning blunder involving the Red Sox. In 1975 in the bottom of the ninth of Game 6 with the game tied 6–6, Boston's Denny Doyle tagged up from third on a fly ball to short left field. He ran home—and Cincinnati's George Foster threw him out. Doyle said he'd heard, "Go! Go!" but Don Zimmer, Boston's third-base coach, said he'd been yelling, "No! No!"

JOSE OQUENDO:
What we did out there on the bases pretty much changed everything. To play well for so long in the season then to have something happen like that? Man, it hurts.[816]

BILL MUELLER:
David has a lot more experience at first base than people give him credit for. He played there in Minnesota. He's played there for us. He's not some guy that just started playing the position, so he has good instincts and he moves around a lot better than most people think. He's got great feet and hands.[817]

KEVIN MILLAR:
Everyone is going to look at that as the reason the Cardinals lost. But you have to understand, the way Pedro Martinez was pitching, that play was not the whole turning point in that game. It was just one of those baserunning plays, and pitchers don't run the bases that much. The way Pedro pitched, I just don't think it mattered.[818]

DOUG MIENTKIEWICZ:
David has good hands. A good arm. He just lacked mobility. I knew David would be fine over there for a couple of days. I joked around, "I wouldn't throw that ball." At that point, there was no way we were going to lose. I hate to say this—and no disrespect to the Cardinals— but the World Series was kind of anticlimactic. At the time it felt like we were playing a Wednesday game against the Astros. After the Yankee series? It was like we were already celebrating in our head, but we still had to finish it. There was no doubt in anyone's mind at that point. It was over.[819]

During the Suppan gaffe, Renteria had been most of the way to third base, but he had to quickly retreat to second. Now there were two outs and a runner on second. Pujols worked a full count then hit a one-hopper to Mueller, who threw him out, ending the inning. The Cardinals had squandered two golden opportunities against Martinez.

LARRY WALKER:
The first three innings, we easily should have put three runs on the board. Perhaps more, but minimum three. We should have had a 3–1, 3–2 lead in the fourth or fifth inning.[820]

PEDRO MARTINEZ:
Once they didn't score in that inning, I said it's up to me now.[821]

ALAN EMBREE:
Third inning. Getting out of it. Just the look in his eye. When Petey has that look, you're not touching him.[822]

And suddenly, Pedro was on. After five of the first 10 Cardinals reached base, Martinez slammed the door, locked it, and became the wily ace Red Sox fans loved. He retired the last 14 Cardinals he faced—only one of those batters hit the ball out of the infield. Martinez ended up pitching seven innings before turning the game over to the bullpen.

BRONSON ARROYO:
Pedro does so many crazy things. Some days, you don't even know he's there, but then the next day he's running around the clubhouse naked, screaming at everyone. Sometimes it's hard for me to believe that guy is the same guy who goes out on the mound and has a look in his eyes like a killer.[823]

ORLANDO CABRERA:
That guy, when he's focused, move on. Let him do his thing. I was telling him, "Pound him! Pound him! They don't even know where they are right now." To this day, people ask me, "Who was the best pitcher you ever faced?" There is no thought in my head other than Pedro Martinez. I feared the guy. Don't ask me why. I was like, "He's going to kill me. He's going to kill me." I could never get comfortable with him. He's got that thing with people—just the way he'd look at you, the way he'd own you.[824]

URI BERENGUER, *Spanish language radio announcer*:
Pedro Martinez told me that Orlando Cabrera was the best defensive teammate he ever had. And the smartest shortstop he ever had. He said, "You have no idea how many times he would be at shortstop behind me and yelling at me, 'Pedro, put it here, put it there, put it here, pitch him this way, because he's coming at me—trust me—and I got you.'"[825]

In the top of the fourth, Bill Mueller cracked a two-out double to left-center. Trot Nixon hit a first-pitch single over Walker's head in right, scoring Mueller. It was the ninth two-out run the Red Sox had scored in the World Series—and they led 2–0.

TROT NIXON:
I didn't feel like I had swung the bat very well in the Yankees series or the first couple of World Series games in Boston. I wasn't happy with how I was seeing the ball. Before Games 3 and 4, my buddy Adam Hyzdu would go to the cage with me, and he would throw me 50 or 60 pitches, and I would bunt. Drag bunt. Jimy Williams used to always tell me that bunting helped your hand-eye coordination when you're swinging. Believe it or not, I found I'd have a lot more success or I'd see the ball a lot better after I did a lot of bunting. I credit Adam for getting me locked back in and helping me get some good at-bats in those last two games.[826]

TONY LA RUSSA:
Two outs, nobody on, double, single. We've given up a lot of runs that way. We need to close out the inning, and we're not doing it. But before we start pointing fingers at our pitching, we missed opportunities to score. We're just getting beat.[827]

In the fifth, Johnny Damon led off against Suppan with a double—again over Walker's head, almost a replay of Nixon's hit in the fourth. Cabrera dropped a single into right field, extending his postseason hitting streak to 10 games. Ramirez sent a run-scoring single through the shortstop hole. After two outs, Mueller's single to right scored another run. Now Boston had a 4–0 lead.

BILL MUELLER:
I felt a little added pressure on myself because I was playing in my hometown in front of family and friends. I was kind of a nervous wreck. I didn't eat for four or five days. I was a mess. I had three errors in the

second game, but I never performed too well in wet situations. One of the really awesome things is that I hit .429 in the World Series.[828]

The Cardinals couldn't seem to do anything right. During the seventh-inning stretch, as Amy Grant began to sing, the scoreboard showed the name of the song as "God Blass America."

For the eighth inning, Terry Francona put Pokey Reese at second base and brought in Mike Timlin from the bullpen. Gabe Kapler, who had pinch-hit, stayed in to play right field. Timlin retired Tony Womack and pinch-hitters Roger Cedeño and John Mabry on three ground balls. Nine pitches and his night was done.

Foulke came in for the ninth. Working in a light drizzle, he struck out Renteria. Larry Walker spoiled the shutout—and Foulke's postgame scoreless innings streak (12⅓)—with a solo home run into the first row of seats in center field. Then Pujols flied out to left, and Rolen struck out looking.

The Red Sox had won again. The final score of 4–1 gave them a 3–0 lead in the World Series. Boston's seven straight wins tied a single postseason record. Everyone now knew that no team had ever come back from a 0–3 deficit to win a best-of-seven series...until rather recently.

Pedro Martinez finished with seven shutout innings, allowing only three hits and two walks, striking out six in 98 pitches. If this was to be his last game in a Red Sox uniform, Martinez had gone out in style.

PEDRO MARTINEZ:

It was a great feeling for me to perform like I'm used to. I got an early lead, a little break in the third, and then after that, I used my experience and threw strikes and kept them swinging.[829]

JOHNNY DAMON:

Just the way they swung the bats against him, you could tell they didn't really know what was coming.[830]

JASON VARITEK:

That could be one of the happiest moments I've ever had for somebody. As much scrutiny as he's had sometimes, with as great a career as he's had, that was phenomenal. I'm real happy for him. I'm proud of him.[831]

THEO EPSTEIN:

Pedro threw extraordinarily well. That was an artistic performance.[832]

PEDRO MARTINEZ:

We're not going to relax. I don't think our team is going to relax as much as the Yankees did. I read something about Sheffield being arrogant. We just shut our mouth and went out there and played baseball. We're going to continue to do that.[833]

MIKE TIMLIN:

We were down in a hole a couple of games ago, and we fought back. And we'll continue to fight forward. That's what we're doing here... and we're not comfortable because we've seen the other side.[834]

JOHNNY DAMON:

We're not taking anything for granted. We know they're a great team. I'm sure they've won four games in a row before. We've lost four games in a row before. But we're going to do everything in our power to make sure that doesn't happen.[835]

MANNY RAMIREZ:

What we learned from the Yankees series is that it takes four.[836]

24

World Series Game 4

Wednesday, October 27, 2004, at Busch Stadium

The Red Sox knew they had four chances to win one clinching game, but they also knew that the same had been true for the Yankees only 10 days earlier.

ORLANDO CABRERA:
You heard some people say, "Man, it would be sweet to win at home." Some guys said that! I don't remember who. And we're like, "He's insane." Schilling said it a lot: "We're not done yet. Don't get confident. We're not the Yankees. We're not them." And I remember saying, "Damn, you know, that's true. This is not just another game. This is like The Game." No! We're not those guys. Win at home? You win anywhere, and they can throw you a party when you get home.[837]

CURT SCHILLING:
Game 4 is the 27 hardest outs we're going to play all year.[838]

JOHNNY DAMON:
A lot of people in Boston are talking about how they can die happy if we win. Hopefully, we make their dream come true. But hopefully,

they don't follow through on their promise. There could be a lot of busy ambulances tomorrow.[839]

ORLANDO CABRERA:
Every game is a Game 7. That's what we're playing. Game 7.[840]

The game pitted the Cardinals' Jason Marquis against Derek Lowe. Marquis had pitched one inning of relief in Game 2.

JASON MARQUIS, *Cardinals pitcher:*
I used Game 2 as sort of a tuneup in my mind. It got my feet wet and let me know what kind of atmosphere I was dealing with. Physically, I feel great. Mentally, I feel great.... We've won four in a row before, and we can do it again.[841]

DEREK LOWE:
The more times you get put in those opportunities and you have success, it gives you more confidence. I love this time of year. You have to relish the opportunity to go out there, not be scared to fail, prepare your butt off to go out and pitch a good game. We came to the park today with the attitude that this was Game 7. We didn't want it to go any further because we know what that team can do. We focused on ending it today.[842]

BRONSON ARROYO:
I couldn't be happier for another person on this team. During the division series, Derek was kind of a fish out of water in the bullpen. It was deflating for him to be put there and not play a major role in the series. If I could have switched places with him and been in the bullpen like I am now, I'd do it because he deserves it more than I do.[843]

On a night that featured a total lunar eclipse, the game began with a bang. Johnny Damon led off and lined Marquis' fourth pitch of the night into the Cardinals' bullpen in right field for a home run. For the fifth game in a row, the Red Sox had scored in the first inning.

JASON MARQUIS:
No big deal. A solo shot to lead off the game. We've fallen behind and bounced back before this year, so I wasn't too worried about that. I just tried to keep us in it.[844]

Tony Womack was the Cardinals' new leadoff hitter; Edgar Renteria had been dropped to sixth in the order. Womack singled over Orlando Cabrera's leap to start the home half of the first. Larry Walker surprised everyone—including his own manager—by laying down a bunt. The power-hitting Walker had only seven sacrifice bunts in his career and none since 1991. But the bunt was successful, Lowe threw him out, and Womack advanced to second.

TONY LA RUSSA:
Larry was upset when he came in the dugout. He had the third base-man off the line, and he was trying to bunt the ball down the line for a hit. We definitely weren't sacrificing there.[845]

DEREK LOWE:
I'll give up a hit to Womack every time if Walker is going to bunt. I was very surprised.[846]

Lowe got two more groundouts, and Womack was stranded at third.

The Red Sox left men at second and third in the second inning. In the third, Cabrera flew out to left. Manny Ramirez singled, extending his postseason hitting streak to 17 games. David Ortiz doubled to the right-field corner, and Ramirez raced to third. Jason Varitek hit a hard bouncer to Albert Pujols at first base, who fired home and cut down Ramirez at the plate. Marquis walked Bill Mueller, loading the bases, and his first three pitches to Trot Nixon were balls. (Marquis had fallen behind to 13 of the first 16 hitters he'd faced.)

TROT NIXON:
I looked at [third base coach] Dale Sveum, and then I looked in the dugout to see if I had a green light. I was feeling pretty good at the plate, but I wanted to make sure. I thought Dale had given me the green light, and I looked over to the dugout. "Are you guys serious? You're going to let me swing away here?" Tito was looking down, spitting on the ground. Brad Mills was clapping his hands— "Let's go, babe. Let's go!"—looking all fired up. So I thought, "All right. They're giving me the green light." It was good fortune that I was able to hit a double. I think Tito's heart stopped when I swung the bat. And it started back up once the ball hit the wall. Dale nonchalantly told me, "Yeah, I gave you a take." I made a

joke out of it. "But I thought we don't take pitches around here. I thought we go out swinging." And he starts laughing. Tito and I had a little moment, laughing, and I told him the same thing, "I thought that was our job, to hit the ball." Things probably would have been different if I had grounded out. I wouldn't have blamed Tito if he'd taken me out of the ballgame.[847]

RON JACKSON:
When Trot got that hit right there, I knew we were going to win the World Series. I had no doubt. We were going to win.[848]

Lowe's most critical inning was the fourth. Boston led 3–0, and St. Louis had its big bats coming up: Walker, Pujols, and Rolen. Lowe set down the three hitters on only nine pitches, including a strikeout of Pujols. Through the first four innings, Lowe's pitch count demonstrated his mastery over the Cardinals: 10, 10, 9, 9. Lowe retired 13 consecutive batters from the first inning into the fifth.

Lowe faced 15 batters before reaching a three-ball count. On 3–2 with one out in the fifth inning, Edgar Renteria doubled to left-center field. There was some miscommunication between Lowe and Varitek on the first pitch to John Mabry, and a wild pitch put Renteria on third. But Lowe struck out Mabry and got Yadier Molina on a routine grounder to shortstop.

In the top of the eighth facing Dan Haren, Mueller singled to right and Nixon doubled into the right-field corner. Jason Isringhausen relieved Haren. Bellhorn walked, loading the bases for the pitcher's spot in the order. Kevin Millar pinch-hit for Lowe and struck out. Isringhausen then got Damon to ground to first base, and Pujols made an off-balance throw home to force Mueller. Cabrera battled for nine pitches but struck out.

In their half of the eighth, the Red Sox put in their late-inning defenders—Doug Mientkiewicz at first, Pokey Reese at second, and Gabe Kapler in right field. Bronson Arroyo, in relief of Lowe, got the first out then walked Reggie Sanders. Tony Womack was up next, so Terry Francona brought in Alan Embree—then La Russa countered with Hector Luna. Embree struck out Luna and got Larry Walker to pop up to shortstop. The Cardinals were down to their last three outs.

CHRIS CUNDIFF:

In St. Louis at the start of the ninth inning, or maybe after there was one out, I looked around the stands and thought these are the last minutes that people can call us losers. This is the end of an era. It's almost the end of a lifestyle. I looked around and thought this is the last two minutes of this. It's going to end.[849]

JOE CASTIGLIONE, *Red Sox radio announcer:*

I was very anxious. I had thought for years about what I'd say if I was on the air when the Red Sox won the World Series. I started to make some notes. Then I stopped. I told myself, *Don't do that. You might blow it. Just do it naturally as it comes to you.* But I had anticipated this moment for 22 seasons with the Red Sox, and I wanted to get it right. I did not want to be trite or to mention the curse, and I did not want to overstate it. I wanted to say something simple that would stand the test of time.[850]

Keith Foulke got the ball for the bottom of the ninth.

KEITH FOULKE:

I was glad to be on the field. It's easier when you've got the ball than sitting in the bullpen.[851]

Pujols grounded a single up the middle—right between Foulke's legs.

Rolen hit a routine fly to Kapler in right. One out.

Edmonds struck out on three pitches. Two outs.

On the Red Sox's bench, everyone was fidgeting, unable to sit down, ready to burst out of the dugout.

KEVIN MILLAR:

I had Schilling next to me. He looks at me and says, "How we going to do this? Which way are you going over the railing?" I wanted him to fall so bad.[852]

Edgar Renteria stepped into the batter's box.

ORLANDO CABRERA:

I wanted that ball hit to me. I don't care if we're losing 10–0 or winning 20–0, it doesn't matter. You always want that ball hit to you. You're not a pitcher or catcher. You want to be part of the game. I wanted that ball. I wished I could be at first base so I could get the ball.[853]

Foulke threw a fastball inside, ball one, to Renteria, and Pujols took second base on defensive indifference.

DOUG MIENTKIEWICZ:

It's the only time I ever stood in the field and started reflecting on how much stuff had gone on in my life. For me, 2004 was an up-and-down year. I got a multi-year contract from the Twins. Wrist surgery. Got off to a good start but then my wrist hurt again. All of a sudden, I got traded to the Red Sox. I thought about all the sacrifices my parents made. I'm looking around and I know what's about to happen. And this is not the Detroit Tigers winning the World Series. This is the Boston Red Sox winning the World Series—it hasn't been done in 86 years. I stood there and thought, *Holy shit! It's here!* I was focused on the game, but my emotions were going nuts. I looked in the dugout, and I saw Schilling hopping up and down. Kevin's hopping up and down. Derek's hopping up and down. David's hopping up and down. It's about to get nuts. It's about to go crazy. It's everything that's good and right about the game of baseball. And it's about to happen in front of your eyes.[854]

Foulke looked in to Varitek for the sign, nodded, and threw his pitch. It was 11:40 PM in New England.

JOE CASTIGLIONE:

Foulke to the set. The 1–0 pitch, here it is. Swing and a ground ball, stabbed by Foulke. He has it. He underhands to first, and the Boston Red Sox are the World Champions! For the first time in 86 years, the Red Sox have won baseball's world championship. Can you believe it?[855]

JOE BUCK, *Fox Sports announcer:*

Back to Foulke! Red Sox fans have longed to hear it—the Boston Red Sox are world champions.... It has been 86 years. Generations have come and gone. And for the first time since 1918, the Boston Red Sox are champions of baseball.[856]

KEITH FOULKE:

It's a play that I've made a thousand times. As soon as I saw the ball hit back at me and I grabbed it, my only thought was, *Don't throw it away*. That's why I kind of double-pumped it, making sure he was there. At that point, everything was so focused, you know, as soon as I started running over there. That was a whole lifetime of joy and a huge release of satisfaction that I'd reached my ultimate goal. It did not happen in slow motion; actually, it went very fast. Once I flipped the ball, as soon as I let go of it, you know it's over at that point. Unless something weird happens. Everything went super fast. I remember turning to Jason and seeing him running out. *Holy cow! There it is.*[857]

CHRIS CUNDIFF:

It was so awesome. I was so excited I started running out—I mean, hell, I would have been like the third guy out there! I might have been in the middle of Varitek and Foulke! I had to make myself slow down.[858]

As had been the case a week earlier in New York, scores of Red Sox fans in the crowd stayed long after the final out, chanting, "Thank you, Red Sox!" Cardinals' management had actually opened the gates of Busch Stadium in the ninth inning, giving Red Sox fans outside the park who had been unable to get tickets the opportunity to witness history. Several Red Sox players came out of the clubhouse and showered the fans with champagne. Pokey Reese emptied the team's bag of batting practice baseballs, throwing them into the stands. Pedro Martinez, the World Series trophy in his arms, took a lap around the field.

TROT NIXON:

This was my dream when I first came to this organization in 1993. When I first got here, people were talking about how long it had been since the Red Sox won, and right then, I said I wanted to be here when we did win it.... I'm so proud of these guys, this organization, so proud of the front office for putting this team together. And it's for our fans that never die on us.[859]

KEVIN MILLAR:

Tears of joy and happiness and all the pain that you go through for the whole season, all the doubters, all the signs and chants you hear of 1918, you can rip all those up now and you can put 2004 Sox. I can't wait for the parade. We're so excited to get on those floats and go, baby.[860]

DAVE ROBERTS:
To be part of the team that re-writes history, it doesn't get any better than this.[861]

CURTIS LESKANIC:
Ending up on this team is a dream. It's like falling out of a dump truck and ending up on a cloud.[862]

DEREK LOWE:
No more going to Yankee Stadium and having to listen to "1918!"[863]

THEO EPSTEIN:
So many people can die happy now. But a whole lot more can live happy.... I hope they're getting that "2000!" chant ready for the Yankees in Boston next year.[864]

KEITH FOULKE:
This is the first time I've ever won anything. Not in little league. Not in high school. Not in college.[865]

PEDRO MARTINEZ:
The ring is meaningless, it's a material thing. But the feeling that the people are going to have in Boston is indescribable.[866]

TROT NIXON:
I bet I've got a full-blown ulcer right now, the way I worry about each and every pitch every time I get to the plate. Every year I bet I lose 10–15 pounds worrying about our club going out there winning games.... The curse? That's nothing now. That's just a five-letter word.[867]

JOHN HENRY:
Teams and kids for the next 20, 30, 40, 50 years will look back and say, "If the Red Sox can do it, we can do it."[868]

Someone said this is the biggest thing that's happened in New England since the Revolution.[869]

CURT SCHILLING:
We are the World Series champions, and no Boston team has been able to say that since 1918. Now we won't have to listen to that chant any more. I'm so happy, so proud.[870]

TROT NIXON:

I'm still kind of in a daze. Did this really happen? I can only imagine what's going on back home right now.[871]

TIM WAKEFIELD:

I think the city is going to be on fire. Not literally. Hopefully that won't happen.[872]

JOHN HENRY:

Last week, we watched the greatest comeback in the history of sports. This week, our fans across the world got what they've waited for all their lives.[873]

BEN CHERINGTON:

The great lesson is do not underestimate what people in the clubhouse can do when they really believe in something. Ultimately, they're the ones who make it happen. We can make moves and sign players and do this and that, but the people in uniform win games. Always have and always will. And that group was a talented group, but they had a lot more than that going for them, too. It was a very unique collection of people who really wanted to win, were talented enough to do it, and were incredibly resilient. . . . They did this with all the weight of the curse hanging over their head. It took a real combination of resiliency, toughness, and talent, but also a sense of humor.[874]

Many of the Red Sox players hugged Johnny Pesky, who had come up empty in his only World Series with the Red Sox 58 years earlier. After his playing career was over, Pesky worked for the Red Sox in numerous capacities, including scout, announcer, coach, and finally, goodwill ambassador. As soon as Derek Lowe was handed the World Series trophy, he sought out Pesky to make sure he had a chance to hoist the hardware.

DEREK LOWE:

People have been waiting for this for a long time, especially Johnny Pesky. We happened to have won the championship, but it's also for a lot of people who played here before.[875]

JOHNNY PESKY:
This is a hell of a feeling. This is the best feeling a ballplayer can have. If I was a poet laureate, I couldn't find the words to describe how I feel.[876]

There is no evidence that Johnny Pesky took off all of his clothes and ran around the field naked. Then again, there is no evidence that he didn't.

The Red Sox scored in the first inning of all four games and became the fourth team to never trail in the World Series, joining the 1963 Los Angeles Dodgers, 1966 Baltimore Orioles, and 1989 Oakland Athletics. In fact, the Red Sox never trailed after the 8th inning of ALCS Game 5, a total of 60 innings.

TROT NIXON:
It didn't feel easy to me. We did this the hard way. We had our backs against the wall against the Yankees. Then we had to avoid the emotional letdown that I think is just an excuse. That's why the Yankees got whacked out last year. We weren't going to allow that to happen to us because we were focused on the bigger prize, the world championship.[877]

GABE KAPLER:
The World Series games felt very comfortable every inning of every game. There were never high levels of anxiety. We were very light, and there was no tightness in our style of play in that series and, to a man, there was an inherent sense that we were going to win. I joked that we all aged 10 years during the Yankees series and were rejuvenated by the Cardinals series. You'll never find anyone who will tell you that the Cardinals series was more important than the Yankees series.[878]

CURTIS LESKANIC:
Do you ever hear anyone talk about, man, in the '04 World Series, when you guys swept the Cardinals? All I hear about is the series with the Yankees. I never heard anything about the Cardinals. I can almost forget that we won the World Series that year. It was so cool the way we did what we did. I don't even know how everyone just didn't fall off the face of the earth after the ALCS and not be able to even make the damn World Series. Because that was the highlight of my career, beating the Yankees, coming back.[879]

During spring training, Manny Ramirez had promised that he would be the MVP of something. It turned out to be the 2004 World Series. Ramirez hit safely in all four games, going 7-for-17 (.412) with a home run, two runs scored, three walks, and four RBIs. He finished the 2004 postseason with 21 hits (one fewer than David Ortiz) and a .350 batting average.

MANNY RAMIREZ:
I went through so much stuff in the winter. So much drama. I just left it in God's hands. And look what happened. We broke the curse. We all pulled apart little pieces. One by one. All of my teammates, we broke the curse.[880]

The championship was truly a team effort. Bill Mueller batted .429 (6-for-14). Mark Bellhorn led the team with a .563 on-base percentage thanks to three hits and a team-high five walks. Keith Foulke pitched in (and finished) all four games, earning a win and two saves. He worked five innings and led all Red Sox pitchers with eight strikeouts. When it was all over, Foulke had thrown 256 pitches in 11 postseason games.

TERRY FRANCONA:
I'm thrilled for Manny, but I think we had a bunch of MVPs. We have a lot of good players who played up to their expectations. We also had some guys that were in role parts that came in and did amazing things to help us win games. If Dave Roberts can't steal second base, I'm home watching this on television. What Keith Foulke did was incredible. That's how you win—when people do special things. We had a lot of special people do special things.[881]

MANNY RAMIREZ:
Schilling, Pedro, D-Lowe, all the pitchers, they are the MVPs here. Without them, we never make it. But I'm blessed to be the MVP and to win a World Series. God is blessing me with a lot of stuff right now.... There's nothing that I can complain about.[882]

After Game 1, the Cardinals scored two, one, and zero runs. The Red Sox starters allowed no earned runs in the final three games. The St. Louis offense was completely shut down. As a team, they batted .190 in the Series with only 13 hits in the final three games. Their trio of potential MVP candidates in the heart of the order came up empty. Scott Rolen was

0-for-15, Jim Edmonds was 1-for-15, and Albert Pujols was 5-for-15 but didn't drive in a run.

TERRY FRANCONA:
We had a great scouting report, very in-depth. Great pitching coach. And, I got to say, two great catchers that took the time to go over the reports and pass them on. But what it comes down to is having really good pitchers who follow the game plan.[883]

GALEN CARR:
There was a lot of objective stuff we broke down. Pujols' ability to absolutely destroy elevated pitches out over the plate was amazing. So we focused on location with him—staying down, down and away, eliminating his ability to do serious damage, keeping him on the ground. He was a great high fastball hitter regardless of the count, and we did a good job of staying away from that. Scott Rolen's swing path did a ton of damage on balls down in the zone on low fastballs. So we focused on staying away from his location strength. With Jim Edmonds, he came into Fenway and all of a sudden he's staying back, letting the ball travel, and using the Wall instead of pulling the ball like a power hitter. That changed our approach.[884]

DAVE JAUSS:
Our pitching had just gone through a pretty good middle of the order with the Angels and the Yankees. That's what preps people to be that good. The AL East in the mid-2000s was a grind. You go through that, and even with veteran pitchers, there's development. You get locked into what you need to do, and can do, against the top hitters in the game. St. Louis had the best hitters in the National League, but we had gone through the best hitters in baseball from August on. Everybody talks about the hitting being so much better in the American League at that time. The pitching became that much better because the good pitchers had to go through those lineups. Every series. That's what I felt really showed in that World Series.[885]

TOM CATLIN, *director of advertising, television, and video production*:
In Game 7 of the 2003 ALCS, after 7½ innings, I went from sitting in the upper deck at Yankee Stadium to the Red Sox clubhouse to shoot video of the celebration. I sat in a front corner of the clubhouse with Billy Broadbent, the video coach, and watched in horror on his

monitors as the Yankees came back and won on Aaron Boone's homer. The Sox clubhouse was silent except for the sounds of Tim Wakefield's sniffles as he sat facing his locker, crying, and teammates coming over to console him. I didn't have the heart to shoot any video. The despair of that loss in 2003 made it so much sweeter when the Sox swept the Cardinals to win the 2004 World Series. That night, I saw Tim crying tears of joy on the field in St. Louis. This time, I was glad to shoot video of Tim's tears. Two seasons, two vastly different finishes, two sets of tears. What a difference a year made.[886]

25

Celebration

TROT NIXON:
We could win an Academy Award, this story is so good.[887]

Generations had come and gone in New England, waiting and hoping for that ultimate victory. Now that it was here, there was an immediate outpouring of exhilaration, relief, and even some disbelief. *"Did that really happen? Did the Red Sox really win the World Series?"*

Everyone across Red Sox Nation—a nation that spans the globe—woke up on October 28 possibly hung over but most certainly smiling. It would take a while for the reality of what had happened to sink in.

CHRIS CUNDIFF:
When we got to the hotel, it was like we were The Beatles. It's only about six blocks away from the ballpark. There were literally people about 10 deep around the entire hotel. They had to bring us in through the kitchen. Everybody was packed inside, too. They had to clear a path to get us to the elevators, and they had to clear a path to get back out.[888]

Back in Boston, fans gathered in Kenmore Square and around Fenway Park in a large late-night celebration. Others greeted the team at the airport or when the players arrived at Fenway Park early Thursday morning. Fans were still sleep-deprived, but it was no longer because of tension. They were just too excited to sleep.

Stan Grossfeld, a Pulitzer Prize–winning photographer for the *Boston Globe*, was on the Delta charter for the flight back to Boston.

> **STAN GROSSFELD, *Boston Globe photographer*:**
> You would think because these guys won for the first time in 86 years they'd be spraying champagne up and down the plane for three hours. But they were fried. They had a champagne toast. Then instead of the flight attendant making the first announcement, we get Curt Schilling. He went into this funny rap about "Why not us?" And then, not long after takeoff, they dimmed the lights and most of the players went to sleep. Pedro was sitting with the trophy like he was a 16-year-old boy and that trophy was his first date. He had the trophy in the middle seat, and he was in love. Johnny Damon posed for a whole bunch of pictures with every flight attendant. Manny was buried under blankets of newspapers or something, and then he walked out all dressed up and looking sharp. After we landed in Boston, Ellis Burks came out and walked down the steps with the trophy.[889]

> **ELLIS BURKS:**
> Pedro, Tim Wakefield, and a couple of the other veteran players thought that I deserved to carry the trophy off the plane. That was a wonderful gesture. It was overwhelming for me.[890]

> **STAN GROSSFELD:**
> There were a ton of state troopers and Logan workers, maybe 100 or 200 people. We all got on the bus to Fenway. It was such a joyous time. Pedro was honking the horn. Trot popped open a beer at 7:15 in the morning. They were toasting people. Truck drivers were getting on top of their rigs and bowing.[891]

A few hours after the players arrived back in Boston, plans for the parade were announced. Boston Mayor Thomas M. Menino announced that the parade would be delayed one day so it could be held on a Saturday.

> **THOMAS M. MENINO, *mayor of Boston*:**
> After 86 years of heartache and disappointment, we can finally say these sweet, sweet words: The Boston Red Sox are World Series champions. We wondered whether we would ever see a World Series

championship in our lifetime. It's a dream passed down from generation to generation. On Saturday, we will celebrate together.[892]

LARRY LUCCHINO:
The Red Sox staged the greatest sports comeback in American history.
It is time for us to celebrate.[893]

The *Boston Globe* printed 1 million copies of Thursday's paper, roughly
twice as many as a normal weekday. Above the fold on the front page was
one word: "YES!" The *Boston Herald* ran three editions with a total press run
of 750,000, the largest run in the paper's history. Fans bought extra copies
of the newspapers and flooded into souvenir shops to buy T-shirts and caps
proclaiming the Red Sox 2004 World Champions. Many fans visited graves to
share the news with departed loved ones, often leaving caps or memorabilia.

TROT NIXON:
Being a lifer with the Red Sox, you tend to become one of the fans.
You realize all the heartache the fans are going through every year
when either we didn't go to the playoffs or didn't win the World
Series. After we won, I can't tell you how many times people came
up to me crying, saying, "I wish my mom and dad were here. My
dad is very sick right now, and now he can go in peace." Those
things are heartfelt. After we won, we drove by a huge cemetery in
Massachusetts—and it was a sea of red. Families had gone out and
they put blankets out there. Balloons. Red Sox balloons. Red Sox
paraphernalia everywhere.[894]

MANNY RAMIREZ:
I couldn't rest. I was so excited about the parade. I've been going
everywhere and people have been telling me, "Oh, my God, you make
the city so happy, you make us all so happy." But they're the ones who
make us happy.[895]

The lead driver in the parade of Boston's famed Duck boats went by the
name of "Captain Foghorn."

GARY MCNALLY (CAPTAIN FOGHORN), *Duck boat driver*:
I remember driving into Fenway Park the night before to store the
Ducks there overnight. We parked 17 Duck boats on the perim-
eter around the field. I drove the Duck through the gates, and the

stadium lights were lit and it was misting out. It was like a religious experience.[896]

The parade began on Saturday at 10:00 AM on Boylston Street and Kilmarnock Street near Fenway Park. Much of the city shut down for the celebration as the Duck boat parade with the team, their families, and Red Sox staff wound through the city, driving past Boston Common to City Hall Plaza. In a stroke of planning genius and a most unusual twist to a championship parade, the amphibious vehicles launched into the Charles River and the parade continued on water, passing massive crowds along the Esplanade and standing on the Harvard Bridge.

DAVID ORTIZ:

When we drove off the road and pulled into the Charles River, I looked at everybody and I was like, "How is this thing going to float, dude?" Everybody laughed. But it was really cold outside and I don't really like the water, so I put on a life vest. Everybody cracked up.[897]

It was a raw autumn day that saw occasional bits of rain, but the crowd couldn't have cared less. The crowd was sometimes 100 deep along the route. People climbed traffic lights, leaned out of apartment windows, stood on rooftops. Fans had flown in from all over the country. There were senior citizens and infants in strollers. Fans carried brooms, a reference to the Red Sox's sweep of the St. Louis Cardinals. They held signs of gratitude, proposals of marriage, and expressions of wonder at what this team had finally accomplished. The official estimate of the number of people at the parade was 3.2 million—more than five times the population of Boston itself.

MIKE MYERS:

All the family members who were holding pictures of their loved ones who never got to see the Red Sox win a World Series, people who had passed between 1918 and 2004. A lot of them were saying, "Thank you," and pointing to the picture. That's something that will always stick with me. You could tell what it meant to the city—not only to the people who were celebrating and having a good time whooping and hollering, but those pictures themselves were pretty amazing.[898]

RAMIRO MENDOZA, *pitcher*:
The experience is something I will never forget. It was awesome and emotional. During the parade, I saw a woman crying and she was holding a picture of a man, either her husband or her father. She was crying as she told us that he never lived to see this. That will never leave me.[899]

DOUG MIRABELLI:
I couldn't believe how loud it was. It's something you never got tired of. I just wanted to keep going.[900]

DAVE McCARTY, *first baseman*:
The whole thing was surreal. So much of it is a blur. There was this deafening noise. The experience was overwhelming. Sensory overload.[901]

CURT SCHILLING:
It was like a four-hour Who concert. It was the loudest thing I'd ever been involved in, for four straight hours.[902]

KEITH FOULKE:
At first, the victory was more of a personal thing. My personal battle with baseball and the years of work and all the sacrifices. It wasn't until the parade that it soaked in. It seemed like everybody from New England was there. It was an ugly day, but there were 4 million people. Even though we'd heard about 1918—every single day—it was during the parade when we really understood. You heard so many fans say that they can die happy. You saw others who were really emotional because parents and grandparents had passed on before they got to see a Red Sox victory. There was a lot of emotion, and that's when you really learned that Red Sox blood runs through these people.[903]

JOE CASTIGLIONE:
One of the greatest thrills was watching Ellis Burks jumping up and down. He was on the Duck boat with us. He didn't play, but he had a big influence. Ellis was a big emotional factor in that whole run.[904]

DEREK LOWE:
It started raining and it was cold and the people didn't even care. They've waited a long time. You'll never see a parade like that with so many people, no matter what sport or what city.[905]

Loew's Theatres at the Boston Common used huge letters to change its name to Lowe's, in honor of the pitcher who won the clinching game in each of the Red Sox's three postseason series.

Pedro Martinez wore a Dominican flag around his neck like a cape. A T-shirt draped on the railing of his Duck boat read, "Hey, New York, who's your daddy now?" Lowe wore Mardi Gras beads. Manny Ramirez held up a fan's sign: "Jeter is playing golf today. This is better!"

DAVE MELLOR:
My dad was born in Rhode Island. When we got on the parade route, right after we left Fenway, I saw someone holding up a sign that said, "Our late parents and grandparents thank you." It gave me chills because that was just so powerful to me, personally, to feel that and then to see other people expressing that, too. After the season, when we ripped up the field, a lot of that sod was saved and sold the following year. A lot of people took those pieces of sod to the cemeteries and put them on loved one's graves.[906]

GARY CORMIER (THE GREAT GARIBALDI), *Duck boat driver:*
Traditionally, we let passengers drive a little on the water—let the kids drive—when they're on a tour. I asked Curtis Leskanic if he wanted to come up and drive. He was having a blast. At one point we're going along the Mass Ave Bridge and there were crowds of people screaming, and Leskanic is in his glory driving the Duck. He got too close to the shoreline, though, and he hit the rocks on the bottom with the tire. I felt us bumping a little, so I said, "Go to the right, Curtis. Go to the right." We got out of the river and I'm driving and I felt something funny. It was a flat tire! So we pull over and everybody else in the parade keeps going. The police escort—they take off, too. At this point, the crowd had swarmed the Duck, and the players were signing autographs. We eventually got on board a replacement Duck. I don't know how the rest of the parade went.[907]

STAN GROSSFELD:
The most joy I've ever seen on Planet Earth was on that Duck boat with Manny and Papi and Millar. I never saw so much unrestrained joy in my life. Papi was jumping up and down with a broom and the music was going and the whole thing was shaking.[908]

BILL MUELLER:

The best part about winning is it will be dissected so you understand that all the pieces came together to make a whole championship. It was an entire staff, an entire bullpen, an entire lineup, the guys that can steal bases, the fourth outfielder, the pinch-hitters, the guys playing every inning. All the guys understood their roles and were, at the right time, the best at their role. And it was good judgment on the part of the front office and Theo and Tito for having the confidence and getting those guys in the locker room.... It was probably the most intense and exciting moments of my career. And I think that whole series, it's one of those things that you'll love to watch over and over again as time passes. Those games will never be old to watch. Standing out there with two outs at Busch Stadium and knowing you're about to win the World Series is the highest point that I could ever have achieved—an awesome thing to experience. I am very grateful for that.[909]

CURT SCHILLING:

I still can't fathom it entirely. We were down 0–3 to the Yankees, down a run in the ninth with Mariano Rivera on the mound. And 10 days later we're world champs? Come on. Who would ever believe a story like that?[910]

Appendix

Part of the Boston Red Sox's extensive World Series preparation were these scouting reports on Cardinals Jim Edmonds and Woody Williams.

EDMONDS, JIM　(L/L)　DATES SEEN:　10/6 - 10/21　CF

STANCE

Sltly closed upright knee-bent stance, feet spread out, hands high above shoulders w/ active bat, 1st mvmnt is to cock front knee rotating it coiling his body in while dropping hands dwn to gd hitting position to below shoulders, no stride.

COMMENTS

Everyday CF, has hit anywhere from 2nd to 6th, appears settled in 5th spot. Very streaky hitter w/ pwr all ovr, LHH built for Fenway, will gear his swing for wall. A swinger but takes walks. Sits on pitches, watch him peeking. Notoriuos 1st-ball swinger, must strtn him up keeping him off plate. See his setup on plate as well as his 1st swing of each AB to read his apprch. Try to keep him on ground, roll him ovr, keep him off balance. Make him think about pulling the ball in Fenway rather than going to LCF. Dangerous late in game as he's swinging, can hit all zones. Stuff doesn't always beat him, location & how you get there are more effective. Handles LHP well (1.013 OPS). Adjusts well to starting pitcher each time thru order (.984, 1.149, 1.206 OPS 1st, 2nd, 3rd time thru order). The MOST dangerous 1st-pitch hitter in the game, was 44-73 (.603) on 0-0 w/ 12 HR this yr, also had gd success on 1-0 (13-24, .542 w/ 3 HR). Need to get strike on carefully, .769 OPS after he falls behind 0-1, 1.128 OPS after he gets ahead 1-0. Much better success w/ none on (1.166 OPS w/ 26 of his 42 HR) than w/ RISP (.894 OPS).

vs. RHP

Try to get sinkers, 2-seamers dwn-away on plate for rollovr. Get ahead DWN-away w/ action tailing away from him, can mix in CHG or SF on 0-0 as well, chg of spds is gd, mvmnt is gd, would not recommend 0-0 strike bckdr CB, cuttr is better. Need to get pitch IN thru out count to prevent him from being all ovr pitch dwn-away in zone (esp in Fenway gearing to LF), does not need to be way in to back him off plate. Location much more important than velocity. CHG a gd pitch when he's sitting hard. Can climb ladder but must get it way UP truly expanding zone when ahead. Front door comeback sinker a gd pitch w/ 2 strikes. Can also spin harder BB dwn-in out of zone as chase, location is important, then chg planes going back well above zone for chase. When behind continue to keep him honest IN mixing in CHG, SF dwn-away.

vs. LHP

Must get balls away chging spds to get ahead, come IN hard to finish. Need to make him aware of BOTH sides of plate thru out count. Avoid pitches up-away unless going above his head. Tough out vs. LHP, will be geared to LF for pwr in Fenway vs. LHP as well, need to make him aware in. Mixing pitches moving off plate away can be effective, can get ahead w/ BB dwn-away early. May want to get ahead hard IN more often than away as he has gd plate cvrge & most likely will be gearing away. If getting ahead away make sure location is gd, when looking away can surprise him IN. When ahead can elevate FB above zone as chase, esp after a BB dwn-away. When behind don't get locked in dwn-away w/ everything or he will stay on ball & go to opp field w/ pwr, need to continue to keep him honest IN.

	Pitcher AHEAD		Pitcher BEHIND	
	FB's	Non FB's	FB's	Non FB's
	.199 (34-171)	.157 (18-115)	.330 (64-194)	.256 (51-121)

FPS - Bases EMPTY			FPS - Runners ON BASE		
Swings	FPS	%	Swings	FPS	%
197	361	55%	214	335	64%

HITTING vs. RHP

AVG	OBP	SLG	AB	BB's	K's
.293	.423	.651	392	88	117

HITTING vs. LHP

AVG	OBP	SLG	AB	BB's	K's
.330	.400	.613	106	13	33

BASESTEALING

SB	CS	HOME to 1B
8	3	4.40, 4.42

BUNTING

TYPE	SAC BUNTS
Occ push vs. LHP	No

SUMMARY

Ran vs. Ocalis Perez on strt steal (may have been missed hit & run), bad jump but still ran. More bent at waist when running. Big turns on bases, Nixon/Kapler can throw behind, be aware of innate ability to react & take extra base. Tags at 1B on routine deep flyballs. Has 3 bunt hits this yr in 3 tries.

POSITIONING	vs. RHP	vs. LHP	vs. Wakefield
INFIELD	Right side exaggerated pull, 3B off line, SS way up middle	Even more to pull	Pull, maybe 3 guys to right side
CROSS CHARGE (RUN SITUATION)	No		
OUTFIELD	Strt up to SS side	Stay honest on everything, play slt SS side w/ RF strt	Pull

ARM	ACCURACY	RANGE
Above average, true + arm, is accurate, aggressive w/ it	Above average	Above average, plays as shallow as anyone in the game

DEFENSIVE ABILITY

Will make the spectacular plays, throws behind runners, dives for balls. Gd CF'er w/ great range, gd feel for where ball is going. Expect him to get to every ball he gets a gd first step on. Can tag up on him when he dives. Can throw runners out, has an accurate, strong arm, is aggressive.

WOODY WILLIAMS (R)

TEAM: ST. LOUIS CARDINALS

ROLE: Starter

ARM SLOT: H 3/4

RUBBER: Middle to 3B side

	OUT PITCH:	Cmnd
	vs. RHH:	.296
	vs. LHH:	.223
	BB/9 IP:	2.75

DATE	w/l	IP	H	R	ER	BB	SO	#P/S
10/18		7	1	0	0	2	4	94/52

VELOCITY

FASTBALL:	87 - 91	88-90 w/ + cmnd, moves ball in-out on/off plate, consistnt strikes, occ gd arm side life.
CURVEBALL:	75 - 79	Bigger OH tight dwn brk vs. RHH, LHH, avg cmnd.
SLIDER:	80 - 85	Go-to pitch vs. RHH w/ RISP, uses more than big CB, occ dwn-in to LHH, chg from cut mid-in.
CHANGEUP:	82 - 84	Occ vs. middle-order guys LHH, will use vs. RHH, rpts vs. LHH, more often 2nd time thru.
CUTTER:	87 - 89	Cut FB, velocity is the same as FB at times.

COMMENTS

Control type 6-inning starter that stays out of the middle of plate, has had a solid postseason (6 ER ovr 19 IP). Aggressive pitching off FB both 2-seam & cutters. Mixes in SL most often w/ occ slow CB, CHG. Gets ahead w/ FB to both sides, esp 1st time thru order regardless of hitter, pulls out his CHG more often to both RHH, LHH 2nd time thru. VG cmnd of FB pitching to corners both in on plate & off plate vs. both RHH, LHH. Quick worker, slow him dwn, take advantage of mistakes on plate as his stuff does NOT get better later in AB or game. A Radke-type w/ out the VG CHG. MUCH better at home (3.36 ERA) than on road (5.01 ERA). RHH get better AB's (.808 OPS) than LHH (.665 OPS) as he has fewer weapons.

vs. RHH:

AVG	OBP	SLG	AB	HITS	HR	BB	HBP	K	SB	CS
.296	.336	.471	399	118	11	25	5	60	7	3

COMMENTS:

A lot of 1st-pitch strikes w/ FB, occ mixes in SL or cuttr away on 0-0, stays primarily away to start. Moves ball around, works off your last swing. Rpts SL, mixes in slwr CB or even CHG to pwr/middle-order hitters. Pitches ins de w/ 2-seamers both in off plate to open up pitches away & on plate to jam. Try to use middle of field, expecting strikes. May not break CHG out very often early but starts throwing it often when he finally does, did so 2nd time thru order vs. HOU. When ahead mixes in heavy dose of offspd, plenty of chase BB's mixed w/ FB running in off plate, sim apprch w/ 2 strikes, goes w/ CB more than SL as chase. Lots of confidence in ability to locate FB when behind.

vs. LHH:

AVG	OBP	SLG	AB	HITS	HR	BB	HBP	K	SB	CS
.223	.297	.368	337	75	9	33	4	71	3	3

COMMENTS:

Similar patterns as vs. RHH, throws strikes trying to get ahead w/ FB, ccc bckdr BB using either SL or CB, LHH often get a FB middle-in to hit. Also mixes in CHG to keep hitter off balance but works off FB in (front door sinker on plate) & out. Generally gets ahead w/ FB sinking away mixed w/ BB to both sides. Will rpt SL, mixes it in dwn-in, also uses cutter middle-in as a put-away pitch, varying the depths of brk, l kes to finish dwn-in w/ chase BB often. Also elevates FB to both sides when ahead. Similar apprch w/ 2 strikes. Works FB to corners when behind, not afraid to come IN w/ it, also spins both BB's to either side, mixes in occ CHG. FB, CB are primary pitches on 3-2, works to both sides.

FIELDING ABILITY

Well above average, does the job on mound defensively, can't really take advantage of any deficiencies.

vs. BOSTON 2003

ERA	IP	HITS	R	ER	HR	BB	K	AVG AG	SB	CS
6.75	6.2	10	5	5	1	1	1	.333	0	0

2004 STATS

ERA	IP	HITS	R	ER	HR	BB	K	AVG AG	SB	CS
4.18	189.2	193	93	88	20	58	131	.262	10	6

In contrast to the 35,547 fans who went berserk at Fenway when David Ortiz hit his 10th-inning home run to win the Division Series, the official scorer's sheet is underwhelming. Chaz Scoggins merely drew four horizontal lines on the scoresheet that is MLB's official record of the game.

Endnotes

1. Mnookin, Seth. *Feeding the Monster: How Money, Smarts, and Nerve Took a Team to the Top.* (New York: Simon & Schuster, 2006), 226.
2. Shaughnessy, Dan. *Reversing the Curse: Inside the 2004 Boston Red Sox.* (Boston: Houghton Mifflin, 2005), 33.
3. Mnookin, *Feeding the Monster*, 164.
4. *Philadelphia Inquirer*, November 13, 2003.
5. Torre, Joe and Tom Verducci. *The Yankee Years.* (New York: Doubleday, 2009), 271.
6. Torre and Verducci, *The Yankee Years*, 271.
7. *Florida Times-Union*, March 2, 2004.
8. Author Interview; *Boston Herald*, October 29, 2004; *Hartford Courant*, October 23, 2004; Associated Press, December 19, 2003; MLB.com, December 19, 2003.
9. MLB.com, December 19, 2003.
10. *New York Times*, February 19, 2004.
11. *Washington Post*, February 16, 2004.
12. *Boston Herald*, March 19, 2004.
13. *New York Post*, February 22, 2004.
14. *New York Daily News*, March 29, 2004.
15. *Detroit Free Press*, October 12, 2004.
16. Author interview.
17. *Fort Myers News-Press*, February 27, 2004.
18. MLB.com, October 28, 2004.
19. Massarotti, Tony and John Harper. *A Tale of Two Cities: The 2004 Yankees–Red Sox Rivalry and the War for the Pennant.* (Guilford, CT: The Lyons Press, 2005), 111.
20. MLB.com, July 21, 2004.
21. *Boston Globe*, July 25, 2004.
22. *Boston Globe*, July 25, 2004.
23. Author interview.
24. Author interview.
25. *Providence Journal*, October 27, 2004.
26. Author interview.
27. Author interview.
28. Author interview.
29. Mnookin, *Feeding the Monster*, 279.
30. MLB.com, July 31, 2004.
31. Author interview.
32. Author interview.
33. Author interview.
34. Author interview.
35. Author interview.
36. Author interview.
37. Mnookin, *Feeding the Monster*, 283.
38. *Sports Illustrated*, September 13, 2004.
39. Author interview.
40. *Boston Herald*, October 1, 2004.
41. *Lawrence Eagle-Tribune*, October 5, 2004.
42. *Orange County Register*, October 5, 2004.
43. *Boston Herald*, October 5, 2004.

44. ESPN.com, October 5, 2004.
45. *Providence Journal,* October 3, 2004.
46. MLB.com, October 8, 2004.
47. *Boston Herald,* October 5, 2004.
48. *Providence Journal,* October 5, 2004.
49. *Boston Globe,* October 3, 2004.
50. MLB Press Conference, October 5, 2004.
51. *Hartford Courant,* October 1, 2004; *Boston Herald,* October 1, 2004.
52. *Hartford Courant,* October 2, 2004; *Boston Herald,* October 2, 2004.
53. *Boston Globe,* October 2, 2004; *Boston Herald,* October 2, 2004; *Boston Globe,* October 3, 2004; *Boston Herald,* October 3, 2004.
54. Author interview.
55. MLB.com, October 4, 2004; *Boston Globe,* October 4, 2004; *Providence Journal,* October 4, 2004.
56. MLB.com, October 2, 2004.
57. *Hartford Courant,* October 5, 2004.
58. *Boston Globe,* October 6, 2004.
59. *Providence Journal,* October 4, 2004; *Boston Globe,* October 4, 2004; *Hartford Courant,* October 4, 2004.
60. MLB.com, October 2, 2004.
61. *Boston Herald,* October 5, 2004.
62. *Los Angeles Times,* October 5, 2004.
63. MLB.com, October 2, 2004.
64. *Boston Herald,* October 5, 2004.
65. *New York Daily News,* September 9, 2004.
66. ESPN game broadcast, October 5, 2004.
67. Sons of Sam Horn, October 4, 2004.
68. ESPN game broadcast, October 5, 2004.
69. *Boston Globe,* October 7, 2004.
70. MLB.com, October 5, 2004.
71. Associated Press, February 20, 2004.
72. ESPN game broadcast, October 5, 2004.
73. *Providence Journal,* October 6, 2004.
74. *Providence Journal,* October 6, 2004.
75. *Boston Globe,* October 6, 2004.
76. *Boston Globe,* October 6, 2004.
77. MLB Press Conference, October 5, 2004.
78. *Boston Globe,* October 6, 2004.
79. *Boston Globe,* October 6, 2004.
80. *Lawrence Eagle-Tribune,* October 10, 2004.
81. Author interview.
82. *Boston Globe,* October 6, 2004.
83. *Boston Herald,* October 6, 2004.
84. MLB.com, October 5, 2004.
85. Boston scored six runs in an inning in Game 5 of the 1903 World Series, Game 1 of the 1975 World Series, and Game 3 of the 1999 AL Division Series.
86. *Los Angeles Daily News,* October 5, 2004.
87. Author interview.
88. Author interview.
89. *Providence Journal,* October 7, 2004.
90. *Providence Journal,* October 6, 2004.
91. *Lawrence Eagle-Tribune,* October 6, 2004.
92. MLB.com, October 5, 2004.
93. MLB.com, October 5, 2004.
94. *Newark Star-Ledger,* October 11, 2004.
95. MLB Press Conference, October 5, 2004.
96. Author interview; *Boston Globe,* October 7, 2004.
97. MLB.com, October 7, 2004; *Providence Journal,* October 6, 2004.
98. Author interview.
99. MLB Press Conference, October 5, 2004; *Boston Globe,* October 8, 2004.
100. MLB Press Conference, October 6, 2004.
101. Shaughnessy, *Reversing the Curse,* 162.
101b. *Boston Herald,* October 11, 2004.
102. Author interview.
103. *Los Angeles Times,* October 7, 2004.
104. Ortiz, David, and Tony Massarotti. *Big Papi: My Story of Big Dreams and Big Hits.* (New York: St. Martin's Press, 2007), 171.
105. MLB Press Conference, October 5, 2004.
106. MLB Press Conference, October 5, 2004.
107. *Los Angeles Daily News,* October 5, 2004.
108. *Boston Globe,* October 6, 2004.
109. MLB.com, October 5, 2004.

110. MLB Press Conference, October 6, 2004.
111. Author interview.
112. *Providence Journal*, October 7, 2004.
113. *Boston Herald*, October 7, 2004.
114. *Providence Journal*, October 7, 2004.
115. *Boston Herald*, October 7, 2004.
116. *Boston Globe*, October 6, 2004.
117. *Boston Globe*, October 6, 2004.
118. Author interview.
119. *Boston Globe*, October 7, 2004.
120. *Boston Globe*, October 8, 2004.
121. Author interview.
122. *Boston Globe*, October 7, 2004.
123. Author interview.
124. Author interview.
125. *Providence Journal*, October 7, 2004.
126. MLB Press Conference, October 6, 2004.
127. *Boston Globe*, October 7, 2004.
128. *Boston Herald*, October 8, 2004.
129. *Providence Journal*, October 7, 2004.
130. *Providence Journal*, October 8, 2004.
131. *Providence Journal*, October 7, 2004.
132. *Boston Globe*, October 8, 2004; *Boston Herald*, October 8, 2004.
133. *New York Times*, October 8, 2004.
134. *New York Times*, October 8, 2004.
135. *New York Times*, October 8, 2004.
136. *New York Times*, October 8, 2004.
137. Author interview.
138. MLB.com, October 9, 2004.
139. Author interview.
140. *Boston Herald*, October 29, 2004.
141. *Hartford Courant*, October 25, 2004.
142. Sons of Sam Horn, October 8, 2004.
143. MLB.com, October 9, 2004.
144. MLB.com, October 9, 2004.
145. MLB Press Conference, October 7, 2004; *Springfield Republican*, October 8, 2004; *Hartford Courant*, October 8, 2004.
146. MLB Press Conference, October 8, 2004.
147. MLB Press Conference, October 8, 2004.
148. *Boston Globe*, October 9, 2004.
149. *Boston Globe*, October 9, 2004.
150. Author interview.
151. *Boston Globe*, October 9, 2004.
152. *New York Post*, October 9, 2004.
153. *Boston Herald*, October 10, 2004.
154. Author interview.
155. *Los Angeles Times*, October 9, 2004.
156. *Boston Globe*, October 9, 2004.
157. *New York Post*, October 10, 2004.
158. MLB.com, October 8, 2004.
159. Author interview.
160. MLB.com, October 9, 2004.
161. *Boston Herald*, October 10, 2004.
162. *Los Angeles Times*, October 9, 2004.
163. Author interview.
164. *Boston Globe*, October 9, 2004.
165. *Boston Herald*, October 10, 2004.
166. Author interview; *Providence Journal*, October 9, 2004.
167. Author interview.
168. *Boston Herald*, October 9, 2004.
169. *Boston Globe*, October 9, 2004.
170. *Boston Herald*, October 9, 2004.
171. MLB.com, October 8, 2004.
172. MLB.com, October 9, 2004; *Boston Herald*, October 9, 2004.
173. Author interview.
174. Author interview.
175. *Boston Globe*, October 9, 2004.
176. Author interview.
177. Mnookin, *Feeding the Monster*, 288; MLB.com, October 9, 2004.
178. MLB.com, October 9, 2004.
179. *Los Angeles Daily News*, October 9, 2004.
180. MLB.com, October 10, 2004; *Boston Herald*, October 10, 2004.
181. *Los Angeles Daily News*, October 9, 2004.
182. *Boston Globe*, October 9, 2004.
183. Author interview.
184. Author interview.
185. *Hartford Courant*, October 10, 2004.
186. Author interview.
187. MLB.com, October 9, 2004.
188. *Providence Journal*, October 9, 2004.
189. MLB.com, October 9, 2004.
190. *Boston Herald*, October 9, 2004.
191. *Newark Star-Ledger*, October 10, 2004.
192. *Providence Journal*, October 9, 2004.
193. *New York Times*, October 10, 2004.
194. Author interview.
195. Author interview.
196. *Boston Globe*, October 9, 2004.
197. *Boston Globe*, October 9, 2004.
198. Ortiz and Massarotti, *Big Papi*, 171.

199. *New York Daily News*, October 9, 2004.
200. *New York Daily News*, October 9, 2004.
201. *Providence Journal*, October 9, 2004.
202. *Boston Globe*, October 9, 2004.
203. *St. Petersburg Times*, October 9, 2004.
204. *Hartford Courant*, October 9, 2004.
205. *St. Petersburg Times*, October 9, 2004.
206. MLB.com, October 9, 2004.
207. *New York Daily News*, October 9, 2004.
208. *Newark Star-Ledger*, October 10, 2004.
209. *Providence Journal*, October 20, 2004.
210. *Hartford Courant*, October 11, 2004.
211. *Hartford Courant*, October 11, 2004; *Bergen Record*, October 11, 2004; *Newark Star-Ledger*, October 11, 2004.
212. Author interview; *Lawrence Eagle-Tribune*, October 12, 2004; *Boston Herald*, October 13, 2004; *Boston Globe*, October 12, 2004.
213. *Boston Herald*, October 11, 2004.
214. Author interview.
215. Author interview.
216. *Boston Herald*, October 11, 2004.
217. *New York Daily News*, October 10, 2004.
218. MLB.com, October 12, 2004.
219. *New York Times*, October 11, 2004; *Newark Star-Ledger*, October 10, 2004.
220. *Bergen Record*, October 12, 2004.
221. *New York Post*, October 11, 2004.
222. *Newark Star-Ledger*, October 11, 2004.
223. *Boston Globe*, October 12, 2004.
224. MLB Press Conference, October 11, 2004.
225. Author interview.
226. *Washington Post*, October 12, 2004.
227. *Washington Post*, October 12, 2004.
228. Author interview.
229. Author interview.
230. Author interview.
231. Sons of Sam Horn, October 11, 2004.
232. Author interview.
233. Author interview.
234. Author interview.
235. Author interview.
236. *New York Daily News*, October 14, 2004; MLB.com, October 13, 2004; *Arizona Republic*, October 14, 2004.
237. *Hartford Courant*, October 13, 2004; MLB.com, October 13, 2004; *Boston Globe*, October 13, 2004.
238. *Hartford Courant*, October 13, 2004; *Newsday*, October 13, 2004.
239. MLB.com, October 13, 2004.
240. Author interview.
241. *Boston Globe*, October 13, 2004; MLB.com, October 13, 2004; *Newsday*, October 13, 2004.
242. MLB.com, October 13, 2004.
243. MLB.com, October 12, 2004.
244. Mussina was the first pitcher to retire the first 19 batters in a postseason game since Boston's Jim Lonborg set down the same number of St. Louis Cardinals in Game 2 of the 1967 World Series. The only two pitchers who retired more were Larsen and the Yankees' Herb Pennock (22 in Game 3 of the 1927 World Series against the Pittsburgh Pirates).
245. Author interview.
246. *New York Daily News*, October 13, 2004.
247. *Boston Herald*, October 13, 2004.
248. *Springfield Republican*, October 13, 2004.
249. *Boston Herald*, October 13, 2004.
250. *Hartford Courant*, October 13, 2004; MLB.com, October 13, 2004.
251. Author interview; *Arizona Republic*, October 14, 2004; *Boston Globe*, October 13, 2004; *Hartford Courant*, October 13, 2004; MLB.com, October 13, 2004.
252. *New York Post*, October 13, 2004.
253. Shaughnessy, *Reversing the Curse*, 170.
254. *New York Daily News*, October 12, 2004.
255. *Boston Herald*, October 13, 2004.
256. *New York Times*, October 14, 2004.

257. MLB Press Conference, October 13, 2004.

258. *Boston Herald*, October 14, 2004.

259. *New York Times*, October 14, 2004; *New York Post*, October 14, 2004.

260. *New York Times*, October 14, 2004; *Providence Journal*, October 14, 2004.

261. *Hartford Courant*, October 14, 2004; *Boston Globe*, October 14, 2004.

262. *Providence Journal*, October 14, 2004.

263. *Boston Globe*, October 14, 2004. MLB.com, October 14, 2004.

264. *Boston Herald*, October 14, 2004; *Boston Globe*, October 14, 2004; *Kansas City Star*, October 15, 2004.

265. *Hartford Courant*, October 14, 2004; *Boston Globe*, October 14, 2004.

266. *Boston Globe*, October 14, 2004.

267. MLB Press Conference, October 13, 2004.

268. *Boston Globe*, October 15, 2004.

269. MLB.com, October 14, 2004.

270. *Boston Herald*, October 14, 2004; *Boston Globe*, October 14, 2004.

271. *Boston Globe*, October 15, 2004.

272. *Metrowest Daily News*, October 14, 2004.

273. *New York Times*, October 14, 2004.

274. *New York Daily News*, October 16, 2004.

275. *New York Post*, October 15, 2004.

276. *Boston Globe*, October 15, 2004.

277. *Boston Herald*, October 15, 2004.

278. *Boston Herald*, October 15, 2004; *Hartford Courant*, October 16, 2004.

279. Author Interview.

280. Author interview.

281. *Boston Globe*, October 14, 2004.

282. *Boston Globe*, October 14, 2004; *Hartford Courant*, October 14, 2004.

283. MLB.com, October 15, 2004; *Hartford Courant*, October 15, 2004; *Providence Journal*, October 15, 2004.

284. MLB.com, October 15, 2004; *Hartford Courant*, October 15, 2004.

285. *Boston Herald*, October 16, 2004.

286. MLB Press Conference, October 15, 2004; *New York Times*, October 16, 2004; *Hartford Courant*, October

17, 2004; *Miami Herald*, October 16, 2004.

287. MLB.com, October 15, 2004.

288. Shaughnessy, *Reversing the Curse*, 196.

289. *Boston Herald*, October 15, 2004.

290. *New York Post*, October 15, 2004.

291. *Boston Globe*, October 15, 2004.

292. *Boston Globe*, October 15, 2004; *Boston Herald*, October 15, 2004.

293. *Boston Globe*, October 31, 2004.

294. *St. Petersburg Times*, October 18, 2004.

295. Author interview.

296. Author interview.

297. MLB.com, October 17, 2004.

298. *Boston Globe*, October 18, 2004.

299. *Boston Herald*, October 17, 2004.

300. MLB Press Conference, October 16, 2004.

301. Author interview.

302. Author interview.

303. *Boston Globe*, October 17, 2004.

304. *Boston Globe*, October 18, 2004.

305. Author interview.

306. Author interview.

307. Associated Press, October 17, 2004; *Boston Herald*, October 17, 2004; *New York Times*, October 19, 2004.

308. Author interview.

309. Author interview.

310. Author interview.

311. Author interview.

312. Author interview.

313. ESPN.com, October 22, 2004.

314. MLB Press Conference, October 16, 2004.

315. Shaughnessy, *Reversing the Curse*, 195.

316. Author interview.

317. *The Boston Red Sox 2004 World Series Collector's Edition* (Major League Baseball Properties, Inc., A&E Home Video) 2005.

318. It had happened in the minor leagues, however. In 1937, the Newark Bears (International League champions, and a Yankees farm team) lost the first three games of the Junior World Series to the Columbus Red Birds (American

Association champions) before winning four in a row.

319. *St. Petersburg Times*, October 31, 2004.
320. Author interview.
321. Ortiz and Massarotti, *Big Papi*, 175.
322. Author interview.
323. Author interview.
324. Author interview.
325. *Four Days in October* (ESPN Films: 30 For 30), Major League Baseball Productions, 2010.
326. Damon, Johnny, and Peter Golenbock. *Idiot: Beating the Curse and Enjoying the Game of Life*. (New York: Crown Publishers, 2005), 198.
327. *Pittsburgh Post-Gazette*, October 18, 2004.
328. Author interview.
329. *Lawrence Eagle-Tribune*, October 18, 2004.
330. Author interview.
331. *Boston Globe*, October 18, 2004.
332. *Boston Globe* (Boston.com), January 24, 2011; Torre and Verducci, *The Yankee Years*, 295.
333. Author interview.
334. Author interview.
335. Author interview.
336. Author interview.
337. Author interview.
338. Author interview.
339. Author interview.
340. Author interview.
341. CBSSportsline.com, October 28, 2004; *Washington Post*, October 28, 2004.
342. Francona, Terry, and Dan Shaughnessy. *Francona: The Red Sox Years*. (Boston: Houghton Mifflin Harcourt, 2013), 116.
343. Comcast Sportsnet Chicago website video, January 14, 2012.
344. Author interview.
345. Author interview.
346. Author interview.
347. *Boston Herald*, October 19, 2004.
348. Author interview.
349. Author interview.
350. Author interview.
351. Author interview.
352. *Boston Herald*, October 19, 2004.
353. *New York Times*, October 25, 2004.
354. Author interview.
355. Author interview.
356. Author interview.
357. Author interview.
358. Author interview.
359. *Boston Herald*, October 18, 2004.
360. Mnookin, *Feeding the Monster*, 294.
361. Mnookin, *Feeding the Monster*, 294; Shaughnessy, *Reversing the Curse*, 198.
362. Mnookin, *Feeding the Monster*, 295.
363. Shaughnessy, *Reversing the Curse*, 198.
364. "Lose Yourself," written by Marshall Mathers, Luis Resto, Jeffrey Bass / Eight Mile Style LLC.
365. Torre and Verducci, *The Yankee Years*, 296–97.
366. *Four Days in October* (ESPN Films: 30 For 30), Major League Baseball Productions, 2010.
367. Author interview.
368. *Boston Globe* (Boston.com), January 24, 2011.
369. Author interview.
370. *Boston Globe*, October 14, 2011.
371. *Boston Globe* (Boston.com), January 24, 2011.
372. *Newsday*, October 19, 2004.
373. *Boston Globe*, August 7, 2005.
374. *Four Days in October* (ESPN Films: 30 For 30), Major League Baseball Productions, 2010.
375. *Four Days in October* (ESPN Films: 30 For 30), Major League Baseball Productions, 2010.
376. *Four Days in October* (ESPN Films: 30 For 30), Major League Baseball Productions, 2010.
377. Author interview; *Boston Globe*, August 7, 2005.
378. *Cleveland Plain Dealer*, June 9, 2005.
379. Author interview.
380. Author interview; *Cleveland Plain Dealer*, June 9, 2005; Dave Roberts: *Ray of Hope* (video) (Boston Red Sox Productions, 2012).
381. Dave Roberts: *Ray of Hope* (video) (Boston Red Sox Productions, 2012).

382. *Four Days in October* (ESPN Films: 30 For 30), Major League Baseball Productions, 2010; Dave Roberts: *Ray of Hope* (video) (Boston Red Sox Productions, 2012).
383. Author interview.
384. Author interview.
385. Author interview.
386. Author interview.
387. *Boston Globe*, October 14, 2011.
388. Author interview.
389. Author interview.
390. Author interview.
391. Dave Roberts: *Ray of Hope* (video) (Boston Red Sox Productions, 2012).
392. Author interview.
393. Francona and Shaughnessy, *Francona*, 115.
394. Mnookin, *Feeding the Monster*, 297.
395. Author interview.
396. Author interview; *Boston Globe*, October 14, 2011.
397. Author interview.
398. Author interview; *Boston Globe*, October 14, 2011.
399. *Boston Globe*, October 14, 2011.
400. Author interview.
401. Author interview.
402. Mnookin, *Feeding the Monster*, 297.
403. Author interview.
404. Author interview.
405. Author interview.
406. Author interview.
407. Author interview.
408. Author interview.
409. Dave Roberts: *Ray of Hope* (video) (Boston Red Sox Productions, 2012).
410. Dave Roberts: *Ray of Hope* (video) (Boston Red Sox Productions, 2012).
411. Massarotti and Ortiz, *Big Papi*, 176–78; *Lincoln Journal Star*, October 19, 2004.
412. Damon and Golenbock, *Idiot*, 204.
413. *Boston Herald*, October 18, 2004.
414. Torre and Verducci, *The Yankee Years*, 300.
415. Mnookin, *Feeding the Monster*, 298.
416. Author interview.
417. *Newark Star-Ledger*, October 18, 2004.
418. *Springfield Republican*, October 20, 2004.
419. *Boston Globe*, October 19, 2004; *Providence Journal*, October 19, 2004; *New York Daily News*, October 19, 2004.
420. *USA Today Sports Weekly*, October 13, 2004.
421. Author interview.
422. Author interview.
423. *New York Post*, October 19, 2004.
424. Author interview; *Richmond Times-Dispatch*, October 24, 2004.
425. Author interview.
426. *Hartford Courant*, October 21, 2004.
427. Author interview.
428. *Four Days in October* (ESPN Films: 30 For 30), Major League Baseball Productions, 2010.
429. Author interview.
430. Author interview.
431. Author interview.
432. *New York Post*, October 27, 2004.
433. *Four Days in October* (ESPN Films: 30 For 30), Major League Baseball Productions, 2010.
434. Montville, Leigh. *Why Not Us? The 86-Year Journey of the Boston Red Sox Fans from Unparalleled Suffering to the Promised Land of the 2004 World Series* (Cambridge, MA: The Perseus Books Group, 2004), 138.
435. Torre and Verducci, *The Yankee Years*, 301.
436. Torre and Verducci, *The Yankee Years*, 301.
437. Author interview.
438. Author interview.
439. *Boston Herald*, October 20, 2004.
440. Author interview.
441. Author interview.
442. Author interview.
443. Author interview.
444. Author interview.
445. Author interview.
446. *Providence Journal*, October 19, 2004.
447. *Boston Globe*, October 20, 2004.

448. *Springfield Republican*, October 20, 2004.
449. Author interview.
450. Author interview.
451. *Boston Herald*, October 19, 2004; *Boston Globe*, October 19, 2004.
452. *Boston Herald*, October 19, 2004.
453. *Hartford Courant*, October 19, 2004; *Springfield Republican*, October 19, 2004; *Boston Herald*, October 19, 2004.
454. Author interview.
455. Author interview.
456. Author interview.
457. *New York Times*, October 19, 2004.
458. *New York Times*, October 19, 2004; *Boston Globe*, October 19, 2004.
459. Massarotti and Ortiz, *Big Papi*, 179–80; *Boston Globe*, October 19, 2004.
460. Author interview.
461. Author interview.
462. *Bergen Record*, October 20, 2004.
463. *Newsday*, October 19, 2004.
464. *Newsday*, October 19, 2004.
465. *Boston Herald*, October 19, 2004; *Boston Globe*, October 19, 2004.
466. *Boston Herald*, October 19, 2004.
467. Author interview.
468. *Boston Globe*, October 19, 2004.
469. *Boston Globe*, October 19, 2004; *Lawrence Eagle-Tribune*, October 19, 2004.
470. *Seattle Post-Intelligencer*, October 19, 2004.
471. *New York Daily News*, October 19, 2004; *Boston Herald*, October 19, 2004.
472. *New York Post*, October 21, 2004.
473. *New York Daily News*, October 19, 2004. *Boston Globe*, October 20, 2004.
474. Author interview.
475. Author interview.
476. Author interview.
477. Author interview.
478. Author interview.
479. Author interview.
480. Montville, *Why Not Us?*, 138.
481. Author interview.
482. *Newsday*, October 19, 2004.
483. *New York Post*, October 19, 2004.
484. *New York Post*, October 19, 2004
485. *New York Daily News*, October 19, 2004.
486. *New York Times*, October 19, 2004.
487. *Boston Herald*, October 19, 2004.
488. *Boston Globe*, October 20, 2004.
489. Author interview.
490. Author interview.
491. Author interview.
492. Author interview.
493. Author interview.
494. Author interview.
495. Author interview.
496. Author interview; *Boston Herald*, October 20, 2004.
497. *Hartford Courant*, October 21, 2004.
498. Author interview.
499. Author interview.
500. *Providence Journal*, October 20, 2004.
501. Author interview.
502. Author interview.
503. Author interview.
504. Francona and Shaughnessy, *Francona*, 119.
505. Francona and Shaughnessy, *Francona*, 119.
506. FoxSports.com, November 1, 2004.
507. FoxSports.com, November 1, 2004.
508. ESPN.com, November 2, 2004.
509. NBCSports.com, November 2, 2004.
510. Associated Press, April 27, 2007.
511. *Kansas City Star*, October 24, 2004.
512. MLB.com, October 24, 2004.
513. Author interview.
514. Author interview.
515. *Hartford Courant*, October 21, 2004; and *Boston Globe*, October 21, 2004.
516. Author interview.
517. Schwarz, Alan. *Once Upon a Game: Baseball's Greatest Memories* (Boston: Houghton Mifflin Harcourt, 2007), 119.
518. Author interview.
519. Author interview.
520. *Providence Journal*, October 20, 2004.
521. Author interview.
522. *Boston Globe*, October 21, 2004.
523. *Four Days in October* (ESPN Films: 30 For 30), Major League Baseball Productions, 2010.

524. *Boston Globe*, October 21, 2004; *Springfield Republican*, October 20, 2004, *Bergen Record*, October 20, 2004.
525. *Boston Globe*, October 21, 2004; *Springfield Republican*, October 20, 2004, *Bergen Record*, October 20, 2004.
526. *Newsday*, October 20, 2004.
527. *Boston Herald*, October 21, 2004.
528. MLB Press Conference, October 19, 2004.
529. Francona and Shaughnessy, *Francona*, 118.
530. *New York Times*, October 20, 2004.
531. *Four Days in October* (ESPN Films: 30 For 30), Major League Baseball Productions, 2010.
532. *Newark Star-Ledger*, October 20, 2004; *Four Days in October* (ESPN Films: 30 For 30), Major League Baseball Productions, 2010.
533. Author interview.
534. Author interview.
535. Author interview.
536. MLB Press Conference, October 19, 2004.
537. Author interview.
538. Author interview; MLB Press Conference, October 19, 2004.
539. Author interview.
540. Associated Press (ESPN.com), October 20, 2004.
541. Author interview.
542. Author interview.
543. *New York Times*, October 20, 2004.
544. Associated Press (ESPN.com), October 20, 2004; *Boston Herald*, October 20, 2004; *Providence Journal*, October 20, 2004.
545. MLB Press Conference, October 19, 2004.
546. Associated Press (ESPN.com), October 20, 2004.
547. Author interview.
548. *Newsday*, October 20, 2004.
549. Author interview.
550. Associated Press (ESPN.com), October 20, 2004.
551. Author interview.
552. Author interview.
553. Author interview.

554. Author interview.
555. *Providence Journal*, October 20, 2004.
556. Author interview.
557. Author interview.
558. *Boston Globe*, October 21, 2004.
559. *San Diego Union-Tribune*, October 20, 2004; *New York Times*, October 20, 2004.
560. *Boston Globe*, October 21, 2004.
561. Author interview.
562. MLB.com, October 20, 2004; *Hartford Courant*, October 21, 2004; *Boston Herald*, October 21, 2004.
563. *Boston Herald*, October 20, 2004; *Boston Globe*, October 20, 2004; *Providence Journal*, October 20, 2004.
564. *Boston Herald*, October 20, 2004; *Providence Journal*, October 19, 2004.
565. *Boston Herald*, October 20, 2004.
566. *New York Daily News*, October 24, 2004.
567. *Boston Herald*, October 20, 2004.
568. *New York Post*, October 20, 2004.
569. Author interview.
570. Author interview.
571. Author interview.
572. *Boston Globe*, October 21, 2004.
573. *Denver Post*, October 20, 2004.
574. *USAToday*, October 21, 2004.
575. Associated Press (ESPN), October 20, 2004; *Boston Herald*, October 20, 2004.
576. *New York Daily News*, October 23, 2004.
577. *Hartford Courant*, October 20, 2004.
578. *New York Times*, October 21, 2004.
579. *Hartford Courant*, October 20, 2004.
580. *New York Post*, October 20, 2004.
581. *Newsday*, October 20, 2004.
582. *New York Daily News*, October 20, 2004.
583. *New York Daily News*, October 20, 2004.
584. *New York Daily News*, October 20, 2004.
585. *Newsday*, October 21, 2004.
586. MLB.com, October 21, 2004.
587. MLB.com, October 19, 2004.
588. Author interview.

589. Torre and Verducci, *The Yankee Years*, 308.
590. Torre and Verducci, *The Yankee Years*, 307–08.
591. *New York Daily News*, October 21, 2004.
592. MLB.com, October 21, 2004.
593. MLB Press Conference, October 20, 2004.
594. Damon and Golenbock, *Idiot*, 213–14.
595. Fangraphs.com, June 22, 2012.
596. Author interview.
597. Author interview.
598. *Boston Herald*, October 21, 2004.
599. Author interview.
600. Author interview.
601. Damon and Golenbock, *Idiot*, 216.
602. Author interview.
603. Fox game broadcast, October 20, 2004.
604. Fangraphs.com, June 22, 2012.
605. *New York Times*, October 21, 2004.
606. Damon and Golenbock, *Idiot*, 216–17.
607. Author interview.
608. *Boston Globe*, October 21, 2004.
609. Fangraphs.com, June 22, 2012.
610. *Boston Globe*, October 23, 2004.
611. Damon and Golenbock, *Idiot*, 218.
612. Fangraphs.com, June 22, 2012.
613. Fangraphs.com, June 22, 2012.
614. MLB.com, October 21, 2004.
615. Fangraphs.com, June 22, 2012.
616. *Boston Globe*, October 22, 2004; *Boston Herald*, October 22, 2004; *Providence Journal*, October 22, 2004.
617. Fangraphs.com, June 22, 2012.
618. *Springfield Republican*, October 21, 2004.
619. Author interview.
620. *New York Times*, October 22, 2004; *Boston Herald*, October 22, 2004; *Boston Globe*, October 22, 2004; *Providence Journal*, October 22, 2004.
621. *Hartford Courant*, October 22, 2004.
622. Author interview.
623. *Four Days in October* (ESPN Films: 30 For 30), Major League Baseball Productions, 2010.
624. Author interview.
625. Author interview.
626. Author interview.
627. *Lawrence Eagle-Tribune*, October 21, 2004.
628. Author interview.
629. *Hartford Courant*, October 21, 2004.
630. Author interview.
631. Author interview.
632. Author interview; *Newark Star-Ledger*, October 21, 2004; *Boston Herald*, October 21, 2004; MLB.com, October 21, 2004.
633. Massarotti and Harper, *A Tale of Two Cities*, 231.
634. *Palm Beach Post*, October 22, 2004.
635. Author interview.
636. *Newsday*, October 21, 2004.
637. Mnookin, *Feeding the Monster*, 305.
638. *Newsday*, October 21, 2004.
639. *Pittsburgh Post-Gazette*, October 22, 2004.
640. *New York Daily News*, October 21, 2004.
641. MLB.com, October 21, 2004.
642. ESPN.com, July 13, 2010.
643. *Hartford Courant*, October 21, 2004.
644. *Hartford Courant*, October 21, 2004.
645. Massarotti and Harper, *A Tale of Two Cities*, 231; MLB.com, October 22, 2004.
646. *Boston Herald*, October 21, 2004.
647. *Hartford Courant*, October 21, 2004.
648. *Hartford Courant*, October 21, 2004.
649. Associated Press, October 27, 2004.
650. *Boston Globe*, October 21, 2004.
651. *Boston Herald*, October 21, 2004.
652. *Boston Herald*, October 23, 2004.
653. *Hartford Courant*, October 21, 2004.
654. *Hartford Courant*, October 21, 2004.
655. Author interview.
656. *New York Daily News*, October 21, 2004; *Boston Herald*, October 21, 2004; *Hartford Courant*, October 21, 2004.
657. *USAToday*, October 21, 2004.
658. *New York Daily News*, October 21, 2004.
659. *New York Post*, October 21, 2004; *Lawrence Eagle-Tribune*, October 21, 2004; ESPN.com, October 22, 2004.

660. Author interview.
661. *Springfield Republican*, October 21, 2004.
662. *Boston Globe*, October 25, 2004.
663. Author interview.
664. Author interview.
665. Author interview.
666. Author interview.
667. Author interview.
668. Author interview.
669. Author interview.
670. Author interview.
671. Author interview.
672. Francona and Shaughnessy, *Francona*, 121.
673. *Hartford Courant*, October 23, 2004.
674. Author interview.
675. MLB.com, October 22, 2004.
676. *Boston Herald*, October 22, 2004.
677. *Newsday*, October 23, 2004.
678. *Providence Journal*, October 23, 2004.
679. Author interview.
680. Author interview.
681. Author interview.
682. Author interview.
683. Author interview.
684. *Providence Journal*, October 23, 2004.
685. Author interview.
686. Shaughnessy, *Reversing the Curse*, 219–20.
687. Author interview.
688. MLB.com, October 22, 2004.
689. *Providence Journal*, October 23, 2004.
690. *Hartford Courant*, October 23, 2004.
691. MLB.com, October 22, 2004.
692. MLB.com, October 22, 2004.
693. *Boston Herald*, October 23, 2004.
694. MLB.com, October 22, 2004.
695. Author interview.
696. *Newark Star-Ledger*, October 23, 2004.
697. MLB.com, October 22, 2004.
698. *Boston Herald*, October 24, 2004.
699. MLB Press Conference, October 24, 2004.
700. MLB Press Conference, October 24, 2004.
701. Author interview.
702. *Boston Herald*, October 24, 2004.

703. Author interview.
704. *Boston Herald*, October 23, 2004.
705. *Boston Herald*, October 23, 2004.
706. *Providence Journal*, October 23, 2004; *Boston Herald*, October 23, 2004.
707. Author interview.
708. *Boston Globe*, October 24, 2004.
709. Ortiz became the 28th player in MLB history to homer in his first World Series at-bat, and only the second Red Sox player to do so. Red Sox pitcher Jose Santiago did it in Game 1 in 1967 against the Cardinals' Bob Gibson. Santiago was at Fenway that night, broadcasting the game to his native Puerto Rico.
710. *Boston Globe*, October 24, 2004; MLB.com, October 24, 2004.
711. *Boston Globe*, October 24, 2004.
712. Author interview.
713. MLB.com, October 24, 2004.
714. Author interview.
715. Author interview; *Hartford Courant*, October 24, 2004.
716. MLB.com, October 24, 2004; St. Louis Post-Dispatch, October 24, 2004.
717. MLB.com, October 24, 2004; ESPN.com, October 23, 2004.
718. *Boston Herald*, October 25, 2004.
719. *Boston Globe*, October 24, 2004.
720. *Hartford Courant*, October 24, 2004; *Boston Globe*, October 24, 2004.
721. *Boston Globe*, October 24, 2004.
722. *Providence Journal*, October 24, 2004; *Boston Globe*, October 24, 2004.
723. *Boston Globe*, October 24, 2004.
724. *St. Louis Post-Dispatch*, October 24, 2004.
725. *Orange County Register*, October 24, 2004.
726. Author interview.
727. *Boston Globe*, October 25, 2004.
728. Shaughnessy, *Reversing the Curse*, 219.
729. *Boston Globe*, October 24, 2004.
730. Author interview.
731. *Providence Journal*, October 24, 2004.

732. *Los Angeles Times*, October 24, 2004.
733. *Los Angeles Times*, October 24, 2004.
734. Author interview.
735. MLB Press Conference, October 24, 2004.
736. *Denver Post*, October 24, 2004.
737. Author interview.
738. *Boston Globe*, October 24, 2004.
739. *Boston Globe*, October 24, 2004.
740. *Boston Herald*, October 24, 2004; *Boston Globe*, October 24, 2004.
741. *Newark Star-Ledger*, October 24, 2004.
742. ESPN.com, October 23, 2004.
743. *Los Angeles Times*, October 24, 2004.
744. *St. Petersburg Times*, October 25, 2004.
745. Author interview.
746. Author interview.
747. MLB.com, October 24, 2004.
748. MLB Press Conference, October 23, 2004.
749. Author interview.
750. The full story of The Standells and their relationship with the Red Sox is detailed in *Love That Dirty Water! The Standells and the Improbable Red Sox Victory Anthem* by Chuck Burgess and Bill Nowlin (Burlington, MA: Rounder Books, 2007).
751. Author interview.
752. MLB.com, October 23, 2004.
753. MLB.com, October 24, 2004.
754. MLB.com, October 25, 2004.
755. MLB.com, October 25, 2004; *New York Daily News*, October 25, 2004.
756. *Boston Herald*, October 25, 2004.
757. Author interview. (Varitek was not officially named the team captain until December 2004.)
758. MLB.com, October 25, 2004
759. Author interview.
760. *San Francisco Chronicle*, October 25, 2004.
761. Author interview.
762. *Orange County Register*, October 25, 2004.
763. MLB Press Conference, October 25, 2004.
764. *Boston Herald*, October 25, 2004.
765. *Boston Globe*, October 25, 2004.
766. MLB.com, October 25, 2004.
767. *New York Daily News*, October 25, 2004.
768. *Providence Journal*, October 25, 2004.
769. *Boston Globe*, October 25, 2004.
770. MLB Press Conference, October 25, 2004.
771. *Los Angeles Times*, October 25, 2004.
772. *Los Angeles Times*, October 25, 2004.
773. MLB Press Conference, October 25, 2004.
774. *New York Post*, October 25, 2004.
775. *Boston Globe*, October 25, 2004.
776. *Newsday*, October 25, 2004.
777. *Newsday*, October 25, 2004.
778. Author interview.
779. *New York Daily News*, October 25, 2004.
780. *Hartford Courant*, October 25, 2004.
781. *Boston Globe*, October 25, 2004.
782. MLB.com, October 25, 2004.
783. MLB.com, October 25, 2004.
784. Author interview.
785. *Metrowest Daily*, October 25, 2004.
786. *Boston Herald*, October 26, 2004.
787. *St. Louis Post-Dispatch*, October 25, 2004.
788. *Springfield Republican*, October 26, 2004; *Boston Globe*, October 26, 2004.
789. *Boston Herald*, October 2, 2004; *New York Times*, October 26, 2004; MLB.com, October 25, 2004.
790. *Hartford Courant*, October 26, 2004.
791. *Boston Globe*, October 26, 2004.
792. *Boston Globe*, October 26, 2004.
793. *Boston Globe*, October 26, 2004.
794. *Boston Herald*, October 26, 2004.
795. *Boston Herald*, October 26, 2004.
796. *New York Post*, October 26, 2004.
797. *New York Times*, October 23, 2004.
798. Author interview.
799. MLB.com, October 25, 2004.
800. MLB.com, October 25, 2004.
801. MLB Press Conference, October 26, 2004.
802. Author interview.

803. Author Interview.
804. *Los Angeles Times,* October 27, 2004.
805. MLB Press Conference, October 27, 2004.
806. MLB.com, October 26, 2004.
807. MLB Press Conference, October 27, 2004.
808. MLB.com, October 26, 2004.
809. *Boston Globe,* October 27, 2004.
810. Author interview.
811. *Boston Herald,* October 27, 2004.
812. *New York Times,* October 27, 2004.
813. *St. Louis Post-Dispatch*, October 27, 2004.
814. *Detroit Free Press,* October 27, 2004; *Fort Worth Star-Telegram,* October 27, 2004.
815. MLB.com, October 27, 2004.
816. *Los Angeles Times,* October 27, 2004.
817. *Boston Globe,* October 27, 2004.
818. MLB.com, October 27, 2004.
819. Author interview.
820. MLB.com, October 26, 2004.
821. *Boston Globe,* October 27, 2004.
822. *Lawrence Eagle-Tribune,* October 27, 2004.
823. *Boston Globe,* October 27, 2004.
824. Author interview.
825. Author interview.
826. Author interview.
827. MLB Press Conference, October 27, 2004.
828. Author interview.
829. *San Francisco Chronicle,* October 27, 2004.
830. *Washington Post,* October 27, 2004.
831. *Boston Herald,* October 27, 2004; *Lawrence Eagle-Tribune,* October 27, 2004.
832. Author interview.
833. FOX game broadcast, October 26, 2004.
834. *Boston Herald,* October 27, 2004.
835. *Lawrence Eagle-Tribune,* October 27, 2004; *Boston Herald,* October 27, 2004.
836. *Springfield Republican,* October 27, 2004.
837. Author interview.
838. *Hartford Courant,* October 27, 2004.

839. *Orange County Register,* October 27, 2004; *Boston Herald,* October 27, 2004.
840. *Hartford Courant,* October 27, 2004.
841. MLB.com, October 26, 2004.
842. Associated Press, October 26, 2004; MLB.com, October 28, 2004.
843. Associated Press, October 26, 2004.
844. St. *Louis Post-Dispatch,* October 28, 2004.
845. *Star Tribune,* October 28, 2004.
846. *New York Times,* October 28, 2004.
847. Author interview.
848. Author interview.
849. Author interview.
850. Castiglione, Joe with Douglas B. Lyons. *Can You Believe It?: 30 Years of Insider Stories with the Boston Red Sox.* (Chicago: Triumph Books, 2012), 59.
851. *Providence Journal,* October 28, 2004.
852. FoxSports.com, November 1, 2004.
853. Author interview.
854. Author interview.
855. WEEI-AM game broadcast, October 27, 2004.
856. Fox game broadcast, October 27, 2004.
857. Author interview.
858. Author interview.
859. *Boston Globe,* October 28, 2004; *Boston Herald,* October 28, 2004.
860. MLB.com, October 28, 2004.
861. *New York Times,* October 28, 2004.
862. *Kansas City Star,* October 28, 2004.
863. Associated Press, October 28, 2004.
864. *Boston Herald,* October 28, 2004.
865. *Boston Globe,* October 29, 2004.
866. *Boston Globe,* October 28, 2004.
867. *Boston Globe,* October 28, 2004.
868. *Boston Herald,* October 28, 2004.
869. *Boston Herald,* October 29, 2004.
870. *Providence Journal,* October 28, 2004.
871. *Boston Globe,* October 28, 2004.
872. *Arizona Republic,* October 28, 2004.
873. *Chicago Sun-Times,* October 28, 2004.
874. Author interview.
875. *Boston Herald,* October 29, 2004.

876. *Providence Journal*, October 28, 2004.
877. *Lawrence Eagle-Tribune*, October 28, 2004.
878. Author interview.
879. Author interview.
880. *Boston Herald*, October 28, 2004.
881. MLB Press Conference, October 28, 2007.
882. *New York Daily News*, October 28, 2004.
883. MLB Press Conference, October 28, 2007.
884. Author interview.
885. Author interview.
886. Author interview.
887. *Boston Globe*, October 29, 2004.
888. Author interview.
889. Author interview.
890. Author interview.
891. Author interview.
892. *Boston Herald*, October 29, 2004.
893. *Boston Herald*, October 29, 2004.
894. Author interview.
895. *Boston Globe*, October 31, 2004.
896. Author interview.
897. Ortiz and Massarotti, *Big Papi*, 205.
898. Author interview.
899. Author interview.
900. Author interview.
901. Author interview.
902. Author interview.
903. Author interview.
904. Author interview.
905. *USAToday*, October 30, 2004.
906. Author interview.
907. Author interview.
908. Author interview.
909. Author interview.
910. *ESPN Magazine*, 2005 Baseball Preview.

Sources

Books

Castiglione, Joe, with Douglas B. Lyons. *Can You Believe It?: 30 Years of Insider Stories with the Boston Red Sox.* Chicago: Triumph Books, 2012.

Damon, Johnny, and Peter Golenbock. *Idiot: Beating "The Curse" and Enjoying the Game of Life.* New York: Crown Publishers, 2005.

Francona, Terry, and Dan Shaughnessy. *Francona: The Red Sox Years.* Boston: Houghton Mifflin Harcourt, 2013.

Massarotti, Tony, and John Harper. *A Tale of Two Cities: The 2004 Yankees–Red Sox Rivalry and the War for the Pennant.* Guilford, Connecticut: The Lyons Press, 2005.

Mnookin, Seth. *Feeding the Monster: How Money, Smarts, and Nerve Took a Team to the Top.* New York: Simon & Schuster, 2006.

Montville, Leigh. *Why Not Us? The 86-Year Journey of the Boston Red Sox Fans from Unparalleled Suffering to the Promised Land of the 2004 World Series.* Cambridge, Massachusetts: The Perseus Books Group, 2004.

Ortiz, David, and Tony Massarotti. *Big Papi: My Story of Big Dreams and Big Hits.* New York: St. Martin's Press, 2007.

Schwarz, Alan. *Once Upon a Game: Baseball's Greatest Memories.* Boston: Houghton Mifflin Harcourt, 2007.

Shaughnessy, Dan. *Reversing the Curse: Inside the 2004 Boston Red Sox.* Boston: Houghton Mifflin, 2005.

Torre, Joe, and Tom Verducci. *The Yankee Years.* New York: Doubleday, 2009.

Newspapers

Associated Press
Arizona Republic
Bergen (NJ) *Record*
Boston Globe
Boston Herald
Cleveland Plain Dealer
Detroit Free Press
Florida Times-Union
Fort Myers (FL) *News-Press*
Hartford (CT) *Courant*

Kansas City Star
Lawrence (MA) *Eagle-Tribune*
Lincoln (NE) *Journal Star*
Los Angeles Daily News
Los Angeles Times
New York Daily News
New York Post
New York Times
Newark (NJ) *Star-Ledger*
Newsday

Orange County (CA) Register
Philadelphia Inquirer
Pittsburgh Post-Gazette
Providence Journal
Richmond (VA) Times-Dispatch
Seattle Post-Intelligencer

St. Louis Post-Dispatch
St. Petersburg (FL) Times
Springfield (MA) Republican
USA Today
USA Today Sports Weekly
Washington Post

Magazines
Sports Illustrated

DVDs/Videos
The Boston Red Sox 2004 World Series Collector's Edition. Major League Baseball
  Properties, Inc., A&E Home Video, 2005. DVD.
Four Days in October. ESPN Films: 30 For 30, Major League Baseball Productions, 2010.
Dave Roberts: Ray of Hope. Boston Red Sox Productions, 2012. Video.

Websites
baseball-reference.com
fangraphs.com

sonofsamhorn.net

Interviews by Authors
All interviews were conducted in 2013, unless otherwise noted.

Terry Adams—September 20
Marilyn Bellhorn—June 6
Mark Bellhorn—June 23
Uri Berenguer—July 21
Billy Broadbent—June 28, August 28
Ellis Burks—July 17
Orlando Cabrera—June 20
Galen Carr—May 13
Joe Castiglione—August 17
Tom Catlin—May 6
Ben Cherington—September 2
Joe Cochran—May 26
Gary Cormier—June 1
Chris Correnti—September 16
Chris Cundiff—June 1
Walt Day—July 23
Leo "Skip" Dervishian—August 19
Christian Elias—July 12
Alan Embree—September 2
Theo Epstein—September 9
Keith Foulke—June 19
Stan Grossfeld—May 29
Adam Hyzdu—October 7
Ron Jackson—July 18
Bill James—August 18
Dave Jauss—May 14
Lynn Jones—June 27
Gabe Kapler—April 22, May 1
Curt Leskanic—April 22, July 3
Dana LeVangie—June 7

Derek Lowe—September 12 and 17
Randy Marsh—July 11
Dave McCarty—April 29
Tom McLaughlin—August 16
Gary McNally—June 5
Dave Mellor—May 22
Ramiro Mendoza—July 12 and 13
Doug Mientkiewicz—September 17
Kevin Millar—June 28, July 24
Brad Mills—May 25
Doug Mirabelli—May 17
Dr. William Morgan—March 27
Bill Mueller—May 17
Mike Myers—August 13
Trot Nixon—September 28
Brian O'Halloran—September 6
David Ortiz—May 24
Pokey Reese—July 9
Dave Roberts—June 18
Euky Rojas—May 10
Jim Rowe—August 17
Curt Schilling—April 18
Bob Tewksbury—July 22
Mike Timlin—June 19, 2006
Tom Tippett—September 5
Jason Varitek—June 21, 2006
Tim Wakefield—May 8
Tom Werner—August 16
Kevin Youkilis—April 19

About the Authors

ALLAN WOOD has been a Red Sox fan since 1976 and has written about sports, music, and politics for more than four decades. He is the author of *Babe Ruth and the 1918 Red Sox* and has contributed as both writer and editor to seven books published by the Society for American Baseball Research (SABR). He has been writing The Joy of Sox blog since 2003. He grew up in northern Vermont, enjoyed 2004 while living in New York City, and now lives on Vancouver Island (Canada) with his partner, Laura Kaminker, and their two dogs.

BILL NOWLIN grew up in Greater Boston as a Red Sox fan, and though devoting most of his time to his music company, Rounder Records, he began to write about baseball in the latter half of the 1990s. He's written or edited more than 100 books, many of them Red Sox–related. He has been on the Board of Directors of the Society for American Baseball Research and has written more than 1,000 biographies and other articles for SABR and edited a SABR book on the 2004 team to be published in 2024. He's seen the Red Sox play in the U.S., Canada, the Dominican Republic, Japan, and England. And now he's seen the Red Sox win the World Series four times.